with islands in mind

Earlyworks Press fiction

GW00728877

With islands in mind

Earlyworks Press fiction

ISBN 978-0-9553429-4-3

Printed in Latvia by

DARDEDZE HOLOGRĀFIJA

Published by Earlyworks Press
Creative Media Centre
45 Robertson St, Hastings
Sussex, TN34 1HL

www.earlyworkspress.co.uk

Editor's Note

Most of these stories are from the authors short listed in our November competition. The book opens with the £100 first prize winner, *His Boots* by Alexandra Fox. All the authors in this anthology had work on the short list. Three were also short listed entrants to our recent Novel Idea Competition, so look out for the names Norman Blake, Manus McDaid and Bella Govan in the 'new novels' section of your bookshop in the next year or so.

Why do we have islands in mind? The unifying feature of these stories is a search for perspective on potentially fatal issues for individuals, cultures or for the whole planet. Some deal with these issues through realism, others through fantasy or projection into possible futures. Looking at the stories together, the reader is left with the awareness of a choice - when Nemesis approaches, do we think on a planetary scale or look inside ourselves for the answer? Can one person save a planet, a culture, or even their own skin? Do we find more strength by working together, or by withdrawing into ourselves, as battered and unreachable as islands in a storm?

Once more, we offer our thanks to Catherine Edmunds. She provided the cover illustration for our last short story anthology, *Survival Guides*. She has now come up with just what we needed for *with islands in mind* – a design which we felt reaches, as these stories do, from the embryonic to the planetary.

Kay Green, December 2006

Some will come down in India and some in China. Some of it will go all round the world and fall on us too – no-one will escape... In people's lives, there are only islands of happiness.

- from *Phragma* by David Dennis

Contents

His Boots

by Alexandra Fox

His boots are too big for you. They rub, sore behind your knees. You can remember a time when you'd put them on and they'd come right up to the top of your thighs like waders, and your soft feet would pull straight up the legs of them.

When you unburied those boots in the mud-room this morning there was a smell inside, of perished rubber, socks, old sweat. How can that be? It must be months since Dad last wore them.

You can feel ripples of packed sand through the soles. You slide across worm-casts but cannot feel the squish. You'd have to take the boots off for that, go bare, and it's too early, too cold.

Margaret's waiting ahead of you. She's stopped, looking out to sea, but the sea is grey, the sky is grey. It's as though a broad thumb has rubbed across the horizon, blurring one into the other. The sea washes into the grey beach. There is no boat, no sun.

She's smaller than you remember; of course she is. You've grown up. But she's still solid, her shoulders tense, not shaking. And you want to stretch your arms around that heavy waist, to lean, to rest your head against the muscled walls of her strong back. But you're taller than she is now.

She told you to call her Margaret, but you only want to call her Mum.

She's wearing a green Barbour, old, soft, waxless. She always said she hated the wearing-in of a new jacket, that she couldn't bear the stiffness against her skin. Her hair's pulled back from the whipping wind, but long strands stick to her salt-wet face; brown cords tuck into black wellies.

She puts her hand deep into the poachers' pocket, and for one long moment you forget how to breathe. Is she going to bring it out heaped with grey ashes, let the wind scatter them across the sand, the sea? Will she ask you to dig your hand in too, to wallow in the greasy talcum softness of his crumbling body-flakes, to come out, open up, let go? You can't. It's not the touching that bothers you, but the washing him off you afterwards, the scraping of the last sad scraps of him from under fingernails.

1

"Here, Beth." Mum turns with a smile. She's holding out an elastic band. "Why not tie your hair off your face, before you start chewing it again."

Beth.

You've been Lizzie for seven years.

~ ~ ~ ~ ~

Cockle-pickers carry a plank of wood with them with a handle on each end. They put it down and rock it. It's meant to soften the sand, bringing the cockles to the surface. They call it a "jumbo".

Dad made you one of your own, when you were about three, not long after you were placed with them. He mounted a little seat on it, like a rough saw-horse. Mum took the leg off an old pair of cords, stuffed it with laddered tights, and pinned it to one end as a trunk. You'd ride your jumbo on the sand, happily rocking while they worked. There's a black-and-white photo of you sitting there in a floppy white sun-hat and a silly frilly swimsuit. It's the first picture where you're really laughing.

Photos. That was another forgetting-how-to-breathe moment, going into the lounge yesterday. You expected to see toys on the floor, maybe a doll's cot in the window bay, a jumble of someone else's books and schoolwork on the coffee table.

But, no. It was like an old theatre where the curtain had come down on the last scene of a play, they'd locked the doors, and everything had stayed the same. That salty wet-rot smell was mixed with lavender polish, and the cushions on Dad's chair were plumped. That was your job, after school, to tidy round the lounge and make Dad's armchair comfortable. Who plumped it this time? Why couldn't they leave it alone, hollowed by the last leaning of his back?

There were photos everywhere, in little frames on the piano, mantelpiece, the window sill, in that multi-frame on the wall you'd bought mum for Christmas when you were eight, with different shaped cut-outs, and you'd sat together with the scissors trying to find which picture would go in the round frame, which in the shape like an egg … you, Dad, Mum, Jimmy the old Norfolk terrier. There's still a ring on the table where you stood the glue-pot.

"Where's the pictures of the new kids?"

"New kids?"

"You've got photos of me and the fosters that came before me, but what about the new ones?"

"We never had any more children, Beth. Not after you. We didn't know, you see. We didn't know how it would work out. If we'd fostered a new child, and you'd needed to come back, they mightn't have let us have you. So we waited."

"If you didn't think it'd work, why did you let me go?"

"We had to, Beth. We had to."

~ ~ ~ ~ ~

You're carrying Dad's rake and riddle. The old sieve's been soldered where it's rusted with the rub of sand and seawater.

Mum's tipping the riddle, swishing, no wasted energy. She beats egg-whites into peaks like that, with hardly a twitch of her wrist. Your arm aches to watch her.

You pick up dad's riddle. You run your hand around and around its curve, like a boy at the steering wheel of his first sports car. You look out to the grey sea, grey sky. A little black tugboat chugs its way out of the smudge, and suddenly you can see the line where one starts and the other stops, as though it's been there all along, but you just didn't notice, couldn't see it.

~ ~ ~ ~ ~

You think back to that hot, still night when a sheet was too heavy but the air wrapped you like an itchy blanket and you couldn't breathe. As you turned your pillow for the coolness the bed-head clanked against the wall. You moved the silence with your sighing.

Dad came in, said, "Come on, Bethie. No good wasting the night. The tide's turned."

You pulled on shorts and a T-shirt. You crept down the wooden stairs barefoot, hopping over the creaking step, latched the back door quietly. Dad took your hand in his huge one, skirted you by the tangled brambles, lifted the sticking gate onto the dunes.

There was no wind. Thick darkness was peppered with stars. A half-moon glowed creamy-white, its reflection lying on the water, edged with pinking shears. Dry couch-grass tickled your thighs. Puddles of yellow light flickered on the shoreline.

"What are those, Dad?"

"Bait-diggers, Beth. Hush. Wait." Dad sat on an upturned bucket, took a notebook from his pocket, a torch.

3

You heard a low rumble, saw twin eyes coming towards you, mouse-eyes, cat-eyes, owl-eyes, till the eyes became headlights and the old tractor dragged its trailer onto the sand. And from around you rose quiet figures, caravan doors clinked shut across the car-park, and you smelled hot sweat.

Dad numbered them off.

"Erin, boss."

"One."

"Bob Thistlethwaite."

"Two."

"Mornin, boss. Jack Porter."

"Three. You're leading twelve to the West. Watch that channel under the cliff. It's running fast."

"Right y'are."

"I've got the nipper here along this morning, so don't count me in the tally. Let's see what you can do before the day hots up."

"Aye."

"Zelenka."

"Four."

He filled a page with names and numbers, then stood you square in front of him, shone a torch in your face.

"And who's this, then?"

"Elizabeth, boss."

"Twenty-seven. And me, twenty-eight." He drew a black line.

It was a long way out to the shoreline, through clogging powdery sand, shard-banks, hard ripples with a sliding film of water on the top.

"Dad. Why do you count them all like that? They're grown-ups."

"It's a dangerous beach, Bethie. Remember the wash-away last summer, that new deep channel? We lost a good tractor in it, and where a tractor can go, a man can disappear too. You can't ever trust the sea; she runs faster than you can, and she tells lies. While folk work for me, I'll take care of them, count 'em all out, count 'em all back again."

"And you count me, too?"

"Yeah, my Bethie. You may be only nine, but you're worth a half a number, so."

And you ran ahead, giggling, skating across the surface water. There was a hint of lightness at the horizon, pink fingers scrabbling. Dad swung his torch, looking for standing water, for dimples in the sand. He stopped, set the lantern.

You had Mum's craam, its prongs twisted through years of use, and you started digging, not too deep. Dad raked the surface sand away, opening up the cockle-bed.

"Beth," he said. "I've got to talk to you, about your mother."

You scooped a forkful of cockles into the sieve.

"My real mother? Is it time to see her again?"

"She's coming out next month, Beth. The social worker rang me yesterday. They're letting her out a few months early."

You dug, twisted, ripped, tipped.

Dad had told you about the Romans, how they used to gather cockles two thousand years ago, just like this. They'd found the rims of their sieves, forks with three curved prongs just like your craam.

He tipped another rake-full of cockles into the riddle on the sand between his feet, picked it up, twirled it gently. They watched together as the smaller cockles trickled though the mesh, back into their cockle bed, tiny seed shells, the "spat". Dad would pick them up in gleaming handfuls. "When you see spat like this you know you're good for another year," he'd say, letting it stream through his fingers. "I could go to the bank manager with this and ask him for money, and when he'd ask what I could offer as a guarantee, I'd point to this – my spat."

Up and down the beach in pools of yellow lantern-light the cockle-pickers raked, scooped, riddled, trickled the little shells back into their beds, leaving them to grow. They filled sacks and baskets with larger cockles, dragged them to the trailer for weighing. They worked to an ancient rhythm.

Dutch fishermen weren't allowed here. They'd bring dredgers in, vacuums, gobble up everything, all sizes, stir and scatter the spat, till the cockle-beds would fall apart, leave the babies rolling, vulnerable.

"But I don't know her, Dad."

5

"You've been to see her twice a year. We've sent her copies of your school reports, photos, let her know what you're up to, about your friends, your music."

"That's not *knowing* her. I couldn't get to *know* her in that visitors' room, on the other side of a table. Is she coming here when she comes out? Have you got room for her? I can move into the box-room …"

"She's looking for a place in London, Bethie, and a job. It'll take her a while to get sorted. The social workers won't let her rush into anything while she's on parole. I just thought you ought to know what's happening, before she sends for you." You looked into Dad's face, his face weathered like burnt bacon. You felt the weight of his leathery hand resting on your shoulder, the heavier weight when he took it away.

You'd missed the dawn. The sun was up already, hard, bright. It turned the beach to sheet ice, scarred where strips of sand had been raked away, exposing the cockle-beds beneath.

~ ~ ~ ~ ~

Mum's only brought one bucket. You're gathering some decent-sized ones today, for tea and for the freezer.

A skirl of oystercatchers lands, piping, on the mud-flat. You and Mum smile at one another, hide a hand behind your backs, bring them out together. She's made a fist; you're pointing one finger. It's a game you've played as a child, watching the birds, guessing if they'll be hammerers, bludgeoning shells open with their beaks, or stabbers who snip delicately through the powerful muscles.

Mum's won. These birds are hammerers; you can see their shorter, blunter bills. But how do the baby birds know what to do? Do they learn from the adults? Are they born with shorter beaks, or do they grow short with the hammering? Oystercatchers are rotten parents. Their nests are open scrapings in the sand; the chicks have to run as soon as they've hatched.

"Mum. What did you think when you saw me yesterday, when you opened the door?"

She stirs the cockles in the riddle, picks out the biggest ones.

"I thought how well you'd grown, how I'd still know you anywhere …"

6

"How well I'd grown? How gross I am, this hair, these glasses … how fat, you mean."

"No. I looked at you, saw someone who was almost a woman. I was torn, torn with longing for the little girl again, but wanting to know this Beth, this … this person who looked like someone worth knowing. I was pleased with what I saw."

"I'd have come back sooner, Mum. I didn't know. I'll never forgive her for it."

"I wrote to you last year, when he first fell ill. When I didn't hear from you, I thought you didn't want to know … that you'd forgotten that part of your life. I was glad for you, that you'd settled so well, but sad for Dad. I wish he'd seen the Beth that I'm seeing now."

"I never got any letter. I'd've come. Course I would. I'd give anything." Where you wipe your eyes with sandy fingers you leave grit, and the grit makes your eyes weep.

A herring-gull lands on the sand in front of you, stabs its wicked beak into the uncovered cockle-bed. You throw a pebble at it. It jumps back, carries on stabbing, watches you.

"It was the silicosis that got him in the end, from his chimney-sweeping days. They say that sweeps are lucky, but I don't know … D'you know they used to give cockle-juice to the miners in Wales, thought it helped protect their lungs?"

"It didn't work for Dad. Did he ask for me?"

Mum stands, straightens, one hand pressing into the small of her back. You pick up the bucket, take it to the edge. You rinse, swish, swish, rinse, till the grit's been washed away.

"He talked about you all the time, pet. You were the one great gift of his life. After you left, when we realised that you weren't getting our letters, that you couldn't visit … he closed up. He started getting the London papers, looking through the news for murders, rapes, missing children. He worried so. He'd watch the cockle-pickers till he got no work done himself, feared that he'd lose one, that somebody would be carried off by the undertow, that the sea would sweep in faster than they could run. He made Jack Porter master in the end. Sold his permit. He couldn't bear to do it any more."

7

His boots were clean and shiny at the water's edge. They're clogged again now, heavy with dry sand, thistle-burrs. You lift the sticking gate. The brambles have grown, woody stems creeping, winding across the path. They cling to your jeans as you walk past, tear with tiny beaded rips.

You take the bucket into the scullery. The bag of oat-flakes is on the same shelf. You scatter a few onto the surface.

"I can't believe you remember to do that."

"What, Mum? Feeding the cockles? Give them a few oats, change the water every day, and in three days they'll plump up and drop their sand."

"It just seems so strange seeing you doing it."

"I remember everything."

~ ~ ~ ~ ~

"Will you tell me about the funeral?"

"One day I will. I can't think about it now. It's like a hole. It's deep, and I don't dare look down there. Right up to the last minute I was hoping to open the door and see you standing there. When you moved round London your file got handed from one agency to another. And you're not eighteen … nobody could help."

"You're not going to let him have that gravestone, are you?"

"You remember. … 'Trevor Hopkins. Gone up his last chimney.' No. I'm not."

… Later.

"Oh Mum, I miss it so much, the wideness of it all here, the space. Where we live, it's a thin place … thin walls with noises coming through, thin curtains, skinny people with thin noses and sneery high voices. There's narrow alleyways to walk through. I don't fit there, Mum. I never did. I don't talk right. I don't look right. I don't bleedin' think right."

"Beth. I'm so sorry. We spoilt you for it."

You could sit in Dad's plumped armchair, but you don't. You sprawl in your old place on the floor, on that same squishy cushion, rest your head in the corner made by Mum's legs and the padding of the chair seat, lean your cheek against her soft trousers, soft leg.

She strokes your head, ruffles the frizz of your hair, scratches like it's behind the dog's ears. You know that feeling in the hairdressers when the girl's washing your hair and her fingers scratch your head just where it itches? You tip your head back, look at Mum with an upside-down smile, wet eyes.

"You never spoilt me, Mum."

"It was too easy to give you everything. You were such a waif when you arrived. Those big brown eyes had seen so much, so hurt, but much too quiet for a tot. And it wasn't like you were dumped on us for just a couple of weeks and we'd have to give you back. We knew your mother had gone down for a good few years. No sign of your real dad. You were so exactly the little girl we'd always dreamed of having."

"Ma told me you'd got another little girl after I left, a baby, that you were adopting her."

"Oh, Bethie, pet ..."

"She was so jealous of you. If I mentioned you or this place she'd start spitting poison. But you and Dad, here, you'd been my life. I kept wanting to tell you things, about stuff I saw, stupid things people said to me. It was like being cut in two, keeping her happy but not forgetting. It's why she never gave me your letters, I s'pose."

"We had a message, saying that we were upsetting you, making you unsettled. That you were home now and we should leave you alone. It wasn't a nice letter."

"What a lot of people hurting."

"Yes."

~ ~ ~ ~ ~

You run yourself a bath. The water still splurts from the hot tap, faintly brown. It's tight on your hips now, the white enamel cold against your spine. You make islands in the water.

Your wrist is scraped and scarred, but even in this past day, it's started healing.

You think of Ma, how her eyes stick out like one of those myxy rabbits you used to find on the dunes sometimes, the ones that staggered around, tipping to one side. Dad would say, "I've got to do the kind thing, Beth. Don't watch," and he'd pick the bunny up. It'd wriggle for a minute in his great hand, and its mouth would open like it was screaming, but nothing coming out except whistle-breath.

9

He'd gentle it behind the ears. Then it'd stop struggling. Dad would take it behind a tree.

That's what Ma's eyes are like, sort of wet, but not normal wet, more oily.

Sometimes you watch a toddler out shopping with her mummy, grabbing the cloth of her skirt with damp fingers while her thumb's plugged into a pink mouth. Ma grabs like that. She does it all the time now. You've taken to wearing long-sleeved T-shirts, because she grabs your left arm, scrabbles it, and if there's no sleeve to hang onto, she'll grab your skin instead. You're getting bruises, scratches from her nails. You have to stand and let her hold, gentle her. Then she'll let go.

You let the drips fall. The towel isn't big enough. It's been line-dried, harsh against your skin. The roughness of it feels good.

~ ~ ~ ~ ~

"Beth, there was a phone call while you were in the bath.... Your neighbour ..."

"Angie. Yeah. I phoned her from the station when I left, said keep an eye on Ma for me, gave her this number. I left a note for Ma, too. It was dead lucky the Social woman rang when she was out, that I got the message myself, or I'd never've known about Dad. I just put some knickers in a bag and ran. I'd got some money from working in Tesco's over Christmas ... I was saving to go hostelling in the summer with a couple of mates. ..."

"Your mother's going to be all right, but she's in hospital, love."

"An accident?"

"Sort of. ... Probably. A kind of overdose."

"Oh my God."

"You didn't know she was using again?"

"Yes ... but she's not dealing. I'm sure of it. She took stuff once before, a couple of years ago, but that was pills and she was sick. I went to a sleepover party, and came back, found her. She was okay. She made me promise not to tell. I haven't left her since. Oh shit, what have I done?"

"You, Beth? You? Don't you *dare* blame yourself for this. We never should've left you there."

10

Suddenly you think of Dad, of the tiny pearls of spat trickling through his fingers, rolling safe into their beds, and the other question you asked him.

"Dad ... what about the bigger ones you're taking? Don't they need to stay home too? How do you know when they're big enough?"

He answered, "Bethie, they're never old enough to want to go, but if we don't give them all space to grow, their shells'll burst. Then the mussels move in, feed on them, and it ain't a cockle bed any more."

"I don't know what to do, Mum. I don't want to go back, but I've got to."

"Was it all so very bad?"

"It wasn't like some slum. No-one hurt me; I had enough to eat. It just felt wrong and headachy after being here. I didn't fit. Ever. Like at school, what am I? Am I a yokel, a townie, a chav? White, black, Paki? I'm not a geek or even clever. I'm not thin. I'm not in anyone's gang, but I'm not a freak. And Ma, she got on this honesty kick, told everyone she was an ex-con ... she thought it was brave. Are you sure she's going to be all right?"

"A psychiatrist's coming to see her tomorrow. Maybe they can get her into treatment. What do you want to do?"

"I can't leave her on her own. She'll just try again. ... But I don't want to leave you either. How are you going to cope without Dad? And I need to finish school. Oh God, I can't lose Dad and Ma, not both."

"Stay here, for now. It's not your responsibility any more, not alone. We'll work it out together, for the best. I'll send for your things, buy you a pair of wellies that fit."

"You mean I'll never grow into Dad's old boots."

"You don't need to. You're my Beth. And that's enough."

"But I'm *not*, Mum. I'm your Beth *and* I'm her Lizzie. Don't you see?"

"I know, and you're Dad's Bethie too, and stronger for it all. Just wait. Stay here where there's room to grow. You'll just have to learn how to be your own Elizabeth."

11

The Rumour of the Knife

by Jenny Adams

The girls sit side by side on a bench. They're made of ice for coldness. They're made of steam for shape-shifting. They're in a fish eye lens, pumped up big and stage centre. Their hair is ponytailed, stretched and polished to their skulls. Their clothing is crinkled and huge. Their legs stick out into the path like traps. If you were to walk past them you'd have to banana round them. You'd have to get ready to be not listening in case they said something, something rude, something girl gang.

"I'm sorry about last night," says Trish. "Were you okay?"
        "Yeah, fine, I didn't even know you'd gone," says Jess. She keeps her tears in their ducts and it takes backbone to do that. *I didn't even know.* Especially when you're fifteen and you've not got much more than greenstick bone. *Didn't even know you'd gone.* And you were left on your own at a party where the boys were older and over-excited. "Where d'you go?"
        "Here," among the gravestones.

There are dead coal miners here, in the graveyard. And some of them are boys and it's the boys that Trish and Jess most wonder at. Beautiful boys with muscles like boat rope and smiles that go off like fireworks, like flashbulbs, on faces marbled with coal dust. The dates on the gravestones show some of them died younger than Trish and Jess are now. Trish and Jess kneel to read headstones and picture ghostly tears that make their own seem stupid and spoilt kid. The girls don't work underground all day where there's nowhere to run if the roof falls in, they don't dig anything up with picks and ponies, they've never buried their brothers in a place like this. But they're great great grandma's brothers, means they're made of the same stuff as Trish and Jess so they can't be dull. They can't be all goody goody just because they're poor, the boys, just because they worked hard, just because they're dead. This fascinates the girls. They make it their fantasia in the graveyard. Trish and Jess wander for hours and hum spooky tunes and make up stories about which boy was reincarnated and as which cousin. Which one sang in the choir, was buried alive, was gay and how that worked down the pit. Then again, it's an easy enemy, hardship, maybe that made those days easier in some ways, made for fewer difficult decisions. Maybe boys were better in the olden days. Does more backache mean less heartache? Were they too busy to be bad? The girls haven't made up their minds.

It turns two o'clock and feels like all of a sudden they're surrounded, Trish and Jess, feels like by a crowd, but it's not.

Grave-tenders. All buttoned up they are, diligent, walking with small truncated footsteps. Half a dozen women wearing short coats and smelling of scent and solvents. Solvents used for spraying hair and touching up paintwork, not for getting high.

Trish and Jess, they're blocking the proper doings of this place. Here isn't a place for simply sitting. You need more of a reason to be here than sitting. Might look like a park but it's not. The girls don't think they have much idea about proper in any of its guises – where you buy the right daffodils for a graveyard, how often you mourn and for how long. Proper place for Trish and Jess would be school, but hey, there's more important things on this earth today than school.

The women tighten their teeth, watch their own feet walking. They'll be all right though, the women, if they keep to themselves, leave the girls be, and don't shout and flap their arms. Same as you're supposed to be with wasps.

The girls know there's disapproval lurking, but they're well practiced in ignoring. Trish and Jess can exist beyond their surroundings like kings among pyramid builders, vampires among mortals, twenty-first century girls among their ancestors. They know all they have to do is hard stare and nobody'll say nothing about being too unusual in a graveyard. They lower their talk to a whisper to keep their business to themselves, but it doesn't work. They're drowning out nature's noises, breezes and birds, drowning the afternoon in issues.

"Who with?" says Jess. *Who with* did you come to the

graveyard where girls are scared to go on their own even in the daylight?

"Nobody concerns you," says Trish. "I had stuff to do."

"Stuff?" says Jess.

"Yeah, private stuff," says Trish.

The first ever private stuff.

Trish and Jess, they'd always helped each other through the bad nights. Even if they'd been on family holidays, miles away from each other. Even if the bad nights were in the daytime.

Trish can't spell well enough for her teachers to respect what she writes. Her bones are long and light and her skin is as transparent as if it doesn't see sunlight. But she can jump hurdles and throw javelin better than most of the boys. At school girls stand in groups of three or four and whisper how Trish is hard even though she doesn't look it. They say she'd use a knife. She'd stick you with a knife, they say, if you look at her wrong.

Jess looks healthy, blossoming, vitamin rich. She tells Trish the kind of things they'll do in America, Japan, Russia, when they're old enough, when they've got money. She tells about genetics and how it's not your fault – genetics. About how many galaxies there are and that's one over there even though it looks like a star.

The planet Jupiter is so big it attracts comets and suchlike that would destroy the earth. Trish and the rumours of the knife do the same thing for Jess. Without Trish, Jess, like the earth, would be an easy target.

"I'm sorry, I shouldn't pry," says Jess. She puts her head on Trish's shoulder. *I'm sorry,* rests her head on Trish as if Trish is made of something strong that can carry the weight, *I shouldn't pry.*

"It's not a problem." Trish closes her eyes.

The women deepen their working, banging about as if the graveyard is a filing cabinet for the dead. When they're duty to be done their own selves are unimportant. They work backs bent, legs straight – must hurt. They get to arranging daffodils and plastic daffodils – bagging up the old ones, plumping up the new ones. The municipal lawnmowers don't mow right up to the edge and more than one woman has brought shears so nobody can say there's a slovenly inch

14

at her verge.

It's hard to concentrate on the job in hand, though, with so much going on in the background. It's as if there's smoke billowing out your exhaust pipe or sniper fire over the street. The more the women blur the girls, the bigger and brighter they get.

"Was fine last night," says Jess. "I got off with somebody,"

"Yeah?" Trish grins and throws her words off the palm of her hand. "Yeah – who?"

The miners died when the roof fell in, when the gas exploded, when the water came in, and so did the pit ponies. The coal trucks were pulled by ponies who emerged half blind into the sunlight when they retired. Jess knows about blind ponies and pneumoconiosis and pumping machinery and who invented it. Trish knows underground's not the only thing that's dark.

I got off with somebody, could've been the most momentous thing Jess had ever said.

Who?

"Simon," and Jess tries not to giggle in the graveyard. Because Simon is Trish's older brother so it's more than wild she kissed him. It's disloyal she kissed him. She can't see why but it is. *Simon*, shouldn't have said it, can't keep bloody quiet when needs be. *Simon*, all the time her heart an apple for all and sundry to take pot shots at.

Simon wouldn't have said it. Simon knows not to say much. He knows even fewer long words than Trish does, but he knows what naïve means so he can make sure not to be it. His muscles are embossed, his smile is criminal and all the girls watch him pass by. Simon is physical. He too stands out.

At the party everybody was so pissed and everybody was so big and Jess was all on her own. Music thumped like two thousand heartbeats and even the smoke was loud and people pushed into each other until they bruised. "Look at you! How did you get that bruise?" The pushes were the stealing of a sliver of sex, or a peppercorn of a fight, or the only way some young men can dance.

When Trish disappeared so did the magic wall that didn't let other people's elbows through. Jess was left dancing with Erica, hell knows who Erica was. Jess was in a pinball machine, bounced off other people's bones and sometimes three or four times on the trot and sometimes the hits were deliberate. She didn't want to give up though, to be a baby, so she kept her spot in the middle of the dance, clacking off ding dongs, fighting to keep up top, until – and it had to happen – she couldn't hold her own any more and got sucked down the hole that waits under the feet of every loser, where the rhythm goes dyslexic and you can't dance any more even if you want to. Jess left the dance floor then.

After Trish had gone Jess didn't leave the party even though she craved home, air and night birdsong through the bedroom window. Too long a walk home on her own. Home was along streets with bushes around the gardens and corners and parked cars where even worse bruisers can wait. And Trish might need her later. Trish might turn up any time and she might be crying, too drunk to get home on her own, hurt by the boy she'd left to be with, something like that.

After apologizing to Erica for quitting the dance, Jess stayed at the edge of the party, holding a drink to her chest, leaning against a corner and weighing up. If she ran all the way along the white line in the middle of the road? If she kept her thumb on her phone? If she texted Trish and said she'd make coffee any time, just call. Vodka nearly had her screwing caution and then she saw Simon.

He came up from under the crowd.

He came up from under the crowd, something volcanic about Simon.

Jess zoomed in on Simon because he was Trish's brother and that was blood and he would look after her. She forgot how popular Simon was, how fit, how losers don't talk to Simons.

"Hey, Simon!" Jess still leaning, being cool as dark blue.

Simon didn't ignore Jess or push past. He smiled and his smile cut through heads and smoke. He gathered her up by the elbow and took her to the back room where the music crawled through doors and walls pretending to be just a memory of music. He sat her down away from the crowd and then he sat down beside her. He passed her a bottle and she drank, touching its neck with her teeth and lips. She suppressed a weakling smile when Simon sat beside her. She widened her eyes and soft pouted her lips. Because this kind of thing happened every day, nothing to be gleeful about, nothing to warrant any display of emotion.

It's hot and Jess is pissed and Simon's arm is round her shoulder and her head is on his shoulder and it's safe because in a way he's not a stranger.

It's hot in here, it's tight, and the front room might as well be over the ocean. Jess's senses are intense. Simon, he smells sweet, salty, musky, like an animal. She can hardly breathe for wonder. She can hardly breathe for sex that's working on her like a steel corset with spikes on the inside.

He says, "Close your eyes."

Simon's arm is round her neck now, squeezing hard enough to hurt. She can feel he's got a hard on and she must've done that and she didn't know she could. His hand is on her breast and his mouth is on her neck, making a mark. He nuzzles under her chin and moves his mouth onto her mouth, not making a fuss, and he kisses her. He kisses like he really means it, like he's saying she too is beautiful. Wide kisses that'll hurt her jaw tomorrow. That'll turn the skin around her lips raw and swell her lips. You'd see the swelling and you'd know what caused it. You'd see if you turned the lights on. Good thing it's night so she can keep his kisses hidden. Even if Trish comes back, Jess can keep his kisses hidden.

Sitting on the floor, wedged between furniture, feels to Jess like time's not there. So when Simon stops to look at his watch it's an icy blast right through her. She opens her eyes slowly and sits up slowly and makes no sign of her shock. He smiles with a glint and strokes her hair once and nips up her cheek like to bolster a child. And he doesn't look back when he goes.

The women, they reach a kind of a crisis. You see, the birds are singing, the wind's full of sea and it's whipping through the boughs and if you look in the right direction there's nothing nasty in the graveyard. They can't help themselves, the women, they start to feel a sort of joy. And it's not new this, they've felt this way before. Years ago.

17

The women don't know where to put themselves in a graveyard that does this kind of thing to them of an afternoon. They look away from the treetops, to ground level, towards the dry stone wall that borders the graveyard and there's the girls sitting on a bench, shouldn't be there, should be in school. Seeing the girls like that makes the women feel normal again, angry. They look at each other, the women, gather strength. They're all wearing the same facial expression, bell metal. With mouths ashamed of their lips they say – I'm paying for their education – when I was that age I'd never have – sitting about in plain view, skipping school in plain view. Bigger than plain view. Showing off. Saying how rebellious we two can be of a weekday afternoon.

The women get to work again. Some of them wearing heavy gardening rubber gloves to keep sharp and staining grass from their fingers. The working is meant to distract them, to keep the drama at a distance. It doesn't.

The girls are head to head now, there's something going on that's fierce between them. The wind is made a gale by whatever it is that's going on between them.

The women can't maintain their efforts any more. They stop, sit on stones, light cigarettes. They're magnets for the turmoil, sponges for the story, and they hear, "Don't go! What's your problem? What's going on?"

Trish stands up, blows into the word, "No."

"Excuse me?" Says Jess.

"No, I can't be having that," Trish shakes her head hard and a hair frond falls onto her face. She twists it into a string and tucks it back into its elastic band.

"Why not?" Says Jess. "Not that it's any of your business."

"You're not streetwise, you think you are but you're not, you're ..."

"Just fuck you Patricia Starling. And you know what? Your twat faced brother too. He kisses like a twat." Had it been anybody else Trish would have smacked her in the face for that. Hard in the face with curved fingers and fingernails that would gouge.

When Trish said, "You're..." Jess guessed she would've said, had she had the words, naïve, vulnerable, socially unintelligent, something like that. Virgin, something like that. Whatever. All insults. All the kind of thing that could end a friendship.

Jess gets up to go.

"Don't go!" Jess stops and Trish says it again. "Don't go."

Jess comes back to the bench and leans forward into her words. She's in Trish's face. "What's your problem? What's your fucking problem then? Why you dissing me like a bastard? You might as well tell me coz I bet it won't be worse than what I think." Trish looks down, looks away. "I think you're feeling guilty coz you went off for a shag in a graveyard and left me like I'm nothing, and then you've got the cheek to be pissed about me and Simon. Hey, it gets worse the more I think on it."

And the women don't say anything. Normally they'd be outraged enough to correct loud girls who swear in front of the dead. *What's your fucking problem then?* But they're hungry for the story, starved for the secret, the secret they can hear behind the shouting.

And back home Simon is washing his clothes while his mother's out at work. Washing out the grass stains and the dried-in blood.

"It's not that, is it? Come on, I know there's something else going on. What's going on?"

"Trust me," says Trish. "You don't wanna know."

"Yes I do."

Jess has never been hurt badly enough to be streetwise but she valiantly tries to be. She knows what probably started the First World War, the difference between Picasso and Monet, the difference between a virus and a bacterium, and she guesses one day that will help. Right now, talking like Trish and knowing what Trish knows, that would help more.

Jess doesn't believe in the supernatural. Trish and Jess would lay their ears on the graves and scare themselves – *Can you hear them? They're whispering down there.* Jess wasn't really scared though, she knew it was adrenaline doing it and adrenaline is fun. Sometimes she wishes she could feel without filters, without as many words talking sensible as much of the time.

Trish left the party with a torch because she knew she was going to

19

the graveyard and she knew there was only one streetlight working there and she knew that even before she got to the party.

She sat on the bench in the graveyard, pressed into herself, listening. It was cold and she shivered. It was as dark as she'd thought. The silence and the night wouldn't let time come easily, they dropped grains of time from a great height, dropping ten seconds into Trish's world for every one in the rest of the world. The ancestors watched from under the grass. Nobody else was there.

Trish listened for the bad lads who were on their way. And they wouldn't be worried about the law or anything, the law wouldn't be interested, not like if they were beating someone up or robbing. They'd said so, the boys. They'd also said, "Sounds like a hoot – I'm in, see you there twelvish, yes, I know, that old church down the Meadowbanks Lane." She listened for them coming to dig the graves, paint the graves, crack the stones, pour beers on the grass, and she mouthed out to herself, "Might be wrong, I might be wrong, I might be wrong, I hope I'm wrong."

Trish had expected them to come up right in front of her, she'd expected an explosion of boys so close she could touch them. But whatever was going on was further away and even louder and more raging than she'd thought.

She heard the screaming before she'd had time to turn on her torch.

It was high pitched, the screaming, and so human.

In the field next to the graveyard Simon and his friends were sticking metal and glass into the sides and the eyes of ponies. "Whoa," they said before they hit. "Whoa, we won't hurt you."

In the field next to the graveyard, Simon and his friends were cutting into the sides and eyes of ponies. And when the ponies began to run they were ready with their bows and arrows and air guns.

Trish scaled the dry stone wall between the graveyard and the field, bruising herself, slipping on loose rock, tripping over brambles and snagging her clothes on their thorns.

She ran at the boys. She switched on her torch and got herself between bows and arrows and air guns and the ponies. They didn't need a torch, the boys, they could have as much fun by moonlight.

She shone light so blue-white circles of the scene flashed

into view like under disco lights, like under police lights, like they were on a stage. Spotlighted glimpses of ponies rearing and kicking and bleeding, and pushing and clawing at the fence, breaking their legs with their struggling, cutting their necks on barbed wire while the big boys laughed big laughs. And bigger than all the rest when the spotlight hit was Simon. Because he was her brother and it was supposed to be she loved him and what was in him was in her. No matter how much she knew genetics wasn't her fault, she couldn't get rid of the nagging that the same as was in him was in her.

His face drew the torchlight, held it fast on his face. He'd always looked such an angel, she'd always taken the flak. It was the face of a familiar stranger, rough with a young man's stubble, pock-marked with the still-wet blood of horses, back-lit with the cold blood of Simon.

When he saw who was behind the torch, Simon lowered his crossbow. He lowered his crossbow slowly, in time with a pissed off sigh and he ordered his mates to do the same. What he said was, "Oh hell! It's Patricia." And that was enough to stop them. It was an order in thumbnail, in code. Everybody here was local and knew everybody else's sisters.

Seconds later than she'd meant to, Trish yelled out, "Stop it!" *Stop it, stop it, stop it.*

Simon ran at her and he was a battering ram. He pushed the front of her shoulders, once, twice and she went down.

Her legs folded under and she went down and she landed on grass that was spongy and muddy and cold. She sat on lumpy pony meadow and felt nothing except the wrack of crying. It didn't feel proper, felt selfish. Felt like she shouldn't be attending to herself, not right when she should be mourning, crying for somebody else. Not a grown up enough for all this, not sure if the same was in him was in her, not sure, not right, not right to leave Jess on her own at the party where anything could happen with nobody to make sure the bastards stayed back. Trish was crying like a big baby on the ground in front of her brother and his friends and she wasn't helping the ponies who were still suffering, quiet now, pressed against walls and fences, breathing noisily and breathing steam that made a mark on the clear night air.

"Shut up your whingeing before you wake the dead," said

Simon. The other boys laughed at his clever joke.

She dried up her crying then, their laughter dried up her crying, got her to be angry through it. "You're all sick, that's what you are. Jealous that horses got bigger dicks than you've got, wouldn't have to be that big though, would they?" Without getting up she told them if they left right now she'd come home with them like a pet lamb and say nothing. "And you all don't even think about starting on them horses again now, coz I'll be right back at you and when I've done I'll have a bigger dick than yours." Simon held his knife above his shoulder, flicked it and mouthed - 'whoosh'. "Fuck your evil, point that at me if you like, better than pointing it at dumb animals who never did you no harm, I'll not let you do that again and I really am not caring what you do to me." And if she heard of any more ponies being hurt tomorrow or the next day, she'd know it's them and she'd blab bigtime. "Don't say nothing else no, don't you dare defy me Simon." She looked up at him and she was looking down at him. Her with long muddy stripes up and down her jeans, him with his blade dark with the blood of animals. "We're all gonna piss off right now or I will phone the police and I really am not caring what they do to you."

"Yeah, yeah right, I get it, but I'm thinking here, you just might care about your friend," Simon tilted his knife till it was at an upward angle then stabbed it up and down in the air. "I got my hand with her tonight, aha, at the party, after you'd gone. Just you imagine what we could get up to, me and Jess, when there's nobody else in the house. You think she's a virgin? You think it might hurt?"

There's the smell of cut grass and the sound of cawing in the rookery and a quiet of cars well away in the distance. There's outrageous girls who should be at school but who have a mystery. There's events in this place, there's sensations. The sensation of being finger stabbed in every body cell, cells being bullied into waking up. The women feel they're being stabbed back to life again. Remembering that everything doesn't have to be middling all the time. Didn't I have a mystery one time? Can't I helter-skelter with emotion? Can't I be scared and survive it? Haven't I just done that?

It had been enormous for Trish to come back to the graveyard in the morning. Horses might've still been there, suffering, maybe nobody had checked on them since last night. Maybe Simon had sneaked back and the field would be full of dead horses. It was all her fault, if she'd listened properly, got there faster. Like Jess would've done. Her finger had been shaking as she'd tapped out a text to Jess – gyard in 30 talk.

Trish and Jess sit side by side on the bench. Lips are pursed in a hard kiss. Hands are smooth, bone china hands. They make fists and stencilled fingernails cut into their palms. Their clothes touch where the wind lifts. They lean forward. They frown.

"I'm sorry I said you're not streetwise," says Trish. "It's nothing to do with that really."

"Then what is it?" Says Jess.

"It was Simon, he said he was going to hurt you."

Trish looks over at the field. There isn't anything obvious there. There's traces.

A broken fence. Some of the ponies had managed to break through fences and run away. A couple of the bigger ones had jumped.

Kick marks in the grass. Blood in the grass. Some ponies were unhurt and their owners had cried with relief.

The footprints of policemen in the grass. Some ponies were too injured to run. Some hadn't seen where the fence was down. Three had died and one was put to sleep by the vet.

Trish is too far away to see the marks in the grass. It just looks like any old field where the farmer hasn't fixed the fences. It doesn't look anything out of the ordinary.

The wind picks up grass cuttings and the women tending graves hear an echo of being peeved that there's mess around their tidy plots. Then they relax. It's all right, if the wind blew them there, then the grass cuttings are where they should be.

The wind picks up Trish and Jess's hair. All that smoothness and all it takes is a breeze to make there rough edges. And neither of them tuck hairs back in.

"I'm sorry an' all," says Jess. "I thought you were saying I wasn't good enough for your brother."

"No, that wasn't it." Trish, the friend, the sister. Telling lies

23

for the best. "Other way round if anything. And I came here last night coz, coz…"

"Oh God, don't cry," Jess puts her arms around.

And the women tending graves see the hugging. They're thinking – suppose we'll never know now, what the secret was. But that's okay. Seems to have ended okay. It's been a different kind of a day and they drive off not in a hurry.

Phase Two Scenario

by Elizabeth Sarkany

Steven wakes up on his forty-seventh birthday and decides to call the woman he met on the plane over from Sydney. He can't stop thinking about her. She reminded him a bit of Diane Keaton. Her hair, when she dozed off with her head on his shoulder, smelt of lilacs. Of course, it's partly to do with being alone in a strange city, but he's started fantasizing to an embarrassing degree. At night, in bed, he whispers terrible love-scene dialogue between the two of them. It makes him blush to think of it, but he even kisses his pillow.

Forty-seven, he thinks. Not seventeen.

There's a message from his daughter, Jess, when he switches on his mobile.

'Happy birthday, Dad,' she says. 'I hope you've made some friends in London to spend your birthday with. It took me longer than three weeks when me and Mum moved, do you remember? But you do already know Duncan. And it's probably different with teenagers. Things are – you know - OK… I miss you loads…Mum's OK… really…I wish you weren't away for so long…six months … seems pretty much like forever doesn't it?' Now he can hear her trying not to cry, taking a deep breath, remembering it's about him, not her. She's only eighteen, it should always be about her, but somehow, he knows, it never is. She sighs. 'Anyway, gotta go Dad. This is costing. Love ya so much… Happy birthday. Love you.'

He could sit on the bed and slump his shoulders and indulge himself with weeping. But then he'll be late for the Monday meeting with Duncan. And, after an entire weekend spent alone, trudging through the drizzle between art galleries with only *Immunology Bulletin* for company, it's a relief to be expected somewhere.

And it's good to have a plan of some sort.

'Louise – hi there,' he says out loud in the shower. 'We sat next to each other on the plane? Steven? Steven Bremen?'

He turns it over in his head while he towels himself dry. It might put things on a better footing if he at least sounds as though he expects her to have remembered him. After all, they talked about anything and everything on the plane: his ex-wife's postnatal depression that never really went away, Jess's Krohn's, Louise's job as director of a family therapy clinic.

Louise told him she hadn't chatted so easily for ages. It turned out they both love 'When Harry met Sally,' and Pink Floyd's 'Wish you were here,' and a fry-up with bacon, but only if it's crispy. When he added, "snowflakes that stay on my nose and eyelashes," she laughed as though it was the most hilarious thing she'd ever heard. And even when they were only discussing the plane food she spoke as though each word had been carefully selected to get to the heart of the matter. Clarity, that's what came over. Precision. She doesn't need to be with a loser.

'Hi, Louise,' he tries, more breezily. 'Steve Bremen here.' He puts on the kettle in the kitchen he hasn't yet cooked in. He pictures the two of them holding hands on the London Eye at night, over the sparkling city, and throwing bread for the ducks on Hampstead Heath, Louise wearing his sweater.

'Just wondered if you'd be free for dinner,' he says to his reflection in the dark glass of the oven door. 'It's my birthday.' No, he thinks. Way too needy. Not the birthday.

"Call me," she told him at the luggage carousel. She handed him her boarding card with her phone numbers on it. He was still waiting for his case but he watched her as she pushed her trolley towards customs. She was wearing a denim skirt with purple ankle boots, a mixture of suede and shiny leather. He hadn't noticed them on the plane.

'Sample recruitment,' sighs Duncan, lighting a cigarette. 'That's why you're here, Steve.' He has grey stubble and a big white stain on his suit trousers. Steven met him in Boston, twenty-five years ago, when they were both part of one of the first groups to identify molecule tumour necrosis factors. Duncan was a damn sharp dresser then. It was one of the few standing jokes among the bearded, diffident researchers in their musty viyella shirts. It surprised no-one when he went home to Twickenham and set up Apex Therapeutic Antibody Technologies. That's where the money is and Duncan has always had a certain lifestyle to fund.

When Duncan got in touch last year and asked him to come over and run phase two of the *Undevimab* trial, Steven thought a few uncharacteristically hedonistic months in London, expenses paid, might be just what he needed. 'We'll have a ball,' was what Duncan promised. But, in the event, there's no ball to be had. Duncan's third wife, a glossy-haired, long-limbed fine arts graduate in her twenties, became pregnant in the interim and has recently given birth to twins.

'Obviously, things won't have been helped by the sodding, bloody mess *Praxis* made of their phase one this year,' says Duncan. 'I don't know if you saw the coverage over there?' His mobile phone rings. He closes his eyes and doesn't answer it.

'Some of the subjects were Aussies, Duncan. Young guys, travelling, who did the trial for a bit of cash. So, yes, it was everywhere. For weeks.'

'Then you realise what we're up against,' says Duncan. 'Couldn't have been worse timing. Distraught blonde girlfriends on every front page. "Witness tells how victims screamed in agony". "Our heads are about to blow". I don't have to tell you about recruitment for phase two studies at the best of times. Always dodgy when you move into a patient population. Always uphill convincing the GPs not to be over-protective. But this time, with the appalling press for monoclonal antibodies...' His mobile rings again. He grimaces. 'Steve, you're going to have to go all out with the GPs. That's our only hope. You speak their language. They don't trust someone at the commercial end like me.'

He walks over to his desk and takes a bottle of whisky and two glasses out of one of the drawers. He waves the bottle at Steve, who points at his watch, raises his eyebrows at Duncan and shakes his head. 'You're a clinician,' Duncan says, pouring himself a drink. 'So you've got that authentic decency – but you're a scientist, too. You *know* rheumatoid. And disease demographics are the way in. If we can show them that we've pinpointed a population likely to derive benefit from the drug ... if we can demonstrate those disease markers which predict safe response...' His mobile bleeps and he fishes it out of his pocket, frowning, and squints to read the text message.

'She wants me back at lunchtime,' he says.

'Not easy,' says Steven. 'Those early days with a baby. Twins, I can't imagine.' He shakes his head. 'Go on then,' he says. 'Pour me a shot. It's my birthday.'

27

'God, Steve, I'm sorry. I'd love to do dinner but we eat on the hoof. Sometimes Carly hasn't even managed to dress.'

'I went to Helsinki when Jess was three weeks old. I presented the encapsulation studies, and then I kind of hung around there. Nobody seemed to think it was odd.' Duncan hands him his drink. 'Apart from my ex-wife,' says Steven, raising his glass in a toast then downing it in one. 'She never forgave me.'

They arranged five o'clock on the phone and it's only six minutes past when he gets to the café but Louise is already there, sitting near the back. She sees private patients on a Monday evening, so dinner's out, but she suggested tea in Swains Lane. Her eyes flick straight up at him from her book as soon as he walks in and she reddens and waves across shyly. She makes a big deal of marking her page and self-consciously fiddling with her bag to put the paperback away. By the time he reaches her, he's realised how awkwardly her nose sits in her face. Her hair is puffy and shorter than he remembers. Her smile is like a plea. It dawns on him that they sat side by side the whole way on the plane, mostly facing forward, like making confession or having psychoanalysis from a couch. She half stands, he bends towards her, her hand clutches at his upper arm, and they kiss on both cheeks like old friends.

'I've ordered you a chamomile tea,' she whispers, as if sharing a lover's secret. Along with everything else he told her about himself, he mentioned he was trying to give up coffee. He realises that Louise, too, has been reliving every moment of it. She, too, has been counting the days until she sees him again.

He sits in the chair next to her rather than the one opposite, in a bid to recreate what happened between them. The languid intimacy of long-haul, so close to a stranger. The discarding of reading material, the cosying under blankets in the darkness. The freedom of being nowhere, of defeating time. The stripping away of everything except themselves and each other. Fitfully sleeping, waking up together, unwashed and tousled. But there's a self-consciousness to things now. And, of course, on the plane, they'd both been drinking.

'I told my mother about you,' she says. 'I said, I feel I've known him for years.'

He wishes she hadn't.

'So,' he says. 'This is nice.'

She turns to look directly at him. He can tell that her eyes are used to seeing disappointment.

'It really is,' she says. He thinks, her nose looks like someone made it from putty and stuck it in the middle of her face.

'It's a nice place,' he says, looking around at the wood-panelled walls with framed prints of musical instruments, the chrome and glass counter, the platters of home-made cakes.

'It's nice to be here with *you*,' she says.

'How's your daughter doing?' she asks him. 'Without you there.'

'It's hard for her,' he says. 'But she understands.'

'I get the impression she always does.'

'What do you mean by that?' he asks.

'This is a child,' she says, 'where the roles haven't been clear from the start. Wouldn't you say? Where there's always been some confusion about who is looking after whom?'

How dare she, he thinks. "*This is a child...*". Who does she think she is?

'Her mother expects a lot of her,' he says out loud. 'That's true I suppose. Her mother has always leaned on her. But I've done my best, given the circumstances. The two of us, Jess and me, we're very close.'

'But are you helping her to spread her wings?' says Louise. 'She should be travelling, spending time with her peers.'

There's a woman trying to read a letter at the next table and Steve notices she's got her fingers in her ears.

'She does have friends,' he says, 'but she prefers to vacation with me. She reads, she lies in the sun, we cook out. She feels safer that way, in case she has a flare-up.'

'She's eighteen,' says Louise. 'She needs to find her own way.'

He feels like telling her to give it a rest. He hadn't noticed the other time how shrill her voice is.

She rummages in her briefcase and brings out a document.

'You might find this helpful,' she says. 'It's the latest thinking on these issues. Adolescent separation and individuation. The development of healthy autonomy. You can give it back to me next time.'

He doesn't want it, but he looks politely at the front cover. It's called *She's leaving home.*

'You don't have children,' he says, quietly.

'You're right,' she says. 'And I'm forty-three. You think that's straightforward?'

He calls the waitress over, an Eastern European girl, with jeans so low he can see the fuzz of her pubic hair.

'A cappuccino please,' he says. And he asks her to bring a couple of serviettes. He's torn his into tiny shreds while they've been talking and he wants to blot the sweat from his forehead.

He looks at his watch.

'I have a dinner appointment after all,' he lies, 'with people from work. It's my birthday.'

'I could have shifted things around,' she says, 'with a little more notice.'

'It's fine,' he says, looking at his watch again. 'But I should make a move soon. I don't want to be late. Not on my own birthday.'

A few tables away, a little boy slithers off his chair and goes round to his father, who's deeply engrossed in the newspaper.

'Finished my cake now,' he tells him. He rests his hands on the man's huge leg and dances a hoppy jig. His father grunts and turns the page. 'Want to go outside,' says the boy. The father's hand absent-mindedly rests on his son's whole head, gently crushing the blond curls. 'It's raining,' he mumbles. 'Not now. Wait.'

'I'll put my raincoat on,' the boy tells him and he moves both hands over his whole body, to show where the raincoat will go.

'Next Monday's a bank holiday,' says Louise. 'Even *I'm* not going to work. I thought I'd take myself off round London, like a proper tourist. See some sights.'

The little boy is trying to put his coat on upside down. He takes his arm out of the sleeve and studies the coat for a minute, frowning, then has another go, a different way.

'It's the old story,' says Louise. 'Lived here all my life and I've never even been to the Tower of London.' She laughs. 'We could go together if you like,' she says. Steven mimes to the waitress to bring the bill.

'I have to keep moving, you see,' says Louise. 'People think I have everything sorted. Professional success, financial security, emotional intelligence, the freedom that independence brings…'

The little boy has his coat on, and is trying to fasten the popper buttons in the front, breathing hard with his tongue stuck out. Frustrated, he stands again in front of his father, shifting from foot to foot, and starting to whine.

'But don't you worry,' says Louise. 'It's not so bloody easy. I'm on the edge of my own big black hole plenty of the time. And, you know how it is, Steven, if I don't keep moving I might fall right in.'

'You've not done a bad job there,' says the father. He folds his paper up and turns his chair and brings the boy to stand between his legs, facing him. He tugs gently on the boy's sleeves and clips the poppers together.

'You see how he's managed,' says Louise to Steven. 'He found a way, without any help, that kid, because he wanted it enough and no-one told him he wasn't up to it. He found what he needed inside himself because he was given the chance.'

When they're leaving the place, Louise walks right up to the little boy, who's lolling against his father, waiting for him to finish counting out the change to pay.

'Aren't you *just great* at putting on your coat,' she says to him and he looks up at her with solemn eyes and gropes behind him to find his father's knee.

'Isn't he, Steven?' She smiles over to where she thinks he is, in the other aisle, separated from her by a line of tables. But Steven pretends he hasn't heard. He's already at the door. He's pushing it open and going outside, hurrying off along the street in any old direction without looking back. There are still a few hours left of his birthday. He hunches his shoulders and turns his jacket collar up against the rain. It occurs to him that if anyone were watching they'd think he had somewhere to get to.

31

The Birthday Party

by Rachel Moses

It's funny, because at first she didn't want to come.

'Why do I have to go?' she asked, moaning that way girls moan.

'Why, Gran? Can't I stay behind?'

Eleven years old and she wants to stay home alone. Well of course her mother lets her, she is used to getting her own way.

Did I ask such questions when I was her age? Did I complain? Things were different then.

'No-so, young lady, you're coming with me.'

'But aren't you going to change your clothes? It's a party after all.'

She is wearing jeans and a grey sweatshirt with GAP across the front. What she always wears, except to school or mosque.

'Grey doesn't suit our skin tone,' I tell her. (Haven't I told her a million times?) 'We Punjabis should wear yellow, orange, red; colours of fire and sun. How pretty you looked in your red suit at Eid!'

But my grand-daughter cares nothing for pretty these days. Twelve months ago everything in her bedroom was pink - walls, curtains, bed spread, posters, toys. In the last few weeks everything has changed. Dolls and teddies, gone. Begged her mother, who has more money than sense, for new duvet and window blind (blue with silver moons and stars), then covered the walls with posters of pop bands ripped from magazines. Clothes now all black and grey, and only three suits of shalwar kameez. *Three*! Even these I had to hunt to find, they weren't hanging with her other clothes but stuffed into a Morrisons bag on the floor.

What is this GAP they all have written across their chests? Surely its meaning is space, or hole?

'It will be such fun-bun, the two of us,' I say, unlocking the car. 'Like old times.'

I used to fetch her from school every day. Every day we went to the park across the road. Fed the ducks and played together on the swings. Now the park is boring. She doesn't want to go. She walks to school alone.

'Nice English birthday party.'

'Thought it was meant to be Indian? Isn't that the point?'

'Indian theme, yes. Vivienne likes our culture very much. She's been so kind to your Mama, helping her with studies and what not. Her daughter's the same age as you.'

But Mina only sighs and checks her mobile phone.

Sometimes I feel my family want to erase every trace of their culture, dig up every one of their Indian roots. I don't know why. It's Western clothes, Western music, American food in the freezer, and Allah knows what rubbish they watch on TV. English names for everything, even me. Gran. An ugly word. Man, pan, van; it rhymes with nothing beautiful at all.

Now my daughter-in-law has given up her job. A good job. A dream job. When I think of what she has done, tears spring into my eyes. Working in British Home Stores, in childrens' clothes, what could be nicer than that? Flexible hours she had, free lunch in the canteen, and ten per cent discount on anything she bought. Ten per cent! On anything at all! School uniform, winter coat, pyjamas, underwear…so many things we got for Mina, as well as sheets and towels and what not for the house. But is it enough for Roxana? No-so. It's back to college, she wants to be a teacher now. IT, or is it ICT? What the difference is, I don't know.

She has plans, that one. She thinks it's secret, but I see how the wind blows. Don't I hear her talking to Arif? Upstairs the walls are thin. Always, it is her words I hear, her words I listen to as I lie awake at night.

'A garden,' Arif says next morning with his sheeps' eyes and his chin on his chest. 'Somewhere safe for Mina to play.'

She wants to take my son from this place where he was born, where I am living more than thirty years. She wants to leave these terraced streets with their backyards of Indian washing and rainbow painted steps. She wants to live where the white families live, independent and semi-detached.

33

Vivienne lives in a terrace. (Does Roxana know that?) It's a surprise, driving over to Bailey, I didn't know Bradford could be so nice. Mina's supposed to be navigating but when I stop for the third time she gets all huffy puffy and leaves me to study the map. Bailey looks like it was a village in the past, with its rows of stone cottages and steep cobbled streets. Behind Vivienne's street there are fields.

'Mind the rangoli,' Vivienne says when she opens the front door. 'Don't smudge the chalk.'

I hadn't noticed the pattern on her step.

'Why don't we do that?' Mina asks, kicking off her trainers in the hall.

'The custom is Hindu,' I explain.

'Pritam doesn't do it.'

'The tradition is an old one. Things change.'

Vivienne's living room is full of girls. They dance to sitar music blaring from the CD player, wiggling their hips and holding the palms of their hands together in imitation of the dancers on the Bollywood DVD at the side of the room. CD, DVD, these days they're the first sounds a child learns to make. Vivienne's living room is painted red, with its colourful rugs and ornaments from around the world it is so nice, so cosy-rosy and warm. In my son's house Roxana has everything white.

'I just love Indian things,' Vivienne shouts above the noise of the dancing girls. She points to the scarves and fringed shawls draped over coffee tables and chairs, incense burning on the mantelpiece beneath a picture of Krishna as a small boy. Next to the incense there are statues of Vishnu, Kali and Ganesh.

'Just love India, don't you?'

'Oh, yes,' I say, avoiding Mina's eye.

Actually, as Mina knows (haven't I told her many times?) I spent my first sixteen years in a village in eastern Pakistan. Until I came here as a bride I had scarcely travelled to any other place. Islamabad, Karachi, Lahore, I haven't seen even now, never mind Delhi or Bombay.

Vivienne is unaware of this, of course. She doesn't notice the pinch Mina gives my arm. Haven't I told Mina, sometimes you have to pick and mix your words. You can't always rush in with the truth. But my grand-daughter cares nothing for courtesy these days.

'Benares silk,' Vivienne says, showing off her sari with a twirl. 'Haggled for it on a stall behind the railway station in Calcutta. Got a good price.'

'The quality is there for all to see.' Of course it's polyester mix.

Esme and her friends have dressed up too. They wear sarongs and scarves around their waists, flowers in their hair, and bracelets which tinkle like bells around their wrists. Some of them look like they're going to the beach, but they make a pretty sight. They laugh a great deal and wave their arms about and seem to be having lots of fun. Mina can't take her eyes off them, but each time I nudge her forward she presses herself more firmly to my side. I wish she had changed her clothes. She looked so pretty in the suit she wore at Eid.

Vivienne points to a chair in the corner of the room. 'I thought we'd do the henna over there.'

Before my brother was born we were five girls. My poor parents, they really believed Allah was punishing them and they were often away on pilgrimage or at some holy sight. My sisters were left to run the house. In my tenth year there was a wedding in the village, and Hamida Auntie came to stay. Hamida Auntie's belly was like a water melon beneath her kameez and when she walked her movements were stiff and slow. The other women who came to live with us at that time, aunts and cousins on my father's side, were very bossy about what Hamida Auntie must do and what sort of food she must eat. They made her lie on a string bed in the shade. If she got up to go for a walk, or even just to stretch, one or other of the cousins or aunts came and pushed her back down. 'Rest,' they said, 'while you have the chance.' My sisters brought tumblers of fruit squash for her to drink, they cooked special savoury snacks and sugary puddings to try to tempt her to eat (apart from her melon belly Hamida Auntie was thin, with arms and legs like twigs) and though they were busy with all the guests demanding food, they stopped frequently to stroke her hair or rub her feet.

No-one had time for me in those weeks before the wedding. I was too small to be useful, too old to be cute. It was my brother who drew the affection of our visitors and won their praise. Usually my sisters sent me on small errands in the village, or they asked me to fetch things from the bazaar, but in these days there were plenty of uncles hanging around the place who took charge of such affairs. So many people, so much activity, yet I was desperately bored. Then one day Hamida Auntie beckoned me to her side.

'I've been watching you,' Hamida Auntie said. 'We are the same, you and I. We have nothing to do. The others are busy, we are no more than a nuisance to them. We must solve this matter ourselves.' Then she laughed, and the sound was like music floating through the air. I hadn't heard laughter much before then.

She patted the space beside her on the bed. 'Come, sit next to me. Not like that,' for I had lowered myself carefully on the edge of the wooden frame. 'Make yourself at home. This belly will make a nice cushion for your back.'

Her hair was long, longer and lighter in colour than hair I'd ever seen, a sweet chestnut brown. She played with her hair as she spoke, twisting it round slim fingers, tying it in a knot behind her head. It leaped onto the back of my hands as it swung down, with a kitten's soft bounce.

'Talk to me,' she begged.

A terrible shyness overcame me when she said this and I felt my cheeks burn. What should I tell her? I wasn't used to conversation with grown-ups. Besides, my life was the same each day, there was nothing interesting to describe. If Hamida Auntie noticed my inhibition she didn't seem to mind, for she hummed a tune quietly to herself and played with the gold bangles on her wrist. Her fingers slid the bangles up her arm, one bangle after the other, then slid them, one by one, back down to her wrist. She did this several times and then she stopped humming and started to quiz me with a series of questions instead.

'Savoury or sweet, which is best?'

'Four sisters! Which one do you hate most?'

'Autumn or spring, what do you prefer?'

'Imagine, if you woke in the morning a boy. Rich. You could do anything. What would you do?'

I answered her questions with no more than a few short syllables at first, but soon curiosity made me bold and my answers grew in length.

'Now it's your turn to question me.'

We compared tastes in seasons, sisters, fruit, swapped fantasies of what we would do if we were free (just thinking it made my head spin). The words flowed easily now, like sweat in summer heat. Thoughts buried deep inside my head I brought out for her to share, and so many dreams unknown until that moment even to me. When I stopped Hamida Auntie sighed, scratched her belly, shifting the weight of hair from her right shoulder to her left. Then we sat quietly, nibbling the sweets my sisters brought, the baby pummelling my back hungrily with its fists.

In the afternoon, Hamida Auntie was too tired to talk. While the courtyard filled with my sleeping relatives' snores, she put henna on my palms. I had seen henna before - ugly orange stains on the fingers of servants and beards of village men and my mother's grey hair. Hamida Auntie's henna was not like that. It flowed like liquid across my hands, delicate calligraphy in brown ink. For days I refused to wash. When the henna started to fade, I begged Hamida Auntie to do it again. Better still, would she teach me how to use the magical paste? She thought about this, smiling at me sideways before she made her reply. She would teach me, she said, but in return I must talk. That way neither of us would be bored.

When the festivities were over Hamida Auntie returned to her house. I went on practising what I had learned, desperate to impress Hamida Auntie next time we met. But I never saw my aunt again. Her baby died in the eighth month and Hamida Auntie lost her own life in the long struggle of the birth.

My sisters grew impatient with me in the weeks after the wedding. Exhausted by the demands of so many extra mouths to feed, they were cross before I begged them for coins to buy henna, beating me about the head as I tried to paint their hands and feet.

'Don't we have work to do? No time for sitting about.'

Then I ran off and hid behind the water tank, watching for Sunny to come back from school. When Sunny did his homework, I sat near him at his desk. While he was busy writing letters in long lines from right to left, I took his hand (the hand that wasn't holding a pencil) and drew squiggles across the back of his palm.

'Every day is like a wedding in this house,' the sweepers used to joke. 'Even the air smells of henna paste.'

Vivienne brings a cup of tea. It's too sweet - 'I know,' Vivienne says, 'how you Indians like your tea' - there must be six spoons of sugar in it at least. She has a big voice, Vivienne, discipline will be easy for her in school. I wonder what she's studying to teach? IT like Roxana, I suppose. (Or is it ICT?) Esme and her friends crowd round as I unpack the contents of my bag. They are like parrots in their brightly coloured clothes.

'Birthday girl first.'

I take out some of the pictures I carry with me, photos and cuttings from magazines that show different styles of henna art. Some are elaborate patterns that fill most of a hand or foot, others are simple, geometric designs. It depends on the occasion, and the preference of the girl.

'What will you choose?'

It's a question I always ask. More often than not the girl shrugs her shoulders. 'I don't know,' she may say, 'I leave it to you.' But I like to ask the question all the same.

Esme is big boned like her mother. Compared to Mina she's a giant, it's hard to believe they're the same age. Small breasts like plums already push out her vest.

'That,' she says, pointing to a picture of a bride, and drops both arms in my lap. Her hands are broad, the flesh thick like fudge. She seems confident, this one, but I can't help noticing her sore bitten nails.

The moment I squeeze the paste from its thin plastic tube, I fall into a trance. I forget about the long drive back, Mina's moods, or my son's hints that they plan to move to a bigger house. I forget about Roxana quitting her job. Henna demands concentration, to do it properly you can't think about anything else. I breathe deeply, close my eyes to shut out the distractions of the room. When I open them again I am conscious only of the hand in my lap, the fingers slightly curled. I start with a small dab of paste. The possibilities are endless; different directions, a myriad of shapes. Some shapes open like a flower. Others close. The henna spreads like water on her wrist.

As the energy flows, I start to dream. In my dream I am a girl. Too young to be useful, too old to be cute. A girl at a good age, curious, imaginative, free. All around there is excitement in the air, the excitement of a wedding. I am old enough to feel the romance of it, young enough not to look ahead. No other wedding will be like this, without the bitter taste of grief. Which sister did I hate most? The truth was I loved them all, but it was a love I discovered late, when marriage split us and stole the only family I knew.

But all this lies ahead, in a future I cannot see. For now there is Hamida Auntie, and a miracle of friendship and words. It is a miracle that comes once. My heart won't open in such a way again, and I will never speak such words. Not to my husband, nor my child. I don't know this then. All I know is that the words leave me empty and complete, with a sadness I am too young to understand. But Hamida Auntie is happiness itself, with her smiling face and quick, ready laugh, her baby hiding in a water melon for me to hug as we doze in the afternoon heat.

Before long Esme has gloves of finest lace on the back of each hand. She leaps up to show her mother, and a girl called Julie takes her place.

'What will you choose?'

Julie is unsure what she wants. Square hands like spades hang down by her side, fat fingers twisting the cuffs of her sleeves. A simple style, I think, a line of leaves like ivy along the index finger to the wrist.

After Julie there is a girl named Sam. Then Vivienne brings a tray of food; rice, vegetable curry and two kinds of daal. But there is little time to eat. After Sam there is Sarah, Rosemary, Kylie, Bethany, Jade. Then a neighbour pops in and Vivienne asks if I would mind doing her hand as well.

My practice paid off; by the time I was twelve I was making money from my art. The sweepers' words came true, and every day was like a wedding in our house. I grew famous for the novelty of my designs. What would they say if I told them my best ideas came from the back of my brother's hand? Sunny had a place at the mission school now, in a town I had never seen, but he had grown used to my presence near him while he worked. The feel of the henna soothed him, he liked its pressure, cool and light, on his skin; as the only son he had the aspirations of the whole family heaped upon his head. He rubbed the henna off when I had finished; he didn't want his school friends calling him a girl.

Wedding henna I did for each of my sisters in turn. When all four were married and scattered like grains of rice in the monsoon wind, I knew I didn't have long. Sunny kept his ear to the ground and found out what he could. I did my henna myself. Is there anything else a girl can choose? Important decisions have already been made. The women came and had their party, there was *gub shub* and laughter and all the singing custom dictates. His female relatives and mine. They inspected my jewellery and clothes, the dowry gifts prepared for Mr and Mrs Pervaiz. They painted my face with coloured powders, rubbed my hair with oil. And I sat with my dish of henna, letting them do what they must, pulling paste across my body in a thick protective veil.

Fingertips to shoulders, I covered. Toes up to my knees. I was a walking work of art, my design the most original, the most daring, ever seen.

*

I don't recognise her hand at first. After all the hands I've held these two hours past, her brown one is a shock. It is scarcely any weight at all. In this place she seems younger; not the teen queen she is at home, just a little girl.

'My turn, *Dadi*, please.'

How I loved the softness of her palm as we walked to the park after school. When she was happy she swung my arm. Sometimes we sang. All the old rhymes I taught her, Urdu and Punjabi, and English of course. It's a long time since I held her hand.

After all, she is still Mina. She is only doing what we must, each of us in turn. She is growing up, that's all.

My dove. My heart.

'What will you choose?'

'Gran,' she says on the way home, then stops.

'*Dadi*,' she says instead.

Words are important, after all. We should cherish the words we use. *Dadi*. It is my Indian name. What I am properly called.

'May I have an Indian party when I'm twelve?'

The car in front stops at a red light. I slam the brakes on hard.

Indian party indeed! She doesn't even like Indian food.

The Memory Archivist

by Jude Higgins

Annie stood in the centre of her dome and thought about the life choice she'd made at seven years old. If she'd wanted to be an actress or a pianist, she wouldn't be here now. Live entertainment was out in the 2050s. Nobody could put a foot outside the door without getting togged up like old-style Arctic explorers and inside their dome dwellings, the remaining original humans lived separately because of the risk of contamination. She should be grateful to be a 'retained elder'. The government kept saying her services were vital – she was one of only a few people who had such a detailed recollection of life before the Big Freeze.

She must have been a strange little girl to have such determination at seven. If only… she spent a second locking into that moment over a hundred years ago…and there it was displayed on the memory screen in front of her exactly as it unfolded in her mind…*She was standing trying to talk to her grandfather, dear Grampy, but his eyes looked blurred, he couldn't remember who she was, that she'd been to see him just an hour before to show him the paper boat she'd folded. She could remember the expression on her face* – that was the exact moment she'd made the choice. Annie paused the memory and zoomed in. She heard the words inside her little girl head. *'I won't be like you, when I'm old, I'll learn how to remember everything.'*

A bleep sounded from the communication screen on the other side of the room and the Clone Controller's face appeared, smooth and impassive as usual. She was moving her lips into a smile-type shape.

"Time to have a rest, dear," her voice sounded hypnotic. "Your memories are getting stuck again. A nice sleep will sort them all out."

Annie felt her eyes droop. They were using some new voice technique on her. She could feel the heaviness descending more powerfully than last time. She turned away from the communication screen, scanning around for a lively memory. Dancing, that might do it. Yes, she found one – winter with Steven, 1975 – that time in the cottage when they were both so happy. Annie felt her energy lift as the images flooded onto the screen:

Her Steven - only about twenty-five then, dancing in front of the big log fire in the cottage near the Standing Stones. A smell of apple wood – Bulgarian gypsy wedding music playing. He was laughing and beckoning her to join in. Then there they were whirling, clapping and laughing together, her in that brown velvet skirt, the fabric swinging round in an arc. His hand clasped her waist...she could almost feel it...him pulling her closer, now his hand sliding up her jumper. The music raucous and wild in the background. Oh, they'd loved each other so much... She watched herself on the memory screen kissing and dancing, kissing and dancing, repeating the memory again and again, her old body swaying, her feet tapping, the weariness dissolving.

"We might be able to use that memory, to help the teenage clones with their sexuality." It was the Clone Controller's voice again, breaking in loudly. Annie heard her voice drop a tone. "You really do need some sleep, my dear. Remember if you're not producing a good memory sequence to feed the little ones, they won't survive will they?"

Annie felt a familiar pull in her heart. She remembered when they'd first told her why they needed her memories. It had felt so good. She was already eighty-five and although she'd kept herself in very good shape, from the memory training, yoga and pilates she'd been doing all her life, the intense cold and the lack of fresh food was weakening her every day. She'd never had any children and the thought of being like a surrogate parent at her age buoyed her up and made her feel like living again. Since Steven had died in the flood at their seaside home, it had been hard to be alive. Being healthy and living longer than nearly everyone she knew had meant she had to endure the massive climate change when the Gulf Steam packed up in the summer of 2034.

"It's like the world's had a stroke," she told her last old friend, Sally, when they heard the news. "We ignored the small Ischemic Attacks and now this is the big seizure. There's no recovery." And they'd cried together and drank her last bottle of organic wine, under the one surviving tree in Sally's garden, toasting everyone and everything they'd over loved.

43

During that winter, weeks of ice storms weighted the power lines with icicles, brought them snaking down and exploding in flames all along the streets. Oil supplies ran out. Only people living in the government facilities where there were Geotherm systems had heating in their homes. Annie was ready to die in the way she'd always wished, complete with all her faculties, unlike her dear old Grandpa. Sally had already managed it, going during her sleep in her freezing bedroom. It would only have been a few weeks; days even, before the cold finished Annie off too. It would have been fine going out with hypothermia.

But then, they found her.

They'd discovered in the Central Record Dome, some of her old TV programmes where she'd demonstrated her fantastic memory skills – found her and lured her in. "Your country needs you," the clone they sent round said, Kitchener style, sitting in her living room, a huge parka over his quality suit. He'd leaned towards her looking sincere – "We need someone like you, Annie."

Perhaps it was her weakened state that had let her mind falter and agree. And it was flattering to be given a job with such a grand title at her age – the 'Memory Archivist'. She would have a warm and comfortable home, and with the new technology be able to project her memories onto a large screen. The approved ones would be filtered into the clone nurseries to allow the babies a virtual experience of a world full of life, colour and personal memories.

"Then the babies can thrive," Tony had said, "and carry some hope forward into the world. It will be nearly as good as real contact."

Why didn't she think they'd never let her die? Or twig that they'd want to keep her as a perverse and immortal Queen Bee, trapped in the middle of a hive of clones?

Annie realised she'd been letting all these memories and thoughts drift over the screen for the Clone Controller to view. She used to be able to switch her brain to the present whenever she liked, and especially when the Controller logged in. Now it required a huge effort not to return to the past.

"So what do you want to do, Annie?" the Clone Controller said. She wasn't smiling any more. "If you stop yourself sleeping and die, all those children will die too. Remember they need your memories. You should know that by now."

Annie felt the tears well up. They'd let her view the clone nurseries to see the little children as they grew up. She'd seen them singing the songs that she'd learned as a child, drawing pictures of trees and flowers and birds she'd projected into their memories. When they grew older she heard teenage clones talking over things from the past, her version of the past that she'd relayed to them in all its vivid detail. The viewings happened a couple of times a year, just enough to keep her tantalised. And she'd longed to see the children personally. Fantasised abut them coming to talk with her directly. One little boy in particular seemed so much like the way she was at seven. Always asking questions, then totally absorbed in making things, writing stories and poems. It was hard sitting and watching knowing that everything he learned from outside was so carefully monitored. There was no Internet any more, and old books weren't allowed because of contamination fears. Annie had decided to try and send him telepathic messages, something that she'd been good at in the past, but had kept secret from the media in case it looked too wacky. She'd sent messages to him during each viewing for the last ten years. Told him there was more to life than what he was being given, and one day he'd be able to find it out, in his own way. She'd thought he started to receive her signals quite quickly, but hadn't learned to send them back.

"You're thinking about the clone children, aren't you, Annie?" the Clone Controller interrupted. "I'm glad to see you're not always thinking about yourself."

Annie felt panicky. The Controller must have seen random images flashing across the screen again. Thank God, her thoughts weren't transmitted into the speakers this time. If thoughts were fast enough, the sensors couldn't catch them. She really would have to be more careful.

"Maybe it's not good for the clones to be in this world just with my memories," she said. It felt important to say something to the Controller to get her off her back.

"Don't you worry now," the controller soothed, "they'll be fine as long as you *keep feeding* them. That's the important thing.

You have such a rich and varied supply and they get additional information from our current events screen."

Annie started to feel dizzy. She must have been awake for over twenty-four hours this time. She was confused. Her mind had always been perfectly clear. Like purest water, you could see everything, right down to the bottom. It was so hard to let go, to forget things, and be muddled. What if all the clones would die without her input, even the older ones – that boy too, he was about eighteen now. It didn't bear thinking about. She found herself walking towards the bed and lying down.

"Good," the Controller's voice sounded faint. "We'll switch off the memory screen now and let you rest. You know you're so much better after a big renewal."

Hearing the words 'big renewal' jolted Annie back into a clear space. She knew they fed her intravenously and scanned her body while she slept to find any damage, but a big renewal meant one of her organs was wearing out and was going to be replaced. They would keep her under sedation until it had healed. So she'd get up as good as new with everything fixed. Nowadays, when she came round, the sedation made it hard for her to remember anything important she'd been thinking beforehand. And there was something she just had to get clear before sleep washed over her. She kept her body still in case any movement disturbed one of the sensors, and she cast her eyes around the room to check the screens were really off. They were starting to dim the lights now, but there was a chance she could make sure. Annie returned to an innocuous memory – Sunday dinner back in her parents' house, 1960.

Two Way family favourites on the radio and Mum's Yorkshire pudding, as it came out of the oven. A blast of heat and the smell of the beef juices and the golden towers of crisp batter...

There was no sign of the memory on the screen. Good – she just had a few minutes privately before they started the renewal process. She breathed deeply and let the oxygen flood her brain. There was something she'd recalled during that last viewing of the cones, that didn't make sense. She remembered a conversation she'd witnessed between the older clones. It was a heated argument about the last big wars in the Middle East in the early 2000's. They were using her views or opinions she'd read and exactly remembered.

She'd been excited because the boy she'd been sending messages to seemed as if he was expanding his own arguments and not relying on hers entirely. Then another group of older clones who'd been sitting in the background walked over and started to disagree with him even more vehemently. And they weren't referring to any of the counter-arguments she'd remembered. They were arguments from a completely different perspective to hers. Ones she'd never thought about or read. Someone else's memory. And the viewing had suddenly been cut, as if the wrong clones had come into the picture by mistake.

Annie felt her head lolling to one side, the bed was rocking slightly, they were spraying lavender oil into the air, and playing a lullaby she'd loved as a child. She breathed in deeply again and imagined sending the memory to her special safe place, a trick she'd learned years ago. Nothing was ever lost there. She would return to it when she woke up.

Daylight streamed through the aperture at the apex of the Dome. Annie could feel the light on her eyelids. Was she imagining it or was there a faint trace of sunshine?

A memory from 2006: She and Steven on their sun loungers in the back garden. He was reading from UA Fanthorpe. Her eyes were shut and the sun was making patterns on her inside lids.

"Very interesting," the Clone Controller's voice broke in.

Annie opened her eyes, the memory of her and Steven fading away.

"I can download some Fanthorpe on your reading screen if you like," the Controller said. "The poems you don't remember."

"Lovely," Annie tried to make her thoughts stay benign. Perhaps the Controller would be less intrusive if she said a few words to her now and then. She ran her hands up and down her body in order to stay present. She noticed a little ridge scar at her side.

"It was a successful renewal," the Clone Controller said. "You've a lovely new liver now, so as it's your birthday, we thought you could take some fresh food, even a drop of cream."

"My birthday..." Annie suddenly felt sad. They'd woken her up on her birthday, as if she'd want to remember she'd survived another year in this place.

"Fancy reaching the ripe old age of one hundred and ten. We've got a few other special treats in store for you. The clones are going to sing you Happy Birthday and," the Clone Controller sounded as if she was talking to a very small girl, "we're going to let you choose one of the older clones to bring your food over to you. How about that?"

Annie stared. What was going on? Was it a trick?

"I thought they could get contaminated."

"Once they're over eighteen they've enough immunity. We've been testing them on outside expeditions for a couple of years. So this will be the first time they're able to visit an original human. It's going to be a special day for one of them too."

"Thank you," said Annie. She got out of bed and stood up. She needed to feel her feet on the floor to stay present. It was so important to feel absolutely in the here and now because she had an idea. She mustn't let any of it spill over onto the memory screen. She must appear thrilled and grateful.

"Can I have some champagne too if my liver's renewed?"

"I'm glad you want to celebrate," the Clone Controller said. "We knew you'd have a change of heart and stop wanting to die. Maybe your liver malfunctioning was altering your mood."

"Probably," smiled Annie. "Liverish energy, that's what they used to say. So when are they going to sing to me?"

"In an hour's time. We'll have the webcams on so you can see each other."

"I'd hoped you might," Annie could feel her excitement growing. "I hope they won't get a shock when they see me."

"You haven't looked in a mirror lately, have you?" said the Clone Controller.

"Every time you're renewed, we do your face with the laser wand and tighten up your skin in general. Have a look before I come back."

In the mirror Annie saw the face that she knew in her fifties. What an imposition it was to be returned again and again to a younger body and a younger face. That face didn't belong to her now. It should have stayed where it was in the past, in the world of trees and grass and sunshine, the world of people and conversation and laughter, the world she'd taken for granted along with anyone else who'd lived in comfort in the West.

She sat in front of the memory screen and scanned back to when she was eighty-five, when all of this had started. It was a relief to see her white hair and wrinkled skin. The way she'd moved and spoken. She wasn't unfit, but she and an old woman, going about her life in an old woman way. Annie returned to the memory of her and Sally under the tree, drinking their toast.

"I'll toast you again Sal," she said. "Just you wait."

She dissolved the memory, wrapped herself in her old blue pashima and sat in front of the communication screen, steadying her breathing and letting her mind be clear and focussed.

The communication screen bleeped on and the Controller was standing there in front of all the young clones in their dome, the little ones in front, the eighteen year olds at the back.

"Ready Annie?" she asked, standing back.

Annie nodded. She concentrated on the young man she'd been observing all these years. He was in the middle of the back row, looking steadily at her. She let her mind transmit her question to him. Was she the only memory archivist? She saw him register the words as they started singing and felt scared. How did she know for sure he wouldn't stop the singing and tell the Controller what had happened? She managed to smile during the song and keep looking at him. He was shaking his head from side to side and for the first time, she heard his voice saying, 'No – ten of you,' echoing in her brain.

No, she wasn't the only one – nine more. Annie had to pinch herself to believe it. *She wasn't the only one.* Why had she never considered the possibility before? Now she could stop feeling guilty. Now she could die.

"You look so pleased Annie," the Controller said when they'd finished singing. "So now you must choose. Who do you want to bring the food hamper?"

"The young man in the middle of the back row," said Annie, pointing at him. Her hand trembled. He hadn't spilled the beans, but what if he wouldn't do the second thing she'd asked telepathically?

"Adam," said the Controller. "A very good choice. One of our most promising clones."

Adam. Now she knew his name. It seemed so fitting. If he did as she asked he'd have to leave the cloistered world of the clones permanently to learn, as from the Tree of Knowledge, what the world was really like. Not a world of dome houses and control for him. She walked around her own dome. What a strange place she'd ended up living. No windows to see out, just the aperture at the apex to let in natural light and those big screens all around. A bed, but not an ordinary bed – one that became an operating theatre at night, when robots descended from channels in the wall to anesthetise her, take out and replace body parts, give her drugs and vitamins. Only a few of her own pictures, some ordinary chairs, tables and rugs from her previous home as if that would make everything real and homely.

Annie sat in her old chair, the one she'd bought in an auction in the 1980s. At least that was looking its proper age. She let herself sink back into the saggy cushions and waited. After a while, she heard a tearing noise as the outer two doors were opened. Her heart started to beat very fast. Previously it had been robots that'd delivered the occasional fresh food from the Farm Domes. It was years since she'd met a living person in the flesh. And now this living person was Adam. She waited with growing excitement as he unsealed the final door. Then he burst through in a flurry of snow. How fresh he looked – as dark as Steven did as a young man. She hoped he'd be as brave. There was so little time. Annie stood with her back to the communications screen. She opened her arms to greet him. He put the hamper down, took off his gloves and hugged her. She let herself lean into his strong, young body for a moment. The Controller had returned to the screen and was viewing them. They'd have to be careful.

"I've always wanted to meet you," he whispered coming to stand next to her, with his back to the screen as well, "Your life was the best – I won't forget. And when I heard your messages, I believed there'd be something else for me."

Annie leaned forward and kissed his cheek. His skin felt cold and wet from the snow. "Thank you," she said, her voice breaking with emotion. "It's made everything worthwhile."

The Controller's voice cut in. "Adam must go now. He can't be put at risk for too long and there's a storm coming."

Annie moved her eyes towards the door. "You know what to do for me, don't you?" she whispered. "Yes," he whispered back. "I heard your last message. I'm not scared." He reached out and squeezed her hand. 'Goodbye Annie.'

She could feel a cold draught from the crack at the side of the unsealed door as she eased off the Champagne cork and poured the wine into a glass.

"To you, Adam and all the clones," she said, raising her glass. The Controller nodded graciously. She hadn't noticed the door. Annie waited until she'd logged off, put the cork back in the bottle, grabbed a tumbler, then pushed hard at the door with her shoulder until it swung open. The air became colder and colder in the corridor and took her breath away when she emerged through the final door into the snowfields. Huge snowflakes whirled around her. It was now pitch black. She stumbled as far away from the dome as she could and collapsed in a ditch where the snow had drifted. Her limbs were already numb, the cold creeping fast towards her heart when, with stiffening fingers, she poured her second glass of Champagne.

"Here's to you Steven. Here's to you Sal. Here's to you Grandpa." Annie lifted her glass to the snow-filled sky, "...and here's to where I'm going."

No Satellite Signal

by Neil Valentine

He flipped channels, as he always did; as, he thought, he had always done.

The station changed, the generated decals went from Bravo to Paramount Comedy, the home of so many memories. South Park, Frasier, all his friends were here, including them, Friends. Images sprung once again into him, recall replaced the lack of motion on the static screen. Friends with their warmth, the microcosm of happiness, the security of being with them, joining with Chandler and Monica, flatmates with Joey and Rachel; all were there in the room, in his mind.

South Park, the pure comedy of Eric Cartman; and he was there, with him as one of his cartooned sidekicks, both set on destroying Kyle, and on wielding Authorit-eye of course.

But all there was to show for it was the blue; deep chroma blue, definite and bold, bright and mesmerizing, taking him back, to where he wanted to be, with them, as he had done his whole life before the box.

He flipped the channel up one notch, leaving the high-case writing from one page and receiving it again on the next – NO SATELLITE SIGNAL IS BEING RECEIVED. But he ignored that, focusing instead on the smaller writing of the channel, and program schedule, both having received no further details since transmission ceased. Although he didn't care, he had enough program and channel info, more than enough to maintain the memory of comfort.

Now he was on the Sci-Fi channel, the intrigue of Rosanna on Medium, searching the dead and living for answers. Kirk and Spock, the early years, a long-term memory for him with his first taste of them decades ago – and they were still going, as was he as the three joined on the bridge of the Enterprise, bound for yet more adventures in Styrofoam. Apocalypse viewed from a thousand angles, hundreds of spacecraft, dozens of complete worlds, all were here, held within the box and its bright overpowering blue – NO SATELLITE SIGNAL IS BEING RECEIVED.

He flipped again, changed up, this time to the Travel Channel. Voyages in Switzerland on a chocolate box railway, mountains of dew on a roving journey, past pines, fern-laden forests, valleys and plains; always movement, displacement in time and space – well, time at least anyway. Last minute deals to the exotic, ones he'd thought about endlessly as he placed himself poolside in the box, beneath the price embossed over the frolicking masses on their once-yearly reprieve. Hanging with the ultra-cool Globe Trekker team, backpacking with the Dalai Lamas of discovery, sharing their joy, understanding of so many tribes, clans, all connected on this Earth – so horribly connected. He searched the blue for images of his entertainers – NO SATELLITE SIGNAL IS BEING RECEIVED.

Another flip; this time he moved up, punching the worn button dozens of times until the first movie channel arrived. Movies, home or cinema, were the sustenance of dreams, givers of hope to the most hopeless in wonderfully stereotypical scenarios. Mel and Danny chasing down the Orange men, going loco before the man and his coco. Cheech and Chong, slippage of the soul not permitted anywhere else in society other that the small silver screen. Romcom, feelgood, trashy action, comic book capers, drifters and moneymakers, all here, all blue - NO SATELLITE SIGNAL IS BEING RECEIVED.

Now he sought knowledge from the radiating haze of deep blue, flipping again he found it – the Discovery Channel, over a dozen slots of primetime know-how, filling him up with that which he would never need to know, or use, but crammed in with unrestrained wanton nonetheless. He'd learnt to build a plane, an entire small fixed-wing aircraft, from start to finish. He could restore the rustiest of wrecks into a gleaming E-type, fit for a king and queen to take out for a spin amongst the casinos of Monte Carlo, through groves of lemon and olive - or was that him driving with Grace Kelly beside him? He'd seen the Mythbusters break endless urban legends, pump crash test dummies full of rounds in the name of viewer science. He'd witnessed entire aircraft carriers constructed in under an hour, and destroyed in far less by the enemy, whomsoever it might have been. He'd watched dogfights and firefights, storms and hurricanes, super-massive magma overrun the globe; he could still see it, in the blue, hidden within the box of rocks his face had bathed in since the beginning of time.

But war and nature were only part, the legends were his favourite by far; he'd voyaged to Shangri-La, circumnavigated the globe with a member of the Monty Python crew, stood shoulder-to-shoulder with Hannibal as his legions of elephants spanned the Alps, sacking Rome for the umpteenth time, although Rome seemed to bounce back more than any other subject in the small, bright blue box. Best of all he had joined with Alexander, as a certain historian walked in the footsteps of history's greatest general; once he and the great man had scaled an impossible peak, to vanquish an enemy who mocked them with cries of "you'd better go home, unless, that is, you have some soldiers who can fly", bodies of their comrades cascaded down like a flesh waterfall, all to get to the far side, and tell their dumbstruck adversary "you'd better surrender, you see, we found those soldiers that can fly!"

The Pacific Rim, Mongolian savannah, Tibetan plateaus with processional flows – he had felt them all, touched their sense as they attained likewise on his karma.

He flipped up several channels, to the History Channel, prepped for the onslaught of crime, war and recent infamy – NO SATELLITE SIGNAL IS BEING RECEIVED.

Now he went to the same place he usually drifted to on the hour, news stations beaming current affairs from the annals of world interest, the latest stocks, terrorists foiled, and occasionally successful – NO SATELLITE SIGNAL IS BEING RECEIVED. As the blue wrapped his features in its glare he heard the sound-bites, the wonderful titbits that enhanced the senses, enough to prevent flipping for the first few minutes of the world news, 'national tensions, open dialogue, worsening relations,' it was the last that inspired the terrible sense of recall. 'Worsening relations'; there's a bite he'd heard so many times before, so much so he and the world were utterly desensitised to it, as far as he was concerned relations between trading blocks and nations were always worsening, always tense. So what?

The thought moved his head for the first time in hours, or was it days? The man panned his gaze over the dozens of heavy and light duty car batteries littering the floor, piled up several high in places. The batteries powered the television - at least until electricity would return to the power-grid - the small fourteen-inch box could go for several days on a fully charged one. One other luxury though had been added to his improvised circuit, a small electric fan, a heater variant now using only the blades to create a wonderful symphony of white noise, a rhapsody of thought, an accompaniment to his lounging, one that gave the room the comfort and durability of a manmade womb.

Empty food cartons, packs of flour, even wallpaper paste, all dotted about the floor, strewn in piles, attesting to his basic calorie intake over the eons he'd been here, washed down with toilet and bath water, fed from the infinity of the water tank.

But, as the man returned to the box and prepared to flip, the last word from the news caught his trance, shaking a brief clarity, installing him with the need to do something slightly different, ponder, and take stock before he could continue.

The man shakily stood; ever so slowly he raised himself up, grimacing as bedsores squealed in protest, burst and boiled at the unwanted movements, demanding a return to sloth living. 'Worsening relations', the thought bounced around his skull as he finally stood, not erect but in a stoop, unable to straighten up for fear of bursting each and every one of his scabs and sores. The thought pushed his legs, fighting past the cramps and urging a slight shuffling action in them, as they too were now far too underused to simply re-engage at will. The man's body now fought a perilous path to the window, the shower-curtain-covered window, which, like the other three in the room, had been securely taped to the frame, allowing just a faint sliver of wind in through the gaps.

The man with no name except the ones bestowed on him by the box, carefully unpeeled one side of the curtain, revealing the world beyond.

A panorama of shattered twisted and melted glass, steel and concrete greeted him. The scene now seemed so old it was petrified, even the smouldering had finally ceased, after what must have been months, although he honestly had no idea, when you sat or laid before the box, days, weeks, and even months merged – tracking time was a trait of those in the box, not before it.

On the slight hill his house was on he surveyed the wide-screen beyond the cracked windows; houses close to his were relatively intact, with just tiles missing and windows blown in. But beyond the first mile of terraced buildings began the edge of the inner radius; entire streets vaporized, factories turned inside out, girders melted into sculptures. The transformation was absolute; the world he once knew had been completely obliterated in favour of this, the new planning committee the atom had seen to that. He really had no idea who or why, he was watching television when it happened! Although anyone scanning the news would have had little preparation, a few censored and sanitized sound bites could hardly prepare one for this.

At least when he next flipped to the news channel to receive the blue-screen bulletin spitting out 'worsening relations' he would know what it actually meant – this thought caused a lump in his tender throat, one that reminded him never to flip to BBC or CNN ever again.

There was one thing he knew about the scene; the Sci-fi Channel got it right, apocalyptic is mesmerizing, a sight of sights, one that only faded when a new channel entered his mind – PBS Kids, home of Sesame Street, giant pinball with him as the ball, one-two-three-four-five, six-seven-eight-nine-ten, eleven-twe-he-he-he-he-he-he-lve.

The man panned a little, attempting to focus a clarity to his milky mire, scanning the hundreds of cars lining both sides of the road as it curved out of sight, all with their bonnets up. The fruits of his labour were evident in the dozens of spent batteries that cluttered up his front garden, placed there by him back in the days when his limbs held more energy. Had it been days – weeks? The answer eluded him; the number of cars scavenged gave him a window, one that he wished not to explore.

But another window on his mortality opened as he turned to leave – his face. The man caught sight of his reflection as he moved, a hairless scalp recently a lush mane, a toothless gawp from a man barely thirty. He knew it wouldn't be long now, his fading life-force attested to that, although how long was in debate, after all it had been an eternity thus far, and he was still here.

He had often pondered if companionship would have been the way to weather it, the depth of love a greater cure than the bright blue doctor sitting by the bedside. Conjured images of his imaginary partner lying limp in his arms, with him whispering sweet sayings into her reddened ear as she wheezed. He told her how beautiful she'd looked on the first day they'd met, how he tingled from point to point as his heart sighted that most fairest of maidens. He stroked her last tuft of hair as he recounted how it would be alright, declared and reaffirmed his commitment to her soul – and as he did the last patch of hair swept from her head in the tips of his caress.

The box won.

The man closed the curtain and taped it up, clearing the stage for the next act. Wearily he lowered himself back onto the bed, grimacing as his sores found pressure and wailed in protest until settling. As soon as he was suitably aligned he flipped the worn button, scrolling past dozens of channels until he found the one he wanted.

PBS Kids, home to Sesame Street, a backwards journey into a world of BMXs, early morning Monkeys fronted by Davy, and the puppets that inspired so much from the eternity of summer holidays. The Count, cackling as he sent forks of lightening to accompany his joy at learning.

The butcher the baker the great motion makers. They would be his guardians now; they always had, their angelic allure, overpowering, demanded he submit – so he did.

The deep blue washed over him, cleansing all outside woes and immersing him in the e-bible.

NO SATELLITE SIGNAL IS BEING RECEIVED.

Under the Porticos of Solomon

by Norman Blake

"One day the Messiah will come," said the Pharisee quietly to himself as he stood in the temple under the shade of Solomon's Porch. Suddenly, he became aware of a tugging at his garments and was surprised to see a diminutive child looking up at him earnestly.

"Rabbi, which commandment is the most important?" demanded the boy.

"That's a very good question. The most important commandment is: 'You shall love the Lord your God with all your heart'."

"Which commandment is the next most important?"

"To love your neighbour as yourself."

"And the next?"

"To honour your father and mother. And where are your parents, child?"

"My Father is in Heaven."

"I'm sorry to hear that. Has he been long in the bosom of Abraham?"

"I mean my Father is God in Heaven."

"Yes, but where is your *earthly* father?"

"On his way home with my mother and my brethren, I suppose."

"Behold the child!" cried the boy's mother running towards them. She looked hot and flustered but also relieved at finding her son.

"Of course, Mother, didn't you know that I'd be in my Father's house, going about his business?"

The woman turned to the Pharisee in embarrassment. "Rabbi, he's a strange child. I hope he has not been bothering you."

"He appears to be interested in religion," said the Pharisee.

"Yes, but what is to become of him? He wanted to be a shepherd, and he often sat up all night with the shepherds watching over their sheep in the fields around our village. Then he would sleep all day. After that he wanted to be a farmer and observed the men in the fields sowing seed."

"I told the man in charge," interjected the boy, "they were wasting their efforts because as quickly as they were sowing the seed, the birds were eating it. And he was very rude and said he'd feed *me* to the birds, if I didn't mind my own business."

The Pharisee laughed but the boy's expression remained serious.

"Later we went up to Capernaum to visit relatives," continued the boy's mother. "Then he wanted to be a fisherman. He spent hours watching the boats and talking with the men as they mended their nets. They said they didn't mind as he was doing no harm, and they even took him out in their boats. One of the fishermen has two boys of about the same age as my son. They spent the whole summer playing together and fishing out on the lake. Of course, his father wants him to carry on the family business."

"I want to be a scholar in the Law and a teacher," said the boy with enthusiasm. "Our Heavenly Father made us, so we belong to him. Caesar rules the world now, enslaving men's hearts and minds as well as their bodies. But our Father will rule again over the earth, and his kingdom is coming soon."

"Out of the mouths of babes and sucklings..." muttered the Pharisee in wonder. "My son, you should not speak openly of such things. It seems that you plan to lead an uprising against our oppressors?"

The boy thought for a few moments. "If there is no other way," he said.

"Madam, you have a very interesting son. I believe that a great destiny awaits him. In the meantime, I suggest that he learns his father's trade."

"Your father will have something to say when he sees you," said the boy's mother pulling him away sharply by the arm.

"Does he know which is the most important commandment?"

"Enough nonsense! Come along quickly now, Judas!"

Invisible Persuasion

by Pam Eaves

Immediately she awoke Hilary could feel the comforting presence of Tildi – a sense of not being alone - someone caring about her. Snuggling under the duvet and savouring a moment of anticipation, she knew today was going to be good and the familiar silvery voice confirmed.

"Wake up," it said. "I've got plans for you."

Hilary wriggled upright and leaned against the broderie anglais pillows, her eyes wide open now and eagerly searching the room. The golden ball bounced gently at the foot of the white embroidered duvet in a shaft of sunlight, and then took off, dancing hither and thither illuminating delicate blue flowers and green leaves on curtains; sparkling and irradiating the room with a soft golden glow.

"Tildi?"

As the globe settled on the bed, gently undulating and sending slivers of light around the pale walls, the voice announced,

"We're going up to town today for shopping and lunch."

"But Tildi," Hilary hesitated, "I daren't spend any more money; there's so much outstanding already on the credit cards, and…"

"Don't worry." As the sphere swayed Hilary wished she could see the tiny figure inside more clearly, but it transmuted into an oval and glittered when the voice spoke again.

"You'll not meet anyone stuck indoors. You've got to put yourself about a bit – push your barrow out."

Hilary giggled. Tildi knew how to cheer her up. And she was right. Follow your instinct lady, and your fairy.

But sitting at her dressing table later, doubts returned. Hilary peered closely at her long, pallid face in the silver-framed oval mirror, inspecting the lines round her eyes.

"Do you think I look old?" she asked, turning towards the light settling on a pot of white hyacinths. A waft of heady perfume and a faint 'of course not' scotched any lingering misgivings and she rose and turned to the expensive fitted wardrobes. Dad wouldn't recognise the house now – it all looked lovely since that heavy, old furniture of his had gone and every room was beautifully decorated and furnished. Pulling open the wardrobe doors, she sighed with pleasure at the row of smart clothes.

Hilary held a new scarlet suit up, inspecting her reflection in the mirror. Yes, it looks good with the new hair streaks and gives my face a bit of colour. I'm not too bad for my age and luckily we don't run to fat in our family. She scrambled happily into her clothes and turned in front of the mirror, remembering her father's constant warnings against debt. Poor old Dad, always on about looking after the pennies so he could leave me something. At least I don't have to worry about that – I've got no-one to leave it to, but it would be nice to meet someone now he's gone. Her eyes misted as a surge of loneliness overcame her momentarily but, pushing it aside, she ran downstairs following the ball of light dancing ahead hypnotically.

Marching to the station, Hilary felt optimistic. Tildi had made such a difference to her life. She grinned, wondering if other people had good fairies and kept quiet about it. Probably not; most of them looked miserable.

If she had any lingering concerns they soon disappeared in the lively bustle of Knightsbridge and she dived into a boutique, smiling as an obsequious assistant approached. If your clothes look expensive, they fall over you, she thought, fishing out her wallet to pay for delectable underwear. Wishing her father could see her now she smiled, imagining his disapproval of the credit card.

'Can't trust them things. I like hard cash,' he'd said. Poor old Dad - so old-fashioned.

There was one nasty moment in Harvey Nichols when a card was refused, but another was accepted and Hilary, laden with glossy bags staggered out into Knightsbridge and hailed a cab. Where am I going? she thought, dismayed. Then Tildi murmured, 'Savoy Hotel' in her ear.

Thank goodness for Tildi – she'd never dare go there on her own. Hilary leaned back on the leather upholstery watching the ball of light dancing in the corner of the cab and wondered if lunch would be very expensive. Not that it mattered much after all she'd spent this morning and Tildi knew what she was doing. This is the way to live, not watching every penny like Dad.

The Maitre d'hotel, recognising expensive shopping bags, hurried towards her.

"A table for one, Madame?"

Hilary nodded, relieved at not having to approach this aloof gentleman and glided in his sinuous wake towards a table.

The menu was incomprehensible and she felt panicky, but the waiter's murmured suggestions were helpful as she tried to look accustomed to the opulent surroundings; acutely aware of the gaze of an attractive middle-aged man sitting at the next table.

"I'll have the sole please."

"And wine? May I suggest, Madame...?"

Hilary hadn't a clue what he was talking about, but she nodded then hesitated.

"I think a bottle would be..."

"Of course Madame, perhaps a glass?"

"A glass please."

She handed back the menu and wondered if she had the nerve to pour water from the jug perched beside a delicate floral display. If only she had something to read; the way that man was looking at her made her feel conspicuously alone. Inspecting the vase of flowers minutely, she wished she'd gone to John Lewis's restaurant, or even British Home Stores, and jumped nervously as, with a flourish, the waiter placed a glass of wine before her. Taking a tiny sip, she tried to look casually round the restaurant.

By the time the sole arrived, Hilary felt more comfortable but, although she was becoming used to eating alone in restaurants, she still longed for a companion. Can't even talk to Tildi, she thought. People would think she was mad, but at least the fairy was there, although the sphere glinting on the water jug looked dimmer than usual.

"I'll have raspberry meringue with blackcurrant coulis," she announced more boldly to the ever-hovering waiter when he presented the dessert menu.

"Cream, Madame?"

"Please, and coffee to follow." Ignoring the friendly smile of the man at the nearby table as he asked for his bill, Hilary bent and pretended to look in her bags.

"I think he's giving me the eye," she whispered. "It's making me feel awkward. What shall I do?" She looked up quickly to see if anyone had overheard, relieved to see no-one was looking when Tildi's barely audible reply came back.

"Nothing."

The man rose to his feet and Hilary dropped her eyes as he moved towards her, so didn't see what happened as the waiter approached with her dessert. Stickiness oozed through onto her legs as she gazed down at the mess of meringue and crimson fruit spattering her front and nestling in her lap. Red-faced, she tried to scoop it up with a spoon, the buzz of concern surrounding her dreadful, humiliating.

"I am so sorry. Your beautiful suit. I can't apologise enough. You must let me pay for it to be cleaned." The pleasant, deep voice sounded concerned.

"Allow me, Madame," the head waiter was there too with a damp cloth, frowning at the hapless waiter gabbling apologies, most of them in unintelligible Italian.

As red as her suit, Hilary had never felt so mortified, and there was no sign of Tildi to help her. All heads in the restaurant turned at the commotion and people watched as she was escorted to another table, bags and packages borne by a procession of waiters, and settled before a pristine tablecloth and a fresh dessert opposite the attractive stranger, who was still apologising and saying,

"You must allow me to pay for your lunch, it's the least I can do and then please will you have coffee with me, and perhaps a brandy. You've had a nasty shock."

When Hilary felt the flush in her face subside and dared to look up, warm, brown eyes were surveying her.

"How dreadfully embarrassing. I hate public incidents like that, and your lovely suit is ruined. I do hope you were not planning to go anywhere special this afternoon."

Hilary shook her head.

"No. I've finished my shopping," she mumbled.

"Well, that's something. Please enjoy your dessert, it looks delicious, and I'll order coffee." A waiter appeared at the table immediately he raised his hand.

Glad to hide her face, Hilary began eating as Giles – he introduced himself: Giles Campion – chatted easily. He always came to the Savoy for lunch when he was in town. Although he owned a place in Wiltshire, he kept a flat in London in order to visit the theatre. Did she like the theatre?

By the time the coffee and brandy arrived, Hilary was feeling less flustered and was able to look at Giles properly. An irregular set of features, but the brown eyes were sympathetic and he had a charm which put her at ease as he asked where she lived, and chatted about art and theatre. What a cultured man, she thought, entranced.

"I don't really know much about art," she confessed. "I've spent the last years caring for my father, but now he's died I am hoping to go to galleries and the theatre and extend my knowledge."

"You must let me take you to the National Gallery," Giles exclaimed, then stopped. "I'm being too presumptuous. I am sorry. You don't know me from Adam."

"Dad always said to be careful with strangers."

"Quite right too, I would be the same with a lovely daughter like you." He quickly changed the subject, describing the beautiful countryside around his home in Wiltshire.

"I really should be going," Hilary said eventually when the coffee and brandy were long finished and the restaurant nearly empty. Giles signalled the waiter.

"I insist on paying for your lunch," he told her. "And perhaps, to show I am forgiven for my clumsiness, you would allow me to see you to your station. It's such a beautiful day; perhaps we could walk by the river first."

Tildi? But there was no response.

Hilary panicked, then told herself not to be so silly. He's not going to attack me in public. What harm is there in a walk?

Smiling agreement, she allowed Giles to gather up her shopping bags and escort her from the hotel, and as they wandered along the Embankment together, she felt her life was quite perfect.

Far away, a tiny, bedraggled figure was stumbling towards a hole in an ancient oak tree. I'm getting beyond working this hard, Tildi thought, her diminutive fingers grabbing at twigs for support as she made her way unsteadily towards home.

"You skiving off too?"

Tildi jumped as a little voice came from the depths of a moss sofa when she entered the communal sitting room.

"I hoped no-one would see me," Tildi confessed. "What are you doing here Tinka?"

"Pleaded tummy-ache. I couldn't face it today."

Tildi threw herself down beside her friend, closing her eyes against Tinka's brilliant light. There was usually only a soft, relaxing beam emanating from the leaf-lined walls when the fairies rested.

"I can see you've not been out. You're dazzling."

"We all need a rest sometimes."

"I wouldn't mind, but it's so pointless," Tildi complained. "Since that dreadful wizard took over it's horrible. Poor old Queen Mab, she hasn't a clue what's going on now she's blind. She'd have a fit if she knew what he was doing. It's absolute chaos out there."

"What's your latest task?" asked Tinka.

"I think I've finished, apart from keeping an eye on a silly woman. Her father left a little house and a bit of money and I had to encourage her to get in debt. I've done a good job; rounded it off by fixing her up with a con man who'll soon wheedle the house from her." She stretched and eased her aching shoulders. "I've just got to get promotion out of this slave shop so I'm trying to please old Willy Wizard. My next task is a chap who can't stop spending so that shouldn't be too difficult, a nudge here and there and he'll be bankrupt in no time. Probably easier than the woman. She kept having doubts so it was hard work. That's why I'm so tired."

Tinka sat up.

"I'm getting people into debt too. What's the Wizard up to? He's got us all at it."

"He's trying to destroy everything, but he knows Queen Mab would use her last breath to avoid another World War, so he's working on the financial destruction of civilisation. Takes longer, but he can wait. It'll be ages before the little Prince is old enough to take over."

"You are clever Tildi," Tinka said admiringly. "I'd never have worked that out."

"It doesn't take much working out," Tildi said, lying back. "He's got the top brass working flat out on the politicians, spreading greed and corruption. Every Government is in a dreadful mess and their Oppositions wouldn't know which way to turn if they did get voted in, while the goblins are busily distributing drugs everywhere. You've only got to pick up bits and pieces of gossip in the dining room to put the jigsaw together. It's so discouraging after the old Queen's training. We fairies are supposed to help humans improve their lot. Queen Mab's a wonderful woman and done so much good in the past, but now... I can't see any hope."

"It shows. Your aura is really muddy. Get some sleep. We'll be off again tomorrow."

"Yes," murmured Tildi sleepily. "I'll go and see that silly Hilary tomorrow morning and listen to her wittering on about this marvellous man. At least I can make her happy for a bit longer before the crunch comes."

From the White City

by Filipa Kaori

In the late afternoons she walked through the great empty halls and the courtyards wound through with vines and weeds. The crumbling statues cast black shadows and she saw the shapes of half-buried creatures in the bricks. A silhouette flicked at a narrow window, high above – perhaps a lizard, perhaps a ghost.

From the gully far below, Leila heard the dusty gurgle of the river: a man choking on his blood. Two great birds from the plains flapped across the White City, and though no attacks had happened in many years she slid under the shadow of a pillar, tightening her cloak. The birds were giant black fish against the blue stillness of the sky.

Sitting down, Leila glimpsed Osmond gliding out of sight. More often, she just sensed the tinge of his presence in the dry clear air – but usually she was not followed at all. After all, where was she going to go?

He stood for a moment in silence, then flickered across the rosy stones of the courtyard to the marble bench where Leila was casting handfuls of sand, to see what patterns they fell into.

Osmond reached out a long pale hand and swept the just-fallen sand off the bench. The grains had suggested a question mark, or a seahorse.

'Your father requests your presence.'

'And my mother?'

He showed no expression. A soldier-doll. 'I will see to the packing. Perhaps you should take your drink.'

'I have already taken my – drink, this morning.'

The Earl turned on his shiny-booted heel; walked off with a sweep of his white cape; then paused, switching his pale-shining head back. 'I would not like to force the issue.'

Leila tightened her hands, but the nails were too short to do more than dent the palms.

Her hands burned to strike him again, as they had – when was it? – when they had captured her, and brought her here. Because of what she knew. And now – now that they had drained her blood and replaced it with black draughts – they were going to drag her back, for the execution. She knew that her legs were too thin and weak to run – and if she fled into the desert she would only die on the bone-scattered sand. And who would not die tomorrow, rather than today?

Leila watched Mary and Serena slide from the dark jaws of the hall, bearing the jewel-studded skull in which they served the potion. Osmond had his comical moments. Perhaps the skull had belonged to a former prisoner. On the other hand, plenty of skeletons still lay around the stone buildings – unmourned, unburied, softening into dust since the plague. The eyes of the skull were great topazes, tiger-yellow; and they held two tiny Leilas like flames.

Mary pushed Leila's head back and Serena lifted the pearl-patterned silver lid, pressed Leila's chin with her thumb, and poured the liquid down Leila's throat. Leila sat motionless, so as not to choke, as the potion spread through her – thick and black as crude oil, flavoured with mildew and leprous rot from the sides of stagnant drains; with liquid drained from graveyards packed with unquiet dead, with ditchwater clogged with rotting flowers; with hemlock and forgetfulness.

When they let go – their fingerprints red on her arm – she staggered to the fountain and retched into the water now running red.

In the end, Leila did not walk out of the White City. They carried her down the thousand steps of carved bone then put her carefully inside the glittering black carriage built from a hollowed-out giant beetle. It was wonderful how careful people became when you were intended for a sacrifice.

The two waiting-women sat down on each side of Leila and Osmond sat opposite and put his cool fingers on her wrist, chilling her blood, as the carriage hummed forward through the grey desert plains. His face looked drained and grey and she wondered if he felt any regret for his evil.

'Not long now.' Whether he spoke to Leila or the waiting-women was unclear.

'You should ask my father to pay you as much as he gave the people who killed my mother.'

The Earl pressed her wrist between his fingertips, then let go, and her hand fell, dead and frozen, into her lap. Then he hummed: a dirge.

Leila's head dropped towards her shoulder, as the black ink billowed over her brain, and when she raised her lids again the beetle was skimming through the Black City, along the surface of the glassy grey canal, past streets of mushroom-people, their over-grown heads tinted black, blue, red, pink, green; patterned with stripes, dots, or small pictures of cats or daisies; and dripping onto the rain-blurred streets where trapped creatures writhed just under the stone.

When they reached the black castle, they chivvied Leila out of the carriage.

She stood shaky-kneed in the wet courtyard, and Osmond paid the carriage-driver. A few grey-faced skivvies hurried past, pretending not to notice anything. Leila tottered after them but four hands – mendaciously kind but claw-fingered – clamped down and turned her towards the great hall.

The King stood in the doorway – strangely dressed: with neither his crown nor his robes. So she was not to be officially received. He looked old, his eyes dark and cold. Beside him, the Witch stood watching Leila: her face was still as an icicle brushed with pearl-powder and delicate rose-tints crushed from the blood of infants kept from the light.

Leila turned around and stood behind Osmond, who pushed her forward.

'She's had a difficult journey.'

'Her room is ready.' The Witch said with a little extra emphasis: 'We've taken the handles off.'

Leila saw Osmond frown slightly. He looked down at her. 'Leila--'

But she walked past him and into the castle. It should not be said that she could not die like a queen's daughter.

In her quarters, Leila lay down on the bed. Serena, a giant moth, flapped around. So Serena was to stay. The room smelled of dust and sweet chemicals – a smell of death. They had taken away the images of her mother, and the mirror was still smashed. When she had lifted the shawl that covered it, her face had been cut in half.

69

The King's head appeared at the end of the bed. Leila regarded him through eyelash-shadowed lids. He had once been a good man, but now he would do nothing to save her. Without his crown, he looked small, foolish – and bald.

'I hope you're feeling a little better.' He padded round to the side of the bed. 'They tell me you've improved a great deal.'

Leila smiled faintly up at him. Serena had put something into a needle and had jabbed the needle into her skin, and almost no blood was left in her body. She saved her strength for her voice. 'Do you have any message for my mother?'

'I can see that you're tired.'

'I will pass that on.'

The King's eyes sidled to one side – to check that Serena was out of earshot. 'Leila. People re-marry. In this country. Your mother was unhappy before all that. It went back to childhood – having to leave Tehran.'

Murderer. But Leila's lids closed, and she knew that whatever was in the needle had finally poisoned all her blood.

'Sleep, then,' said the King.

And Leila knew she would sleep for a hundred years. Kingdoms would rise and fall; sailing ships would find and start to destroy untouched new lands; castles would be built and crumble into green-veined rubble, and the graveyard where her mother was buried would sink under new buildings, new streets, and feed those poisonous vines that grew above the streets and watched everyone with their shining eyes.

And then, after a hundred years, Leila woke up. No blood was left in her body, and they congratulated her on this.

Her father's wife took her out to get new clothes, and bought what she would want to wear herself. Leila did not resist.

Strangers, their heads obscured by umbrellas, jostled past them on Oxford Street.

Mrs Ansari, Leila and her younger sister sat down with their bags in a café, and Mrs Ansari blew smoke into their eyes.

'So, Leila, looking forward to university?' She brushed a little froth from her immaculately coralled upper lip. 'You're lucky they kept your place for you.'

'I suppose.'

'Indeed.' Mrs Ansari reached over to Sahar, who had twisted her hair into a spiral and was thoughtfully chewing on it. She removed the marmite-dark spiral from Sahar's mouth and it hung, discouraged, by the side of her face. 'Still, at least you won't be wearing your old glad-rags.'

The girls looked down, shoulders sloping, at their coffee.

Mrs Ansari smiled. 'You'll meet some nice boys – Sahar, don't drink, I mean eat sugar from the packet. Mind you, I always did suspect you of harbouring a little ... soft spot for Dr Osmond. But not to pry. Just a hint that you'll do better with someone your own age.'

Leila found that she was nodding.

'We'll get your hair sorted out before you go. You can look through some of my magazines...' Mrs Ansari, caught by some thought, mused in the smoke for a moment. 'Really, I don't know what people expected with that kind of upbringing...' The Englishwoman seemed to lower her lids over a vista of books, the Arabian Nights, and sitting around on cushions eating sherbet and telling dreamy stories. That this vision was not, in fact, so far from the way that things really had been, only made it worse.

But even this implied criticism of her mother did not provoke Leila, and Mrs Ansari, who had watched her with speculation, looked satisfied. She stubbed out her cigarette and Leila watched the silvery-yellow castle above the ashtray tremble into ruins, and then nothing.

Leila and Sahar followed Mrs Ansari out into the wet grey street, and they stepped onto a bus to Lewisham. Through the grimy window, Leila watched the streets pass by, as the bus bore her back to real life.

Maria

by Eddie Gubbins

My heart was pounding in my chest as I looked out of my cabin window across the deck of the Otter and the docks beyond. I was excited because I was waiting for Maria to drive to the ship and take me back to her home to tell her parents that we were to get married.

My mind drifted back to that first time I had met Maria. It seemed so long ago now, that night at a party on the Otter. It had not been an auspicious meeting. I had been sitting on the deck in a corridor, slumped with my back against the bulkhead, trying to regain my senses after too much drink. I was feeling as though I was floating a few feet off the deck, free and above the mere mortals attached to the earth who walked by in a blur.

Then somebody had spoken, breaking through the drink-induced fog and I was looking into pair of dark brown eyes gazing seriously at me through large glasses. The face was round, with a small nose on which her lenses perched. Even through the fog of the alcohol, I was aware that she had a rather large mouth filled with very white regular teeth that smiled at me from very close. The face was framed in brown hair, neatly cut and not quite reaching her shoulders. She introduced herself as Maria Tourvelinen and told me she had come to the party with my friend Brian's girlfriend. Somehow, I had pulled myself together enough to dance with her and ask for a date when the ship was next in Helsinki.

The following time the ship had come to Helsinki, we had met, had a meal and been to a concert. After that, we arranged to see each other at every opportunity and started to make love in her flat whenever I was in Helsinki. After a while, I had asked her to marry me but she refused.

It came to a head one day in April, when the snow had melted and the grass was starting to show green in the parks. We were walking through the park near the sea and it was so sudden and unexpected that I did not know how to handle myself.

Innocently, I had said to her, "I have this feeling we were meant to stay together and grow even closer. I suppose what I am trying to say is that I think it is time for us to talk about getting married."

When I had finished speaking, Maria stopped suddenly. It was as though I had punched her. Roughly, she pulled me over to the rail by the edge of the water. She stood there not looking in my direction but staring out to sea. It was as though she was asking the sea to give her some inspiration, for the words to rise from the waters like a siren and rescue her.

"Its so hard to explain ," she had begun, her voice trembling. "If you were a Finn I would most likely say yes to marrying you. I don't really understand why but there is something which holds me back from saying yes to marrying you."

"I am from this land, this is where I belong," she went on after a pause and I did not reply. "We Finns have feelings which are rooted deep in the soil of our forests and in the history of our people. For all the hard climate, the isolation from the rest of Europe, the snow and the cold, over the centuries, we have built a way of life. All my friends and my parents live here and I am scared to move away. If I married you, I would have to leave my land and my friends."

"Other people have managed," I had replied harshly.

Now, standing looking out of my cabin window waiting anxiously for Maria to arrive, I distinctly recalled her words: "Ah, James you are not like all those other people. Don't you ever listen to yourself when you are talking? When we lie together, our passion spent or as we drink coffee in the mornings, you should pay attention to what you are saying. All the other English seamen I have met talk about the here and now and never give any indication that they ever think about the future. To them the whole purpose of living is for their ship to arrive in Helsinki, what they are going to do while they are in port and whom they will meet. I have noticed, even when we are with other people from the ship, you talk about different things than they do, as though the ship is only a place of work and there are other things to do in life. When you describe England in the spring with the soft rains and the budding flowers, the country bars with huge open fire places and pints of beer, your eyes shine with an inner passion. Though you might not realise it openly, I can see that is where your heart is and England is where you will eventually return to settle down once you have had enough of the sea. James, I have lain in bed listening to you talking about the town you come from, about your friends and family and I know that you have roots as deep in that community as I have here. Your bonds to your family are as tight as my own. Our roots go deep into the soil of the places and into the soul of the people from whom we sprang. I am tied to my past and you are to yours."

"Maria, that may have been true in the past but events change our outlook on life. If we got married, your family would become my family, your home my home. My attitude to England would change just in the act of marrying you!" I had emphasised each word by almost shaking her.

"No, it would be like caging an animal which has always been free to roam and cutting it off from its home. You do not talk about the sea in the same way as the others, as though you are going to spend the rest of your life at sea. Always in the background of what you are saying, I have detected that if the right job came along, you would leave the sea without hesitation. Don't get me wrong, I am not saying you do not like going to sea. All I know is that I am certain that one day you will say to yourself, I have had enough of the sea and then you will find a job ashore and that job will be in England. James at the moment, I don't think I could leave Finland and come to live in England even for you."

A silence had fallen between us after that. It was not the silence of contentment nor of anger but of bafflement at how this divide could have grown so swiftly. No doubt both of us were thinking about how we could rediscover the excitement of being together which we had had before the question of marriage had arisen.

It came as a shock to me when I realised that Maria had inadvertently opened my eyes to the way I thought about a career at sea. For the first time in my life I began to realise that the sea was not everything to me but only another job. The sea which had dominated my life since as long as I could remember, could this only be a passing phase in my life? I asked myself as the doubts about the foundation of my living began to make all certainty crumble. Would I be able to leave the life I had built for myself at sea if I found another job which did not involve going away from home? Was my character so rooted in England that it was obvious to Maria, while not to me, that I would finally settle down in England? Was Maria right in claiming that it would be impossible for me sail to Helsinki for the rest of my life, that in the end the excitement would fade and I would seek a more stable life style?

After our disagreement, the Otter had sailed to other ports than Helsinki and for a long time I had not seen Maria. All through this forced separation, in her letters, Maria had maintained her stand of not wanting to get married.

When I had finally arrived back in her flat in Helsinki, she had told me before we had made love: "Your being away for so long has convinced me that I cannot live without you. As far as I can think, this means we will have to get married. I suspect that nothing has changed between us. Our getting married will mean I have to come and live in England at some time in the future. If going to live in England is the only way I can be with you all the time, I will be willing to leave Finland and come with you."

All I could say was thank you. She had been aware of how I felt towards her for a long time. For me it had been an age to wait silently, hoping each time we met for her to say those words. At the time there was little I could say.

After she arrived on the Otter, we had lunch and it turned into one of those happy occasions which come unanticipated, which I can even now recall in every detail as though it was only yesterday.

Captain Harris ordered a special meal, even going so far as to break out some of his much cherished wine which he usually kept locked in his locker. He played the gracious host, dressed in his best uniform, presiding over the meal with genial competence. Indeed, he appeared to be genuinely pleased that Maria and I had decided to get married. I had shyly told him of our plans on the way round the Finnish coast from Helsinki to Kotka. As I came off watch, he had called me into his cabin for a gin before we went to bed. His normally serious expression had almost changed to a beaming smile and he had insisted we had one more than our usual ration of gin.

All my friends were sitting around the table. Most had delayed their usual headlong rush to leave the ship and catch the bus for Helsinki. We sat in the same saloon where I and Maria had first met, surrounded by memories of the party and my first kiss. Above the echo of my friends laughing and drinking through lunch, were the ghosts of other friends who had been at the party that night.

75

The toasts that lunchtime were for the ship and for Maria who sat in her seat by Captain Harris sparkling and smiling. When the last of the wine had been consumed, all those present insisted on lining up and kissing Maria in turn. As an after thought they all shook my hand and wished me good luck.

When we finally got back to my cabin to fetch my bag, Maria flung her arms round my neck, kissing my lips through the taste of the wine. The warmth of her body and her trembling excitement made my heart beat faster and my body pushed against hers as though I had no control over my behaviour.

"Let us make love here in your cabin before we drive home," she had whispered in my ear. "I have always wanted to make love on board the Otter and in your bunk. You have always come ashore to my flat whenever you are in Helsinki, so I have never had the chance."

We made love slowly and silently, conscious of the people walking past the door of my cabin. It was wonderful. Afterwards we lay in each others arms laughing about how we should have done this that first time she had been aboard the Otter.

Then, after drinking a coffee, we went arm in arm out into the cold, down the gangway and into her car. Even after so much time, I can still see her smiling face as she waved goodbye to Bill who was leaning on the ship's rail watching us depart and, if I think deeply, experience my sense of happiness and the rightness of what we were about to do.

The light was growing dim as we left the Otter in the middle of the afternoon and Maria had to turn on the car headlights. As we sped through the frozen landscape towards Maria's home, the woods on each side of the road looked dark and forbidding. The trees were individually visible close to the road but fading into a dark mass further away. We hardly talked, content to let the dirty snow at the side of the road slip by as the studded car tyres threw little chips of ice into the air. We were still, I suppose, enveloped in the warm relaxing glow of our love-making, in many ways outside of time.

Through half closed eyes I recognised the approach to the village where Maria lived, thinking vaguely that it would not be long before we arrived at her parents' house.

When the car started down the steep slope just before the

edge of the village, there was a bang from the front of the car and I sat up in my seat conscious of a sense of fear creeping into the car. Maria was now fighting the wheel, the gears and the brakes. She was staring straight ahead, a vein throbbing in her temple, her mouth a tight, thin line. The skin was pulled tight across her cheeks in an expression of fear and her back was rigid, away from the back of her seat.

The car was gathering speed down the hill and I looked away from Maria and out of the windscreen. A sharp bend was coming towards us too fast. Everything seemed suspended. I stopped breathing, my mind went blank and all my muscles were stiff and unmoving. It was apparent to me even through my fear that the car was not going to get round the bend at the speed it was travelling.

I must have called out something to Maria but she did not answer. A piercing scream seemed to come from outside the car, a scream which told Maria to hold tight. The frozen snow was flashing past the car, throwing up clouds of spray exactly like a ship in heavy weather. The car was bouncing horribly on its shock absorbers as it left the road and headed for the trees. There was a loud bang as an object hit the side of the car and pain was shooting through my body as the sound of grating metal filled the air.

Another loud bang, more pain as my body bounced off some metal and I felt I was flying through the air. My leg smashed against something rough and hard and my side was being dragged over what felt like broken glass. Another thump and I came to rest.

Events became completely disoriented then. It was cold and I can remember trying to find out what had happened to Maria. I tried to get to my feet but everywhere there was pain and my legs would not hold me upright. My eyes would not focus and all around it was dark. Somehow I was outside the car, even my fuddled brain could work that out. I was lying in the frozen snow slowly getting colder and colder. The cold did not matter too much because the colder I became, the less the pain throbbed through my body.

Then I was surrounded by people and flashing lights. I tried to ask about Maria but all they did was push me back onto a blanket. They were fiddling with my legs and I confess I screamed with the pain. Then I was inside a vehicle travelling at speed through a village with the people in the green coats still leaning over me wiping my face and holding my hand. The vehicle stopped, the doors were flung open and I was being pushed at great speed along a corridor on a trolley. Doors clanged shut in our wake and more people were leaning over me looking at my legs. I heard a voice as though from a long way off moaning Maria's name and then there was nothing.

It was like floating in a tank of liquid, relaxed and secure. There was no sound and the sense of being detached from anything else was very strong. The light was soft but dappled, dark and bright as though I was lying in water under a tree. There was no time and my body did not exist. It was wonderful.

Then the noise started, a relaxing sort of sound as though I was lying, dozing, on a beach with my eyes closed listening to the waves breaking on the shore. A noise in the background, soothing absorbing, helping me sink back below the surface of consciousness, floating, relaxed and secure. It was only in the mind, not in the body.

Then I was rising above the surface and the soothing sensation of floating was thrust aside by the pain. The colour in my mind was now red. I was surrounded by red but I tried to get back to my floating. It was still all in the mind but I was surrounded by pain.

As I broke the surface of the liquid, the pain started to separate. Soon I could identify different parts of my body by the type of pain. Then I was fully conscious and I wished I had stayed in the liquid. My head had been taken over by a trainee drummer who was practising the same phrase over and over again. My leg hurt with stabbing bursts of pain as though somebody was pushing a knife into the muscle and twisting it savagely. As my heart beat rapidly, I could feel my side and arm throbbing as though somebody was hammering to get out.

I opened my eyes slowly but had difficulty focussing at first. Raising my hand, I rubbed my eyes and was surprised to feel bandages. The general whiteness of my surroundings started to come into focus. Trying to sit up proved difficult, if not impossible. The red curtain descended again as soon as I tried to move. Pain filled my whole world so much I wanted to cry out. Steeling myself against the onset of the pain, I raised my head sufficiently to look around and found my leg encased in plaster, raised above the bed on some kind of harness.

Just as I was sinking back onto the bed, sweat beading my

brow, a girl in a white uniform and with a cheerful face crossed the room into the direct line of my vision. She went to the door and shouted something I did not understand. Soon, another girl appeared and between them they managed to raise me into some semblance of a comfortable sitting position. I asked her in a very hoarse voice, what had happened to Maria but she only shrugged and made signs that she did not understand what I was saying. It was obvious she did not speak English or so I reasoned. I told myself I would have to wait until somebody who spoke some English came to see me before I would find out about Maria.

Later a doctor came to examine me but he would only answer question about my condition. With a touch of a smile playing at the corner of his mouth, he told me to lie back and try to relax. I was helpless to do anything else, though I dreamed about walking out of the room. Instead, I lay back and let the nurses deal with my needs. After an injection, the pain stayed in the background and I was able to relax.

A long time passed, or so it seemed to me, when the door to my room opened and Mrs Tourvelinen was standing there looking at me. My heart missed a beat when I saw her. She was visibly drawn into herself but rigid as though trying to hold herself in control. She looked so much like my Maria, I wanted to cry out. She came a few steps into the room and then hesitated for what, to me lying captive in that bed, seemed like hours. Then she pulled back her shoulders with a mighty effort and walked across the floor to stand by the bed.

Suddenly as though all the courage she had stored up had vanished, she collapsed onto the bed and pulled my face into her breasts. She sat like that, rocking back and forth, stroking my hair like a mother with a son she wants to protect from the evils of the world. I could feel the tightness inside, the cording of her muscles as she fought to control her emotions. She lost the private battle with herself. Tears cascaded down her face and sobs shook her frame.

I knew then what she had come to that hospital room to tell me. It was as though her grief had been transmitted without words. There was no need for her to try to compose herself but she fought for control so that she could tell me what had happened. Stiffening myself against the onset of my grief and anger, I strove to make my face appear as unemotional as possible.

When she was able to start, she was very blunt and brutal. I suppose at the time there was no other way in which she could have braced herself to speak.

"Maria died in the crash and the funeral was yesterday." Her face was still wet with tears, the anguish of her expression showing how she was trying to comfort me but finding the right words was proving difficult. "I hope you will be able to forgive me for not telling you as soon as you regained consciousness but the doctor told me that you must not be stressed too much so soon after coming round. In addition, I wanted to tell you myself what had happened. I could not leave that painful duty to somebody unknown to you."

"The car hit a tree on Maria's side and she was crushed against the door," she went on, even though it was obvious she wanted to hide the memory from herself but was compelled to tell me what had happened. "Somehow you were thrown clear of the car because the emergency service people found you lying some distance away jammed between two small trees. The doctors and nurses fought to save her life. They managed to get her back to the hospital but she died the day after she arrived without regaining consciousness. At the same time they were trying to put your leg back together and bring you out of your coma. My husband and I have taken turns to sit by your bed. It has been over a week since you were brought here and when they told me you had regained your senses, I thought it was time to come and tell you what had happened."

While she was talking, I kept my face impassive but my throat was so tight, I could not say anything. All I could do was sit and stare wide eyed at the wall. My mind tried to grasp what Mrs Tourvelinen was telling me. I knew her words were important. I tried to reason out what her words foretold about my future but I could not hold onto the words long enough to understand. My stomach felt as though it had been placed in a freezer. Cold fluid filled my veins. Numbness was rapidly spreading towards my brain. Echoing through my mind was just one refrain and this was not really a part of me. What am I to say to a mother who has just lost her daughter while I lived through the same crash? What comfort can I bring to this vulnerable woman when I feel so empty and bereft of any reason for living?

After she had finished telling me as much about the crash and what had happened afterwards as she could, we sat in that white painted hospital room in silence. We were lost in our own thoughts but the presence of the other brought a feeling of sharing and a great deal of comfort. She held my hand and after a while, quietly left, whispering goodbye as she went out of the door. I did not move but lay still staring at the wall. The silence stretched into my small world. All alone I sensed the white walls crowding in on me, making me feel I was in some sort of snowy hell.

I cried then, deep sobs wrung from the depths of my very soul. The shaking tore at my body until there was no emotion left and I could lay back. I now had to confront the images from the past that rose up out of my mind to join me as though they were real. The nurses frequently bustled into the room and performed their secret rites before leaving to find their next victim. Through this time, I hardly noticed their passage or the passing of the hours or the days. For a while it was as though I was suspended from the bed, looking down at events as they happened, completely divorced from the person lying there. At other times, I was submerged below the oceans of my emotions trying to swim through an opaque darkness that had no end.

What fools we humans are, I kept telling myself in the few moments when I was conscious and rational. We build in detail our future plans in the certain knowledge that what we plan will come to pass. All the time there is lurking in wait the sudden event that shatters all the certainty from life in a fleeting moment. We are then all left naked before the world. All we humans beaver away like ants to construct relationships, to lay the foundations on which we base our lives. But, I kept asking myself as the time floated by as I lay in that hospital bed, what for? Why do we plan and what is the point of making foundations for our future life? Who in the whole universe can answer me that question honestly? At times when the plans we lay are crumbling before our eyes and there is nothing we can do to save them, the whole exercise of living appears such a huge joke. Something or somebody must get a whole lot of pleasure out of watching the manoeuvring and posturing of these earthly beings as all their plans and hopes turn to dust in their hands. How often does the bad appear to triumph over the good? That is true, I hear myself almost shout. Why do the bad win most of the rewards in life? Why do the bad seem to enjoy life much more than the good? Or have I got the meaning of life all wrong? Am I really looking at the bad and the good? It is a mystery to most of us as to why some people always win and yet others always lose. It does not look as though there is any connection to good or evil. It is a mystery of which most of us are not privileged to glimpse the answer.

Do Unto Others

by Clive Gilson

(Loosely based on Charles Perrault's Toads & Diamonds)

A broken home is rarely anything other than a trial for all those who have to live within its walls. Apart from the trauma caused by the breaking up of a previously coherent family unit, subsequent actions and hardships often make life extremely difficult and taxing for each and every one of the unhappy participants in these events. The time when and the place where lives are squeezed and wrung out under such circumstances is, in the great scheme of things, immaterial, but for one such family, living in a small village in one of England's elm-folded western valleys, the struggle for a good life was particularly hard.

Mrs Milligan and her two daughters, Estelle and Hazel, lived in a small redbrick cottage that stood in a forlorn and lonely spot at the far end of an old and dusty village high street. Where there had once been rows of vegetables growing in the front garden and a pretty orchard of neatly pruned and espaliered fruit trees in the back garden, there was now nothing more than a choking of weeds and ivy-smothered, skeleton branches. Ever since the departure of her husband some years previously, the family had scraped a living by taking in washing and ironing, and doing cleaning jobs for some of the village's more prosperous families. The two girls could remember little other than traipsing around after their mother, visiting house after well-appointed house, in a desperate quest to earn money amid fineries and fripperies that they could never hope to afford for themselves.

Of the two daughters, Estelle was the spitting image of her mother, although blessed, thankfully, with the softness of youth, while Hazel, two years the younger, was the very picture of her father. The similarities between mother and eldest daughter did not end in looks. They were both of a similar personality and disposition, being proud and disagreeable to an extreme, convinced as they were that they were the victims of a cruel and heartless man. Because of this undoubted sin perpetrated against them by the ogre, they both believed the world owed them bigtime for all of their suffering and undoubted grace under poverty's iron heel. It was no surprise to anyone in the village that Mrs Milligan had remained single for so many years.

Hazel, on the other hand, was one of the sweetest, kindest and most courteous little girls in the whole county. She had a radiant smile that lit her face up with a pure and natural beauty that brightened the gloom well beyond the physical limits of light. No matter what the hardship or the provocation, she always tried to see the best in any situation and so, despite the tragic circumstances of her family's life in the closeted world of Upper Risington, she remained a shining beacon of happiness when all around was shadowed in darkness and despondency.

Life in the Milligan household was a bleak affair at the best of times and Mrs Milligan suffered unaccountably from her nerves due to the continual reminder of her bastard husband that blazed out from her youngest daughter's face every minute of the day. She would have been quite content for the girl to spend her days out of sight and her nights locked in her bedroom had it not been for the fact that Hazel never complained about chapped hands or ironing elbow. Hazel was quite unlike Estelle, who preferred to spend her time, when not pretending to dust someone's knick-knacks, watching day time television soap operas and reality shows about other people's lives. Mother and eldest daughter doted on each other and regularly shared the little luxuries that came their way when there was a purse full of cash left over from the benefits payments and the hourly wages earned from charring.

Poor Hazel, meanwhile, worked her fingers to the bone in a never-ending cycle of drudgery and domestic slavery, washing other people's clothes and ironing them, cleaning the house, cooking meals and fetching thick, black coal from the back yard bunker. She was never allowed, now that she was blossoming into a beautiful young woman, to leave the house and accompany her mother and sister on their daily errands and cleaning jobs. Her only respite from the drab surroundings of the little redbrick cottage was a weekly trip to visit an aged one time neighbour, a Miss Huddlestone, who had been kind enough to babysit for the girls in happier times before the family had split asunder.

Miss Huddlestone now lived in a sheltered retirement bungalow in the next village, Lower Risington, and every Wednesday afternoon Hazel popped into the village shop, bought a large Bakewell tart and a bag of lemon sherbets, and walked, come rain or shine, the two miles to her friend's neat little home.

One Wednesday afternoon, with the sound of her sister's harsh voice still grating in her ears, Hazel put the usual cakes and sweets into a plastic bag and walked all the way to Lower Risington bathed in bright spring sunlight. She was particularly fond of spring, heralding as it did the lengthening of days and the chance to hang the washing outside to dry in good, clean, fresh air. On this particular Wednesday the world was particularly bright and full of goodness, with the hedgerows sparkling in their blossom coats and the birds busy with their nestbuilding songs. Hazel was in a fine mood when she knocked on her friend's door and together they enjoyed quite the happiest afternoon tea they had ever had together.

As Miss Huddlestone drained the last dregs of her Earl Gray and wiped Bakewell tart crumbs from the lightly sprouting beard that covered her withered old chin, she turned to young Hazel, took her hand and whispered, "You are such a lovely girl, my dear, so pretty and kind, and you've never forgotten to come and see me. I want to give you a gift."

Hazel smiled sweetly and protested that visiting her friend was enough of a gift and that she wouldn't think of accepting anything else, but the old woman paid no attention to her whatsoever.

"I think you'll like the gift," continued the old girl, smiling broadly. "You see, I'm not just any dear old bat, dear, I'm a dear old witch, dear!"

Hazel tried very hard not to laugh because she didn't want to appear rude, but she couldn't help smirking slightly behind her hand.

"I know, I know," said the old woman, "it's all very hard to fathom, especially when you're so young and inexperienced. Anyway, I've decided to reward you for all of your kindness and for taking the time and trouble to come all this way every week. From now on, whenever you smile a real smile, a smile that breaks like sunrise on a clear blue summer morning, you'll find a little pearl or diamond in your pocket!"

Hazel laughed out loud and beamed at the old woman. "Oh go on, Mary, you're so funny," and as she grinned at the old woman with every ounce of her happy, joking little soul, she put her hand into her jeans pocket. No one in this fair land's long history could ever have been as surprised or delighted as little Hazel. Between her fingers she could feel something small and hard and round, and she was sure that there had been nothing in her pocket just a moment ago. She pulled out her tightly bunched fist and opened her fingers out slowly and nervously. Right there in the palm of her hand was a perfectly round, moonshine pearl of such beauty and radiance that the girl was unable to move or to speak for a full five minutes. As the shock and surprise subsided, Hazel realised that she did believe in witches and fairies and she let out a yelp of joy, hugging old Miss Huddlestone so tightly that the old dear thought she would burst her seams.

By the time that Hazel had greeted everyone she met on her way home that evening with a massive smile and wave, by the time that she had expressed her joy to the world a hundred and one times, her pockets were positively bulging with gem stones and pearls. She arrived home a little later than usual to find her mother and her sister waiting impatiently for their tea. As soon as the front door shut they both began to scold her for being so late and so inattentive to their well-being.

"I'm sorry for being late, Mum," replied Hazel, smiling in spite of the hurtful things that were being said. She walked over to the coffee table in the middle of the living room and filled the spaces in between empty cola cans and the over flowing ashtray with a heap of brightly shining diamonds and pearls. "But I can explain…"

"What the bloody hell have you been doing?" screamed her mother as Estelle immediately knelt down by the coffee table and started to pick out all of the biggest diamonds from the pile. "Where the chuffin' hell have they come from?"

Hazel told her mother and her sister the whole story about their mutual friend, about her being a witch and about her wonderful gift. By the end of the story the entire family was beaming. At last their suffering was over and their fortunes assured. Mrs Milligan cuddled her youngest daughter to her ample bosom for the first time in years and called her things like 'darling' and 'poppet' and 'precious'. Every time that Hazel smiled at her mother or her sister she reached into her jeans pockets and added another sparkling gem to the pile on the coffee table. By nine o'clock that evening the family had enough booty in their living room to retire from the domestic cleaning and washing business forever more, and Hazel, tired out from smiling so much with all of the love in the house, went to bed to dream happy dreams of a future where neither the bogeyman nor the tallyman would ever come to get her again.

Once Hazel was safely tucked up in the land of dreams, Mrs Milligan, having allowed her eldest daughter to keep a few of the smaller diamonds, then swept the pile of jewels into a plastic food container. Sharing a bottle of fizzy wine with Estelle, she set about making her own plans for a future far removed from the heartache and stress of her current life.

"Hazel's luck should be yours by right, my girl," she said to Estelle. "From now on we'll keep her here on Wednesdays while you visit that daft old bugger. With a little bit of work you should be able to get her to do the same trick for you. She was half raving when we moved in here and she's obviously gone the whole hog now. Treat her nice for a few weeks and we'll be millionaires by Christmas."

"I'm not visiting the daft crow, ma," replied Estelle with a whine. "She's old and she smells and everything."

Mrs Milligan looked at daughter number one with a hard, ratty stare.

"Do I have to?" whimpered the girl.

"You'll do as you're bloody well told, miss," hissed her mother, and with that, and despite all of the sullen whinnying and misery that Estelle brought to bear, schemes and plans were laid for the following week.

Come the Wednesday afternoon, Mrs Milligan locked Hazel in the under stairs cupboard and frog marched her eldest daughter to the village shop, where she bought the finest assortment of soft centres that the proprietor had to offer. Then she ordered a taxi to take Estelle to Lower Risington. In no time at all Estelle found herself on Miss Huddlestone's doorstep, box of chocolates in hand, forcing the most wheedling of smiles across her barely cleaned teeth. The taxi parked up at the kerb side, Estelle having told the driver that she'd be no more than ten minutes.

Miss Huddlestone opened the door to her beloved Hazel but found there instead the gum-chewing, pony-tailed whine that marked Estelle's presence in the world. She let out a long sigh, but nonetheless she ushered the girl into her home and brought the tray full of tea things through to the front room.

Estelle sloped into one of the armchairs, declining a drink or a biscuit. She chucked the box of chocolates at the old lady and pouted.

"Are you sure you won't have a cup of tea, dear?" asked Miss Huddlestone

"No," grunted the girl.

"Oh well," replied the old woman. She took a sip of Earl Gray and looked at her visitor over the rim of her teacup.

"Would you mind awfully fetching my glasses from the kitchen? I must have left them on the worktop and I can barely see anything without them."

"What am I," complained the girl, "you're bleedin' slave or something? I'm not a skivvy, you know!"

Estelle gave the old bat one of her looks, a look that told you to sod off because you were boring and didn't understand anything important. Miss Huddlestone, who was no stranger to angry young women, having spent many years in secondary education before taking up her current line of work as a white witch, returned the look, eyeball to eyeball, pensioner to youth, and won the contest hands down.

"I'll tell you what you are, dear," she said calmly and quietly, as she put her cup down on the tray. "You're a rude and spoilt little hussy, definitely your mother's daughter. You've all the breeding of the pigsty, but despite your ill manners and your attitude I will give you a gift, just like I gave lovely Hazel a gift. Every time you give someone one of those vacuous and disobliging looks you will find a little present in your pocket."

"Vac…what?" muttered Estelle

"Just leave now, dear, before I get really pissed off."

Estelle had her pride. No one had a right to talk to her like that. She gave the old hag her most vicious, drop-dead stare and stormed out of the little house. She slammed the front door shut and jumped into the waiting taxi, barking orders to the driver to get her back to Upper Risington pronto. That might have been the end of Estelle's ordeal, except that Miss Huddlestone's power to grant gifts was unparalleled anywhere in England's green valleys. The car had only gone a few hundred metres down the road when the driver slammed on the brakes and turned to look at the girl on the back seat.

"What the bloody hell is that smell?" he hissed nasally, holding his nose tightly shut between his thumb and forefinger. Estelle pouted, stuck her hands in her pockets and was about to deliver her best ignoring look when she made a dreadful discovery. Her right hand, rather than being thrust into a soft, warm pocket full of dark, tight nothingness, had actually made contact with something altogether more disgusting. She felt something soft and warm all right, but whatever it was it was certainly of some substance.

"Out," yelled the taxi driver, in a horrified, gagging voice, and out the girl got. She was left stranded in the middle of a country lane on a bright and sunny summer afternoon with nothing to show for her effort but a pocket full of dog mess and a smell that seemed to follow her whichever way the wind blew.

When Estelle eventually reached her home, bedraggled and exhausted after her long walk under a baking sun, she hung around in the front garden, not daring to enter the house. As soon as her mother caught sight of her lurking there in the front garden she rushed out to find out how the afternoon had gone.

"Well?" she demanded urgently, before taking a step back and asking, "Have you trodden in something?"

Estelle stood there dumbly, mouthing words but unable to make any sounds, and so, after a few mute moments during which she could feel her mother's anger rising, she pulled her right hand out of her jeans pocket and let little gobbets of half baked ordure drip from her fingers. At the sight of the awful gift given to her by Miss Huddlestone both mother and daughter wailed like banshees, cursing their ill luck and the name of poor Hazel to hell and back.

"It's all her fault," screamed Mrs Milligan. "I'll beat her black and blue, I'll tan her, I'll strip that smile of hers from her bones!"

Needless to say, poor little Hazel, who had been locked away in the cupboard for the whole of the hot and sweaty afternoon, had finally come to the end of her own tether. When her mother unlocked and opened the door, Hazel burst through the opening like a small

89

hand grenade and ran out of the house, down the road and far, far away, taking her wonderful gift with her. No one in Upper Risington ever heard from her again, although there were rumours that she ended up in London, where, it was said, she married a prince or a famous footballer and lived happily ever after.

As for Estelle, try as she might she couldn't break the habit of her early years and she never learned to smile. Eventually, after suffering many years of ridicule and evil odours, she learned to never wear any clothes that had pockets attached, but by then the following wind that had first assailed her one Wednesday afternoon in her teens had saturated her skin. Wherever she went people called her names until, one summer some years later, she took herself off to a remote corner of the Lake District, lay down in a corner of a field and there, as far as anyone knows, she still remains.

Mrs Milligan, meanwhile, minding the Tupperware tub full of diamonds and pearls taken from Hazel when she had come home from visiting Miss Huddlestone's bungalow, found that a life backed up by a little capital was much more bearable and now lived in genteel respectability in a seaside villa on the south coast with a retired bank manager, which goes to show that happy endings, even with Estelle's tragic and lonely life taken into account, usually have little to do with what some people deserve.

Caring

by Enid Meredith

Today there's a new girl coming from the agency. I expect I'm going to give her a hard time. What do they think they're playing at? Sending out clueless girls to bungle taking care of me? Care agency! - They couldn't care for a row of rag dolls!

She's late - Naomi - the carer who's been here a few times before. The new one's arrived and I have refused to speak to her - so she's slunk off to the kitchen. I can hear her putting plates and cutlery away, bashing and rattling. Now she's come back into the room and she's smiling at me. Soon wipe that off.

'I hope you've not put my things away in the wrong places so the regular girl can't find them.'

She shakes her head, still smiling. I give her my most impressive scowl.

'Where's Naomi? It's after 8.00 o'clock. She's late. I don't appreciate being kept waiting.'

She shrugs, continuing to smile at me. This irritates me even more.

'Are you mentally defective? Foreign? Or just plain stupid?'

This gets to her. She's a thin girl with frizzy, red hair and big, pale blue eyes.

'The middle one. I'm foreign', she snaps. 'From Donegal - that's in Ireland. As far as I know I have all my marbles and a first in German and French from Trinity - that's a university in Dublin. Did you know that?'

I nod but keep my face expressionless. 'I want to be washed', I say.

She fixes me with the pale blue eyes. 'I don't know why Naomi is late but I do know I'm not getting you in the hoist on my own. You'll have to wait.'

I say nothing but meet her gaze.

She is the first to look away. 'Will you be wanting a cup of tea now?'

'No. What I want is a cigarette. Do you know how to roll them?'

Her mouth tightens. 'I don't smoke meself but I can do roll ups. Used to do them for my brother.'

I lift an arm towards the table by the window. 'The machine is there plus paper and tobacco.' The dull ache in my arm grows teeth and goes to work on my nerves. I grimace and let my arm flop to the mattress like a dead jellyfish. The savage, neuralgic pain subsides to the dull ache.

Where is Naomi? My pad is wet and offensive to my nostrils and I want to defecate. I use that word to myself because it sounds more bearable than 'shit'. I can't get to the commode on my own. I need the hoist. To use the hoist I must have two carers. My skin is crawling with the insect irritation of stale sweat.

Naomi - I need you and this hostile Irish girl to wash me, dress me, place me in my wheelchair - upright, braked and ready for the rest of another interminable day. I will be parked in front of my window, the sight of the sea coaxing my mind to roam unfettered and I will commit my thoughts to the recorder, waiting patiently upon the table, since my hands will no longer obey my desire to write. And I will be fed by spoon and will drink through a straw. But none of this can be achieved without Naomi.

The Irish girl is at the table with her back to me. I observe her backbone, forming a thin cross with her bra, through the white nylon tabard she is wearing. I cannot see what she is doing but there are several slim cigarettes by her left elbow, each with its filter. I insist on filters. Curious really since I am not inclined to prolong my life. Smoking is a small pleasure, but it is a pleasure.

'I suppose you have a name, girl.'

She turns, glances at me then turns back to her task. 'Cate. That's Cate with a 'C' and I am called Caitlin in my own country.'

I make a noise. To my ears, it is halfway between a snort and a laugh.

'Well, Cate with a 'C', I suggest you phone your agency, which promises much and delivers little, and which I have named the Wizard of Oz - an impressive front but not much behind - and find

out what has become of my second carer. In short, where is Naomi?'
She nods and fishes her mobile phone from the pocket at the front of
her uniform. She looks at me as she locates the number but, before
she can make contact with Oz, we hear a key in the lock and Naomi
appears, her dark and beautiful face lit with a great, white smile. My
heart lifts. Rescue from my noisome pit.

'Hello there, Naomi, what happened to you?' asks Cate.

I arrange my face into a scowl although really I want to grin
with relief.

'Yes, where were you?' I glare up at the Ormolu clock on the
mantel, kept ten minutes fast on my orders. 'You are thirty eight
minutes late.'

She stops smiling. '*Twenty* eight minutes late. The blame
rests firmly on the bus company. My bus broke down on the cliff top.
We had to wait nearly twenty minutes for a relief bus. I would have
been even later if I had not set out early. And the new bus was so
slow because it was picking up passengers from every stop. Good
that it's such a sunny day.'

Cate nods, 'Indeed 'tis a lovely morning to be stranded on a
cliff top.'

I make an impatient noise - the nearest I can get to
'hurrumph' whatever that may sound like. My head swivels towards
the window. The sun hovers above a grey-edged cloud. 'Sunny day!'
I scoff. 'It's going to rain. Any fool can see that.'

'Okay, okay,' says Naomi, 'and good morning to you - let's get you
feeling more comfortable.' She removes my pad and then motions to
Cate to bring the hoist over to my bed. She trundles it across and
together they arrange the sling beneath me. One, two three they
intone and roll me about like a pale, smelly sausage, until I am
centred in the sling and they can arrange the straps, hook them to the
hoist. I hear the whine of the electric motor as I am lifted from the
bed and swung across towards the commode. The goods are in
transit, ship to shore.

Naomi turns her head and looks out of the window. 'There!
The cloud's gone and the sun's coming out again.'

'I need the commode and I need it now.' My voice is
twanging with anxiety. I wish I could accept it. My helplessness.

But I can't. The operation is complete. I am seated on the commode and the sling has been removed and I am ready, as Naomi says, to move my bowels. Naomi and Cate chat as they make my bed. Their words float across: 'This guy - really fit....d'you go to that club? Cool!...Mum wants me to help out more - but I'm just not earning enough....what a holiday! - on the beach a lot - loads of guys, really hot....the guys?...no the sun, donut!'

'I'm ready to have my wash now,' I bleat testily. They are spreading a waterproof sheet over my bed. Cate goes off and returns with a bowl of water, towel, flannels and my special washing cream. I am back in the hoist and am lowered on to my bed. I poke an unsteady hand into the bowl. 'Too cold!' Cate goes to get a jug of hot water. Naomi adds it, dips her elbow carefully into the bowl as if it is a baby's bath. She nods and smiles at me. 'That'll be fine now, I think.' They wash me thoroughly, turning me this way and that, but with gentleness. As usual, I ask to be towelled dry briskly. I enjoy my wash. A small pleasure, like smoking, but a pleasure. I am sprinkled with talc like a mince pie with icing sugar and then a clean pad, knickers, no bra - no breasts now to speak of - and my best silk kaftan style dress is manoeuvred into place. My feet are encased in sky blue slippers to match the dress. My hair is brushed.

Today my son visits with my two grandchildren and, unfortunately, my daughter in law. I think of her as I am being winched into the wheelchair and the neck brace is fixed to the back of the chair. I am arranged at the table opposite the sea view. India was not my choice, of course. But, as Piers said, 'Not your choice to make, mother. I want to marry her and that's that.' That was that. I felt alone. Was used to having my son treating me with respect and consideration. Used to having Piers around keeping me in touch with the world. She made him buy an overlarge house in Twickenham. Five bedrooms, three bathrooms and a cloakroom. Ideal for the obsessively clean or the terminally incontinent. I was occasionally invited to stay. Christmas, Easter, when Daisy and Charlie were born, odd weekends. Now it's not possible, of course. And anyway, her mother practically lives with them. Always coming down from Manchester, Giggleswick or wherever she hails from to spend weeks with them.

94

Piers seems to put up with her endless visits and India (bet she wasn't born India) loves to be ministered to and have the children minded while she goes off to play tennis, attend coffee mornings, or whatever she gets up to. She doesn't work. Is allegedly writing a book. What about? Flower arranging? Macramé? How to restring tennis racquets? She brings out the worst in me. I hate her over-refined counties drawl. I would prefer it if she spoke like her mother. Northern, and doesn't try to hide it. Doesn't try to hide her dislike of me, either, come to that. Her daughter's propaganda, I expect. I hate the way India repeats everything I say, to Piers, with a catty little spin. Her views get back to me of course when he remonstrates with me. Apparently, I am critical of everything she says - or cooks.

I am brought out of my gloomy reverie by Naomi asking what I want to eat. I reflect. 'First a fag then two soft-boiled eggs. And I mean soft. One piece of marmite toast. Oh and some orange juice. Don't forget the ice.'
　　　Cate goes off to cook and Naomi lights me a cigarette and holds it to my lips. I take a deep drag. She removes the cigarette until I signal with a nod that I want it back. We progress to just above the filter. She stubs it out. My orange juice arrives with an ice-cube bobbing on the surface. I think how much I would like a real drink. Alcohol was always a problem. My false friend. Largely responsible for my illness. Neural degeneration brought on by alcoholism. The specialist's face floats in front of me. Then the rest of him, immaculately tailored in black. A handsome, tanned, silver-haired sod. Sepulchral delivery in finely modulated tones. The bad news given with suave gravity and precision. The other bad news, the huge bill, parchment engraved with copper-plate handwriting, arriving on my doormat two days later.

Kim always handled the bills. I could never open window envelopes. After he died it was my son. Now it is mostly Social Services and Piers looks after any repairs needed in the flat. I like this flat. Big, high-ceilinged rooms filled with old-fashioned furniture. Lots of caramel-coloured wood panelling. A kitchen with walk in pantries - not that I visit the kitchen these days. I spend most of my time in this room filled with Kim's collections from his expeditions and my

95

books. Because I am thinking intensely of him, Kim comes to me and I see him as he was when we were first together. Tall, fair skin reddened by tropical sun, faded blue shirt and khaki trousers. Wonderful, wide smile revealing his big, English teeth which, I thought, made him look very boyish and vulnerable. Kim's eyes were grey and clear. I remember them filling with expressions of interest and curiosity as he bent over his latest botanical find. He unlocked the door of my neat, middle class existence, took my hand and led me into his world. A world of rain forests and wide, brown rivers. He studied bromeliads mostly - great, rootless plants, often high in the canopy, each with a crown of spiky leaves and each a world in itself. A habitat for tiny frogs and their tadpoles, swimming in the tanks of rainwater at the base of each leaf. A living sanctuary for insects, lizards and spiders.

I was of no real help to him as a researcher. My mind moved like the butterflies waltzing around us. Alighting briefly on a thought then off to another. But he seemed to like having me along. He said my delight in the forest was unscientific but refreshing and kept him from getting too obsessively academic. Of all the birds of the rain forest, I particularly loved the parrots. Kim returned from his last expedition with a beautiful, green parrot. He called him Eustace - after an uncle with a huge beak-like nose. Kim was already ill, but we did not know it. He died suddenly, three months after he got back from French Guyana. A heart attack. Piers was away at university when it happened. I gave Eustace to a distant cousin. Kim had taught him to say, 'Hello, Kim. Welcome home!'

The sunlight is dappling my face, diffused by the canopy above my head, and a warm breeze is lifting my hair and breathing the scent of flowers into my nostrils. I open my eyes and look up and there is an endless vista of glistening leaves, an undulating green ocean with bright birds and butterflies dipping and gliding like reef fish in its mysterious depths.

'Wake up Margot! First your pills then your eggs and some brown bread and butter. The toaster's packed up - so no marmite toast, I'm afraid.'

I start and stare with annoyance at Naomi's smiling face. I really don't like carers calling me by my first name.

'I've finished my juice - I need more to wash down the pills.'

'Thought you would.' She is arranging my napkin as a bib. 'Cate's squeezing more oranges.'

I nod slightly, with approval. I only drink freshly squeezed orange juice. God knows what's in the orange-flavoured sludge in the cartons. Now I am to be fed. I watch as Naomi decapitates one of the eggs. First she taps it sharply with the back of the spoon and the shell fractures like an over-thin skull. She pulls away the shards with her fingers and then takes a knife to the white dome to reveal the pool of golden yolk beneath. She plunders the yolk with the end of a brown bread soldier and inserts it in my mouth. Cate arrives with the second orange juice. I take my pills.

I am back in the forest, my face lifted to the scented breeze. The butterflies are swirling around me - rich yellow wings with brown bread bodies and legs. A jaguar slides into view around the trunk of a great tree. Sinuous, and seemingly all black but I can see spots on his velvet hide and his eyes are wide and colourless, like ice. He yawns. I see his long, pointed fangs. Perched on his shoulder is a parrot. At first he is green and I call 'Eustace!' but then his feathers change abruptly to metallic orange and I can see that it is not Eustace and that it's not even a parrot but some sort of Quetzal of a kind I had not seen before. I turn, but not in fear, because I sense Kim is standing behind me. And he is. He smiles and says, 'Not bothering you, are they?' I turn back and the jaguar and the bird are gone and the butterflies are now white with black bodies and legs. Around them, a mist is rising.

'Are you all right, Margot?' I feel a breeze, but it is not scented. Naomi's face comes into focus and she is fanning me with a newspaper. Are you feeling better?'

'Better?' I snap. 'Of course I am not feeling better. Why can't you just leave me alone?'

Cate says, 'We would have done just that, Margot, but you fell forward into your egg and you didn't wake up all the time we were getting the yolk out of your hair and sponging off the orange juice, 'cos that went straight into your lap. Quite a mess so it was.'

I glare at them both. 'I'm not in the mood to record anything. Get me my book and my page turner and then you can both be off. Kim is due here this afternoon, so I don't expect to see you back before six. He'll get my supper.'

'Kim?' says Naomi.
        'Piers. I meant to say Piers - and his family.'
        'Is Piers your son?', asks Cate.
        'He is - not that it's any of your business.'
        'Are you still reading this Elizabeth Goudge?' Naomi puts *Towers in the Mist* in front of me. I nod. She gets the page turning contraption set up. She places the pad to activate it next to my elbow. She puts my glasses on my nose and the cord attached to the earpieces around my neck.

After they have gone, I allow the glasses to slip off my nose. They dangle in my damp lap. All is quiet for a while and then I hear faint whirrings and chirpings and I lift my face to the perfumed breeze.

The Town

by Anne O Dea

I look around. It's a town you'd escape from, not to, but beggars can't be choosers. There's nowhere else for miles, which has pluses and minuses. It means I don't need to spend another night in the open. On the other hand, if they've picked up my trail it also means they won't be needing that rocket science thing to find me. The bus stops on a mean street that's probably the main drag, and disgorges three people, including me. There's a diner nearby and I head there without looking left or right. The men's room is the first port of call for more reasons than the obvious. I haven't seen a mirror since leaving home, and there's every reason to suppose that I'm not a pretty sight. A repair job is top of the list if I want to eat here, and not be remembered.

A quick examination shows that it could be worse. Very short hair helps. The washroom stays empty while I freshen my face, arms and hands. I ache for a shower and those around me will ache worse, but that'll have to wait. A final glance. I'll do.

Thirty minutes later, seated near a window overlooking the street, I push aside an empty plate and signal for coffee. Shock, grief and fear have receded, probably only momentarily, but enough for me to try to clear my mind. I need to concentrate so as to get a handle on exactly when this all began.

I got home for spring vacation on Tuesday, that much I'm sure of, because I've the clearest possible memory of events leading up to that point. I said nothing about these to my mother that first evening, just chilled, enjoying being with her the way I always do. Did. The way I always did.

My plan was to tell her everything the next day, when the two of us were due to go trekking near Clear Lake, a favourite outing, a kind of tradition we've built together these past few years for the first day of vacation. Okay, so this began on Wednesday, which probably means today is Friday. Yeah. Two nights in the open, with little in the way of food or water, and with an awful lot on my mind.

I squeeze my eyes shut. A hot flush of misery swamps me, no less intense than those of the past few days, but even though this dump of a diner is almost empty I struggle to suppress it. I need a clear mind.

My mother, Kate Cahalane, was a private person, the most private I've ever known. I recognised in my soul that there were secrets in her life that she never shared, maybe never would have shared. Like where my father was. Or who he was. And why she, and therefore I, had no family, or none that she acknowledged. Or why she was always so hesitant regarding my talents, though I never for a moment doubted her love for me.

Wednesday was glorious, warm and clear. The trek she and I planned would take most of the day, so we made an early start. My plan was to tell her when we stopped for lunch, to find a way to break the news to her. I was nervous, no question, but it had to be faced, she had to be made to see reason. And besides, the news would be all over the state media when we reached home.

But the words weren't coming. She smiled at me as she dusted the breadcrumbs from her lap. Her eyes were bright. I felt a familiar tug of love for her.

"You've something on your mind, Robbie," she said, dabbing her lips with a paper towel. "You're twitching. You've been twitching since you came home."

"No," I said stupidly, thinking this is crazy, here I am with the best possible news, and I can't find the goddam words. "There's nothing."

She laughed. "Okay. You'll tell me when you're ready. Can you hand me my backpack?"

That was when it happened. As I lifted my mother's backpack, with no sound audible except for a hint of distant birdsong, she keeled over, most of her head blown off.

There are no words I can ever find to describe that moment, or those that followed, even though they seemed to last forever. I made a move towards her, a strangled scream of horror forcing itself from my throat, but there was no doubting that she was gone, even in that moment I knew I'd never see her smile at me in the way that was special between us.

As I moved to hold her I realised that I was next, and with this thought I crouched, swerved, picked a route opposite to where I figured the bullet might have come from, and moved out of there at a pace that equalled my best. This was despite terrain that was a fair bit rougher than I'm used to, not to mention that my mind was paralysed with shock. And somewhere, a peripheral somewhere glimpsed or maybe imagined as I flew across country, I caught a hint of gold, a dullish gold, maybe like the hood of a jeep, but it was blurred, I was moving too fast, I could have got it wrong.

There's no way of measuring how long I ran, or how far. All I remember is that I kept going way beyond my previous records, which is something I might take out in the future and examine, if I still have a future in which I care about such things. Maybe I could have kept going longer and further, but I'd reached some trees, a small wood by the looks of it. Once in there the sense of immediate shock and terror eased a little and I allowed myself to slump to the ground. I looked without seeing at the backpack which lay beside me. I must have carried it completely unawares.

After a while I glanced at my watch, and saw to my disbelief that it was only 2pm. How could my mother be dead – murdered – and me lost and frantic in the middle of nowhere – when only a couple of hours ago she glowed with life and I was on the edge of achieving my life's ambition?

I must have slept because next thing I remember was that night had fallen. Though I'm a cross country runner, possibly the best in the nation, nature's night time face has never appealed to me, particularly under circumstances I couldn't have imagined in my worst nightmares. I made it through till dawn, sleeping some of the time, probably crying the rest. My mother's backpack held cell phone, food and water, but I decided to leave the food till daylight in case it attracted the kind of attention I did not want from nocturnal creatures.

The next morning I pulled myself together some, ate the leftover provisions and fished out my mother's compass. Home was north, unless I'd screwed up totally yesterday, which was not impossible, but for now I had to make some assumptions. So I wanted to go south, east or west. I opted for west on some kind of instinctive sense that they'd expect me to head towards civilisation, not away. Then I examined my mother's wallet, avoiding the driver's licence with its smiling photo. One credit card, which she only used in emergencies. $600 cash. Who else but my mother would go trekking with that much cash? She hated to be low in the readies as much as she hated, or maybe distrusted, plastic.

My mind was freeing itself up sufficiently to start wondering. Why my mother? Was it a random killer? I hadn't heard a second shot as I ran, but then again I hadn't heard the first one. A random killer with a silencer. Right. So if not random, why on earth would anyone kill my mother? And how would a killer know where the two of us would be?

Nothing made any sense to me but one thing I was sure of. I was not about to head home, or anywhere I could be recognised, until I had some grip on what was happening.

Another day and night alone without sight of anyone. On Friday morning when I heard a bus in the distance, I sprinted to the road I'd been paralleling and stuck up my thumb. Rochester West, it said. I had no idea where or what that was but hopefully it could provide a shower, a bed and a phone.

The diner is still like a morgue. Exhausted, I rise to my feet. Signalling for my bill I head to the pay phone near the door. Some instinct tells me to avoid using my mother's cell phone. I dial Directory Enquiries to get Bill Prufeck's home number. His folks should be at work so it's a safe enough bet he'll answer.

"Hey," he says.

Bill's my closest friend, we met up in grade school when we were eleven, but even he doesn't know how I dreaded breaking the news about being selected for the Olympic Team.

"Hey," I say.

"Robbie? For fuck's sake, where've you been?"

"Hey, it's okay," I hear myself saying, which has to rate as the dumbest response in history.

"I've been calling you since Wednesday evening, your cell, home. No one's answering.."

"It's kinda complicated," I mutter. He hasn't said anything about a body being found. The Clear Lake trail isn't Fifth Avenue, but it's used a fair bit this time of year. There's no way she wouldn't have been found. Unless he, or they, took her. Buried her somewhere.

"Rob, you okay?" There's real concern in Billyboy's voice and the tears are one blink away. "And why're you calling me on the home line?"

"Gotta go," I say. "Talk soon." Brushing my eyes, I replace the receiver. If they've taken her body then for sure they're after me. Unwillingly my mind flickers to an SUV I saw a couple of times during the long bus ride. Dullish gold hood. But there's any number of them on the road, surely, so no reason to assume anything. Even less of a reason not to assume, a small voice murmurs in my head.

I slip a twenty from my stash, planning to slap it on the counter and leave, when it strikes me that this will make me more memorable. So I wait while the pudgy blank-faced kid rings up my bill and gives me change without any exchange of words or eye contact.

On a side street some ten minutes from the diner I see a house with a Room to Let sign in the window. This seems a safer bet than looking for a motel. And cheaper maybe, unless they look for a non-refundable deposit. Glad of the backpack, I ring the bell. A skinny little guy answers. He looks up at me nervously through Clark Kent style eye glasses. Maybe husky dusty guys with minimum luggage are not his normal takers.

"I'm here for the room." By now I'm craving a shower and bed like crazy.

"Sure." He stands back to let me enter. Immediately a cat insinuates itself around my leg, and I bend to pick it up.

"That one's Sandy," the guy says. "I h..hope you don't mind c..cats?"

I'm more of a dog person, but my mom never wanted animals. "Cats're good with me," I say.

The guy's smile is okay. Accompanied by two further felines I follow him up the stairs, nearly bumping into him when he turns unexpectedly. He reaches out his hand.

"I nearly forgot. I'm Aaron Walpole."

I totally forgot to have a name ready. Thinking frantically as I gripped his hand it comes to me. The name of my math teach in Junior High.

103

"Marty Colver," I say.

"Pleased to meet you, Mr Colver." We continue up the stairs. Fifteen minutes later I'm asleep. Twenty rifles could have released their loads, and another twenty dull gold SUVs parked outside the rooming house and I'd have slept through it all. When I wake it's dark. My mind is a little clearer and I realise something. The only thing that's different in my life in a long time has been all the fuss about the prospect of winning Olympic gold.

Donning the same clothes again sucks, but there's no alternative. I leave the house without encountering Mr Walpole. The internet café's no more than five minutes walk. I log on, putting in my name and track details. It's then I see the photo of my beautiful mother. I remember how adamant she was about not having her picture taken. But when I left for college I took a photo without her knowing, and for the past three years it's been standing on my desk. The only way it could be on the net is because some journalist looking for a background story on the Olympic hopeful knocked at my door. I think fleetingly of my room-mate, Walt. He's so proud to even know me, he'd see no reason not to show the photo to anyone who asked.

I feel like throwing up, and consider making a run for the bathroom. But after a few moments and several deep breaths I get myself under control, and begin to think about the past. Fifteen years earlier, when I was six, my mother and I left NYC, and we've never gone back, or even talked about our life there. I've only the faintest memory, no memory at all really, of that time or of a man who might have been my father. And because the gates are opening, I recall an evening, eight, maybe ten years earlier. My mother was very upset about something. All she would say was "Kleinbach, talk to Greg Kleinbach. If anything ever happens, Robbie, only trust Greg Kleinbach." She seemed to regret saying this, and would never discuss the matter again. Two days later, maybe less, my memory of that is vague too, both of us were in a new apartment in a new town. Whatever worried my mother then seemed to go away and other than the matter of the photos life became normal enough in the years since.

I google the name. My memory is uncertain, but when I try Gregory Kleinbach I hit pay dirt. It seems that Greg Kleinbach is a senior FBI agent. His name comes up on a dozen and more federal cases. I borrow a pen and some paper and scribble the numbers of the Federal offices he's been connected with.

There's nothing I can do till the morning. I sit back, staring at the PC, seeing nothing. I'm lonelier than I could have believed possible. I call Bill again. This time he's definitely sounding freaked.

"What's up?" I say.

"You've gotta talk to me, Robbie," he says. "I got a call yesterday, some guy says he's a cop, wanting to know if I've heard from you."

"So what did you say? Did he give a name?" My voice sounds calmer than I'm feeling.

"I said no. Not sure why, just felt right. He said he was Lt. McKenzie, that you and your mom seemed to be missing."

I can't think what to say. Is this McKenzie guy one of them? Or a real cop? How can I be sure about this, or about anything? "Listen, Billy, there's stuff happening that I'm trying to figure out. Best say nothing to anyone for the moment, and you've definitely heard nothing from me. And be careful, okay?"

"Okay." Bill sounds scared. What will I do if any harm comes to him? "You take care, Robbie. Let me know any way I can help, okay?"

That night I can't sleep. Nothing makes sense. It all goes around and around in my head like some crazy kaleidoscopic rollercoaster. I hear Mr Walpole coming in around five am. He's a real quiet guy, once the front door closes I can't hear another thing. At seven I crawl out of bed and into the shower. Cold water helps and I stay under it for as long as I can bear it. I'm hungry, but it's probably too early for the diner, and I'm not even sure I can hold food down.

At eight I call Kleinbach. It takes forever to be connected. I tell him who I am. He's cagey. I'm cagey. I won't say where I am. Eventually he suggests we meet in Lanesville, which I know, a small city several hundred miles from my home town.

"Five pm at the Ramada Inn," he says.

A combination of buses gets me there. I stare out at the endless highways, almost hypnotised. I doze now and then, waking with a little jerk. I arrive with an hour to spare and decide to blow some of my precious cash on a change of clothes and a toothbrush. I'm tempted to bin the gear I've been wearing, especially given the stink, but I've grown cautious and thrifty in a matter of days and I leave everything in the men's room at the Ramada Inn, hoping it'll be there on my return.

Kleinbach finds me. He's an ordinary looking guy in his forties, thinning hair, nondescript jacket. I hardly notice him when I scan the lobby. "Mr Cahalane?"

I'm not used to being addressed so formally so I fumble the handshake.

"There's a quiet spot over there." He indicates with his eyes. I nod and follow him to a small booth. A few moments later, coffee cups on the scarred table surface, I finally look directly into his face. It gives nothing away.

"So," he says after a bit. "You called me because years ago your mother said so. Care to fill me in?"

I describe the events of the past few days as best I can, aware how little sense I'm making. He listens without comment or change of expression. There's silence for a while when I run out of words.

"So she never told you," he said eventually.

I blink at him, then frown. "If you know something, Mr Kleinbach, can you please tell me." I hear the edge in my voice and fight to control it. I don't want to alienate this guy, at least not until I find out what he knows.

"Yeah," he nods. "I know some of it. I met your mother before she left NYC with you, back in '91 and I spoke with her a few years later on the phone. She trusted me as much as she trusted anyone. I just can't believe she told you nothing."

I stay quiet. I know I'm about to find out what my mother kept secret for so long. And now I'm no longer sure I want to hear any of it.

"Your father was called Alex Rostov," Kleinbach begins slowly. "He was, well let's say he was a violent man. Your mother knew nothing of him or his family when she married him. He'd been raised in Atlantic City as a boy, part of an extended Russian family, most of whom were wanted by the cops or the FBI for something, anything from weapons to drugs. Alex was small time, not because he was dumb, far from it, but because he couldn't be trusted to keep his temper under control. Or his tendency to inflict unnecessary pain – and we're talking here of an environment where these traits would not normally be considered defects."

I'm getting a sharp pain in my heart, or maybe it's my gut. I'm thinking – I travelled all day to hear this? I want to be somewhere else, anywhere else that did not involve listening to this.

"When you were six your mother, who was a very brave woman, decided that unless you were to end up the same she had to get away. She knew, or thought she did, the risks that were involved. Then, on the night she chose to make the escape Alex found out, he went into an insane fury and she barely escaped with her life..." I'm thinking - this guy's telling me all of this as if it was some of my business... "Your mother's shirt was found at the apartment, splattered with Alex's blood. But she didn't do it, Robbie. She witnessed the killing that night. She didn't do it, but the Rostov family believed she did. Word at the time was that they didn't blame her much, maybe they were relieved that someone had given Alex what he needed."

I say: "Murder? She witnessed it? She never told me that. Is that why she and I have been hiding out?" That pain is getting sharper. It's hard to breathe because now I'm consciously acknowledging that hiding's what we've both been doing, and that it's most likely because of me and that photo that she's now dead.

These Rostov people were after her, but maybe she learned a lot in her years as my father's wife, and maybe that helped her avoid being caught. Till now. Because of me. This knowledge makes me want to die. The pain of what I'm hearing, what I'm realising, is so bad that I really want to die.

Kleinbach looks oddly at me. "Like I said, they thought she did it," he continues. "They didn't hunt her down too hard. They could've found her years ago if they had wanted her badly. But I guess when her photo appeared they reckoned they should deal with her. They wouldn't want to appear soft."

"B...but," I stutter, sounding just like Mr Walpole, "she didn't kill him. My mother couldn't kill anyone, even someone like this Rostov guy..."

"No, you're probably right, Robbie," Kleinbach says. He's looking at me strangely. "But it seems that you could."

Absolutely

by Lynne Voyce

Bernie surveyed the debris from the grime-rippled window of the Number 96 bus. Among the creeping rubble was a square of wallpaper from the Hawaali, a segment of Blake's shop sign – 'Men's Outfitters' it said - and the walnut curve of an old fashioned counter, maybe from McGee's sweets, maybe from Ellen Lay's Ladies' Drapers. He used to come here with Michelle. There was that place that sold Chinese kimonos and silk pyjamas that she loved. Shanghai Surprise it was called. But it was derelict now and so was he.

"Hey Bernie, wake up," Tony nudged him, pointed at the carcass of a building, "look at The Ship: I met my wife in that pub. I wonder why they called it that eh? Round here's about as landlocked as you get."

Bernie lifted his chin in absent agreement and peered through the autumn gloom. The buildings seemed to reform as if the demolition was being played backwards. He remembered the day Michelle had bought that silk negligee embroidered with nightingales and flowers from Shanghai Surprise; then they'd gone to the market across the road to buy fruit. Michelle had insisted on having her palm read in the motorised gypsy caravan by the Caribbean food stall. There was always a queue outside and boards flanked the beaded doorway, showing photos of television game show hosts and all round entertainers, their hands palm upwards in the clutch of Madame Rosa, 'original Romany gypsy'. Michelle had gone in smiling but when she came out she looked sickly and was blowing on her bottom lip, something she did when she was embarrassed.

Later she told Bernie that Madame Rosa had known all about her and Vince; had insisted that she make a decision and set Bernie free; had said her and Vince were destined to be together, for better or worse.

Yes, the place held memories for him.

Ironic, then that once the demolition was completed he'd be the one in charge of rebuilding. 'Site Manager'. Right now he barely managed to get out of bed in the morning. He pushed his hand into his pocket, felt the rolled envelope, let his fingers stick to the gum of the flap. 'Decree Absolute' – such a wonderful title he thought, so irrevocably final: absolutely positive, absolutely over you, absolutely fine. She was all of them now.

"Look Bernie, a clean slate," Tony stood on the precipice, arms outstretched, a rock star addressing a crowd of forty thousand, "It excites me, you know."

Bernie surveyed the missing landscape between Moor Street and St Martins. The demolition was complete, not a brick remained but Bernie's memories seemed to tumble across the raw earth with bitter regularity. St Martin's Church, a landmark, an architectural triumph and often a shelter from the rain for Bernie and his wife in their married days - had been spared. Its foundations clung to solid ground, the limestone spire about to bend its neck and stare into the abyss. "It's a pit. That's all it is, a big ugly empty pit."

"You might see it like that mate, I see it as a new beginning."

"You don't half talk rubbish Tony," Bernie pushed his hard hat off his face, took a swig from his bottle of water, "It's nothing more than a back breaking slog: working in a hole in the ground. It's just a job. OK, the first one since Michelle left. But just a job all the same." He turned his back on the site, swallowed, "So thanks for the pep talk Tony, "he murmured, "but to me this place looks – annihilated."

Bernie stood on the footbridge, looked down through the wide gapped chicken wire at the maze of foundations; pale grey bricks against the dark pit bottom, like an incomplete crossword puzzle. He'd been there at the laying of every single one.
They put the wire there to stop people jumping. It seemed to Bernie that if you really wanted to jump, you'd bring a pair of wire cutters. Or jump off a multi storey car park in the best tradition of urban suicide. He'd thought about it the other day as he drove his Astra up to level nine in the multi storey at the back of the station. What would it feel like falling through the air? How do people take such a

dive? Maybe they're so desperate they don't think. Maybe they believe they can fly.

"Morning boss!" he felt a slap on his back where his wings would be and turned round. It was Tony, two smoking cups in his hands; a brown paper bag hooked on his little finger, "Bacon butties." Bernie unhooked the bag, fished inside for his and took a bite, brown sauce dribbled down his chin. "Michelle's moving to Leicester with Vince."

"So?" Tony shrugged.

"I'll miss her," Bernie licked sauce from his finger.

"You haven't seen her for months."

"I'll miss the thought of her."

"Hello in there," Tony rapped Bernie's hard hat, "you're divorced."

"I know," he lifted the top off his sandwich to inspect the filling.

"How's the new house?"

"It's got damp, dry rot, woodworm, a chocolate brown bathroom suite and a stone clad bar in the dining room."

"So why did you buy it?"

"I thought doing it up'd give me something to do. I'm going to gut the place; get rid of everything, strip it down to the bare brick."

"Can't you just go out and get laid like normal blokes?" Tony handed Bernie a cup.

"Can I make something really clear?"

"Course."

"I'm not interested in women. Not any more. Michelle was my 'wife'," he gave the word extra emphasis and paused, "she left me for a bloody salesman. End of story. So can you just stop interfering?" He put his cup on the floor; pushed the remainder of his sandwich through the wire, watched it fall to the ground. "I'll see you tomorrow," he said and took a stride forward. Then he stopped as if he'd hit an invisible wall.

Someone had caught his eye and he couldn't drag his gaze from her. A petite woman in a black overcoat and neat feather trimmed bowler was coming towards him. As she passed him on the bridge he studied her delicate face. She gave him a brief smile of acknowledgement but her eyes didn't reflect it: she looked as though she had been crying. What was it that made him stare? Had they been at school together? No. Was it the hat? That was unusual. Was it that she walked upright as if invisible strings were attached to her shoulders? Or was it the patent shine of her lace-up shoes? Wasn't it captivating the way she avoided people, stepped out of their way with a little cha cha cha. Then suddenly she was gone. Swept back into the rush hour crowd. "Bernie are you alright?" Tony broke in.

"Yeah I'm fine, I just saw someone I thought I recognized. That woman in the black coat and the hat, do you know her?"

"What woman? I didn't see anybody."

"No bacon," he mumbled to himself, his and Tony's coffee in his gloved hands, (gloves Michelle had bought him last Christmas when he'd really wanted an impact screwdriver). It was getting colder on the site and they all needed hot food. "How can they serve breakfast and have no bacon?" He passed the market traders beginning to rig their stalls – forgetting, for the first time, to check if the gypsy caravan had returned - and stopped before he drew too close to the boards that shielded the site. He looked up at the metal skeletons, emerging from the pit like Adam's rib sticking up from the dust. "I did that," he said loud enough for it to be true, "and," he continued, "I plumbed my own bathroom at the weekend." He wanted to punch the air in triumph but the polystyrene cups prevented him, so he merely bobbed his head with satisfaction and ambled forward. "Hello," said a woman's voice. He turned, expecting to come face to face with someone from the café or one of the girls from wages but the speaker had gone. All he saw was a streak of feathers flit past and then the back of a long black coat. It was the woman from the bridge.

He saw her every morning now and after two months of her smiling at him, and him smiling at her through sips of breakfast coffee, she'd spoken to him. And he'd been too busy wrapped up in his own small victories to reply.

111

The brickie swung his hod to the floor and shuffled the mortar with his trowel. Bernie stood on the newly created ground and watched, fascinated at the way each brick so perfectly fit with the others. The brickie put his spirit level on the fledgling wall and smiled with satisfaction.

Bernie used to be a brickie: he'd had his own business. That's how he'd met Michelle – building a utility on her parents' house. He'd start at eight o clock every morning; Michelle would come downstairs barefoot in her nightie, a little dark blue satin and net thing. She'd make him tea, chat while she leaned on the kitchen door post. At first he thought nothing of it, then he noticed she'd put her legs in this strange, toe pointed position that made them look longer. He knew she did it on purpose. And she used to wear bright scarlet toe polish. Bernie had liked that. A couple of times he had to stop himself proposing there and then. In the end he settled for asking if she'd like to go for a drink up town. She'd smiled and said 'yes.' Bernie had never imagined that a girl like Michelle would ever say 'yes' to him..

The stab of sentiment in his gut coincided with the laying of a new brick. It pained him to think of when he and Michelle first met – they had loved each other.

Maybe he wouldn't tell the woman in the black coat his name today. He had planned to. They had been saying hello for weeks and he wanted her to know who she was saying hello to.

As if his thoughts had conjured her up, she came into view doing that neat tightrope walk with the occasional cha cha cha. Every feature of her face was turned up at the edges in one big smile. It was warmer than usual; she had her coat open, he could see a red dress underneath, the skirt flapping at the front like a rudder. Swinging in her hand was a pair of black shoes suspended from ribbons. Of course, she was a dancer. He let the pleasure of realising something new about her rush to his head and in that instant blurted, "Bernie, my name's Bernie. My mother named me Bernie."

"Beth," she returned, her balance utterly uninterrupted, "my mother named me Beth." Her voice was clear and strong.

"Those glaziers are on a good number," Tony balanced his sandwich on the arm of his deck chair and stared at the eyeless column above

112

him, the unglazed windows empty sockets, "If you call one out in an emergency they can charge you hundreds," he looked over the flat roofs to the cloudless spring sky and said wistfully, "I'm thinking about it after this job."

"Like you were thinking about opening a bar on the Costa del Sol?" Bernie said, distracted, looking over at the board and mesh that circled the site now the ground was level with the rest of the city, "or buying a racehorse or being a flaming water diviner."

"No, I'm deadly serious, it just seems more civilised at my age – putting in windows rather than being a navvy."

"Oh, I don't know," Bernie waved expansively, "we've built this from scratch. It'll be beautiful when it's finished. We're just as responsible for this as the moneymen and the architects. We've changed the skyline, changed the way people walk to work, changed the city for ever." He let his eyes sweep across the reflective edifices, as though surveying his country estate.

"God, you've changed your tune, you were calling it an ugly pit last September."

"Are you free at the weekend?"

"Yeah, why?"

"Need some help to lay the carpet in the dining room. Well, it's not carpet, it's that seagrass stuff."

"I'll come along bring a few beers. The wife'll be fine with it. About what time? Bernie... hey Bernie, are you listening?"

But Bernie was standing, waving his arms. On the other side of the mesh was a woman and by the way her head bobbed it seemed she was on tiptoes. "Beth, would you like to go for coffee?" he shouted.

"Absolutely," she replied, "when?"

"Next Friday, 12 o'clock," his voice was resolute," they're going to put a bench about where you're standing. I'll meet you there."

"Looking forward to it," she jiggled a dancing shoe in each hand and sunk below the line of the boards.

"Who the hell was that?" Tony asked as Bernie sank into his chair with a satisfied swagger.

"Someone I've been saying hello to."

Bernie looked at his watch – 12.45. He looked at the clock on the church spire at the head of the recently completed St Martin's Square to confirm. The same. He loosened his tie and kicked the hard hat he'd taken off and placed at his feet, sending it rocking across the stone paving, like an up turned tortoise. "I should have bought lilies," he muttered looking at the red buds of the roses that lay next to him on the bench, "would have gone better with the décor at home."

A woman walked past, leaving *Anais Anais* in her wake, the same perfume as his ex-wife used to wear. He pictured Michelle and Vince, standing in their Leicester car showroom, smiling, wearing fancy clothes. He felt his spirits plummet.

Easing himself up with both hands, he picked up the hat and the cellophane wrapped flowers, making them crackle. "Bloody fool," he said as he turned to walk to the last remaining site hut, small and ramshackle in comparison to the gleaming freshly built giants. The white June sunlight bounced from window to window, in a big game of pinball, before an ominous cloud drifted to cover the sky above his head.

He felt older all of a sudden and the buildings seemed to crowd him in a way they hadn't before. A first spot of rain fell into the bowl of his hat, and the sound seemed to echo around him. Or was it the sound of a word? Had he heard someone whisper? "Wait." It seemed to be coming from the walls, the very walls he and his workmates had built. "Bernie," they said, "wait." He carried on walking but there it was again. "Bernie wait." He glanced back and suddenly there was Beth, running so hard he could hear the metal studs of her tap shoes, clipping the edges of the cobbles. "Bernie," she shouted, "wait!" Her hair and her long coat blew behind her and he could see the full-skirted red dress she wore, clinging to her chest and legs as she ran through the virgin street. His pace quickened as he walked towards her. "I'm sorry, I'm sorry," she cried.

"It's OK," he called back.

"No, it's not," she gasped, as she reached him, "I was scared."

"But why?"

"Because it's new."

"It's not new," he said as he reached her and led her to the bench, "it's just a beginning."

sky fills her skin

by Martin Ungless

he was not really looking, just gazing in that out of focus way, when his eye, with a life of its own, caught her movement. he did not register her, his eyes simply pointed in her direction. h did not think his thoughts, they happened, he could not have said that he was thinking about anything. but his thoughts were of her. or rather her washing, of the story it was telling. a life lived for someone else. a wife support system, hanging out her husband's clothes.

she was not really thinking either. just pegging out her washing, arms and hands doing their own thing. as they do. she felt the chill in the air and she adored it. she bent to her basket, stood, then smelled the clean wet of her washing held to her face.

no children's clothes to show for all her efforts, what a wasted life he thought. how could she stand to clean and cook, and cook and clean and wash, only for her husband. her dull husband whom he had seen in town with his dull friends, all being dull together. he knew that her husband worked late and that she must be bored, unless she too were dull. surely if she saw her own life as it really was, then she must end it all.

hands pegging, not thinking, she let herself feel. just feel. she felt the cool sky on her skin through her thin summer tee-shirt, worn still in this first crisp early autumn air. she let her head hang back, facing the blue. she tried not to have any thoughts which might smother the touch of the world and its acres and acres of openness.

look, he thought, she is tired, she works hard. he did not believe that the house was big enough to occupy all of her time, what did she do with herself. she went out, but he never saw her return save with shopping from the supermarket. food and things to clean with, he supposed. he could never recall having seen her with shopping bags full of fancy clothes, or even her returning with a smile of simple satisfaction upon her face. what did she do for herself.

sometimes they met in the village shop, nodding as neighbours do, she might be buying stamps or a packet of biscuits. he wondered if she avoided him.

he noticed that she had stopped hanging the washing. he saw that she was standing still, facing the sky, and he felt that he understood her for a moment. not her life, he could not understand her life. he felt that he understood this moment. he remembered what it was like to stand in the wide blue, with fruit on the trees, and feel the freshness of the breeze that turned to the north for the first time as the seasons cooled.

and as she stood there, allowing the sky to fill her skin, she did permit herself a thought. she thought about her life as if she were not herself, as if she were not inside her body with its clear sensations, but outside. she thought for a moment about the life of someone she might see pegging out the washing whilst their husband was at work. and she remembered her husband's tenderness each day, and she saw how much she loved him.

a shadow passed in a moment's cold, as she wondered whether she deserved him, but the great blue quickly washed this thought away. she saw herself beneath the vastness of the flatland sky and knew that her husband loved her too, and that they were happy. as happy as anyone had the right to expect to be.

through his dark window he watched her and thought about the terrible waste. the waste of a life that he saw each day. waste that he could no longer bear to witness. he asked himself if it was too late for her to start a family, and felt dread at the thought that she might be barren. perhaps this was the shadow hanging over their lives. or perhaps, he thought, her husband falls short of the name.

as he watched her peg up the last of her washing, he hoped that she would be fulfilled. he saw that she could enjoy the simple things, with the pleasure that she took in the early autumn air. he thought there was promise in this and fumbled with his zip.

when she turns she sees him pressed against his window. BLOODY PERV she yells, and walks back in to her house.

116

The Crisp New Twenty

by J M Thomas

It so happens that, about thirty years ago, our man is cycling home late at night. His bike is old. The paint is eroded and the maker's name a mere memory of gilt and black paint. If he oiled the chain it would improve the performance. He could strip down and realign the derailleur. That would make changing gear less adventurous. But little he could do would disguise the decrepitude of that bike. Our man is young though, and fit. Lithe and lean. He pedals happily and sturdily through the sodium lit streets. He pedals carefree and whistling onto the roundabout not far from his house; and collides with a car. That is fair; the car was there all along and he did in fact pedal right into the side of it. He lies on the road in a tangle of legs and metal; he is lanky and the bike of generous and sadly unfashionable proportions. So, as he lies there, the driver of the car approaches and looks down at him in the manner of a scary character in a black and white horror movie, face looming pale. The driver, clearly discerning that our man has taken beer somewhat immoderately that evening, and seeing that he seems largely unhurt, decides to chance his arm. He offers him twenty quid to repair the bike and a lift home.

Now twenty quid would have bought the bike some times over and our man is on the dole; happily and voluntarily on the dole, but skint nevertheless. He is less drunk than mellow and is sharp enough to appreciate the bargain he is offered. Of course the driver isn't sober himself, else why take the trouble when he was not at fault?

I'd like to say a crisp twenty changed hands, but thirty years ago a twenty was uncommon pocket change. A scrabbling of rancid notes, green and blue, and some large silver sort the exchange and the bike is manhandled into the back of the car with the grit and determination shown only by drunks on a mission the purpose of which is rapidly fading from view.

The next day, recalling the incident and verifying his recollection by inspecting his knocked elbows and knees, our man decides that this has been an encounter of note. The crossroads of highway 66. An epiphany. He likes to bracket his spiritual leanings just in case. Picking through the detritus of his right hand jacket pocket he assembles the twenty pounds in soiled, though legal, currency and pops off to the Post Office. He is a familiar face there from Giro day. He greets the Post Office man cheerily. He exchanges his motley money for a crisp twenty.

Home again, he folds the note twice. He runs his thumbnail along each fold. They are clean folds. It is an uncirculated note without even a counting crease to mar the symmetry of the edge. He wonders if the designers had known or even intended that folded in this way Shakespeare was pleasingly framed leaning on his writing desk gazing over his shoulder. Is he regarding history in readiness for transforming it to stage or is he seeing his rivals pursuing him in this very aspiration?

Our man looks about the room. It is a small room looking out high over the park. A dark double bed occupies the central position and, serving as an armchair, an old leather dentist's chair reclines in a corner. On a table in the window bay a few small possessions cast low shadows. He picks up a small bible. It is not a beautiful book. It is barely larger than a pack of cards and bound in shabby white plastic. The Gideon crest is embossed on the front and spine. Looking closely it is not a bible but a New Testament. A frayed and greying hand-embroidered ribbon hangs from it weighted with blue beads. The ribbon marks Matthew 14. He opens it at a different page and places the note tight against the seam of the page in Acts 9 and closes it firmly. He seems indecisive but puts the book back on the table straightening the ribbon and touching the embroidered cross.

Pulling it out from the wall he upends his bike and begins to push and pull half-heartedly at the spokes of the front wheel. Where the metal shows through the oily road dirt it is pitted with decay. Nothing about the machine expresses care. It is not an old friend much loved, but a lucky find needing only a new tyre and a hardened backside. He sags at his task, dropping his hands between his knees and thinks about that crisp twenty note. It's not a fortune, but it's more than he is used to having. He keeps looking at the little bible on the table and picturing that note spread out in his hands, displaying that little stage set, the TWENTY POUNDS writ large. He rises from

118

his crouch smoothly and goes to an old haversack laid over the chair. He looks at it, thumbing his nose. He puts a hand into its grubby neck and feels about. An astonishing level of rustling accompanies the movement of his hand, out of sight in the bag. Clearly this is his office, his filing cabinet, a repository for papers of all magnitudes of importance or none. By his fingertips he is able to discern the paper he wants. He draws out a small, only slightly creased, piece of writing paper. It is half a sheet of Basildon Bond Azure neatly torn along a crease leaving a slightly furred edge. He puts it on the table, the side with the small ink smudge facing down. He finds a short well-sharpened pencil in his pocket and sits at the table. He does not write anything, but sits for a long while looking out the window. The cows move about the field in slow deliberate patterns. Now and again someone cycles across the lumpy footpath; a black and white dog, masquerading at this distance as a border collie, trots beside a figure in a green mackintosh too long for it. He looks up at the sky, and down again, rising in his seat to see the road. And still he writes nothing. Our man is a thoughtful type. He never rushes. After twenty minutes he writes on the paper *1. a new dictionary.* Apparently content he rises and turns again to his bike. He knows almost nothing about bikes. He puts his pencil and both his hands in his pockets. In his head he is writing *1. a new bicycle.*

The following morning our man wakes to sunshine on the wall and the remembrance that it is signing on day. As he has signally failed to repair the bike he will have to walk. This is a significantly longer journey and he has to be there at ten. He turns on the radio and hopes for a time check. He doesn't think it is late yet, but knowing he has to leave at 9.30 to get to the dole without rushing makes him anxious. He hears Douglas Cameron introducing Thought for the Day and relaxes into his pillow. He lies looking up at the smooth white ceiling; a strand of long abandoned cobweb moves in a thin high draught. He thinks about his John Mayall records. In his head he writes *2. a stereogram* but crosses it out and writes *2. a record player.* A pause. *3. ticket to the City Hall.*

By ten to ten he is at the dole office. His light jacket for a spring morning was fine whilst he was walking, but now, standing in the overcast courtyard our man is growing chilled. Nevertheless he will not go into the building until ten o'clock. He likes to be on time;

not early, not late, but just on time. He luxuriates in his time. Working he would have no control over his time. He wonders how long he can stay on the dole. It's been over a year now. The warm righteousness of unemployment benefit is behind him. Now on Supplementary Benefit he can, he understands, be pulled in at any time to have his circumstances assessed - Social Security Sus. This threat to the control he exerts over his existence nags him. Waiting at the window for the clerk to find his card he tries to calculate what they would dock from his giro if they know about that twenty snuggled up in his bible. Since he had come out of the Post Office yesterday with that sharp bright banknote in his hands it seems that not a waking moment has passed without his thinking of it. It only seems that way. Often whole rafts of minutes go by without it intruding into his thoughts. But sure enough, back it would come disguised as possibilities and desires. Now in the dole queue it becomes tainted with threat. Our man looks about him edgily. Foolishly; for no-one looking at him can see that he has a crisp new twenty note stashed away at home.

Walking back across town he makes a little detour. So little he can almost convince himself that it happened by accident. He now has to pass the dingy corner junk shop. Not in the window, but behind the counter, are disjointed record players. He looks at them as closely as he can without asking to have them brought down. One of them appeals to him. It has been there a while, its ticket still reading £2.10.0. It was brown woodgrain-effect and had a grey smoked glass-effect lid. It wasn't what he wanted of course. He wanted a stereo. A stereo would have separate speakers to stand at each side. And it would be more than £2.50. Of course he has more than £2.50. He also has more than one thing on his list. But he hasn't actually made his mind up whether the list represents everything he intends to get or only a list to choose one or two things from. And his list is surely not complete. He feels in his trousers pocket and finds only the usual small coins for emergencies. He will have to come back when he has been to the Post Office. He thinks about his John Mayall records. "Empty Rooms" and "Bare Wires". There had been more of course, but his conscience had exerted some belated effect and he had taken only those two. He begins to run through that huge case of records. He would be able to replace only a few, perhaps only one from each artist - Dylan, Renbourn, Jansch... or new people. Why not new people? Not new records perhaps, songs that have stood the test of a few years, but artists new to his collection. Clinking the coins in his pocket he is barely aware of the journey home until he passes the letter box two doors down; an Edward VII pillar box. He has never posted anything in this box.

On Saturday he writes *2. a record player* and ticks it neatly. He opens the window. Raises the lid on the record player and carefully fits the new stylus. Blows softly on the vinyl scrolls of "Bare Wires" and sets it in motion. The volume is higher than necessary and someone posting a letter catches a fugitive strand of sound. The dingy corner junkshop had also been able to provide a motley selection of small tools. A bicycle repair kit apparently. In the market he has been sold, after some debate, a little flask of oil that clicks and has a long narrow spout. And still that twenty snuggles crisp and safe in Acts 9, a fat little lifebelt against all this reckless dole spending. He pulls his bike out from the wall and upends it. He carefully removes one or two components and contentedly scrapes and polishes in time to the music. A few days later he walks into town and buys a little tin of Japlac and a small brush. He is a bit sad to paint over the place that had once had such a fine golden name to it, but the uneven black gloss looks fine.

Our man is booling along in the sunshine. He congratulates himself on the work he has put in on the bike. The cranks turn smoothly and the gears engage after a couple of jiggles. He no longer needs to tussle with himself about adding a new bike to the list. That twenty is looking safe for a bit longer. He puts his back into the pedalling and whistles the Wombles song in breathless spurts. He is happily employed with random thoughts as he shoots onto the roundabout and collides with the car already there. It is the twin to the accident three weeks ago. It is the same car. Truly, it is. It is a different driver though. The original driver, realising just how drunk he had been and concerned that our man might turn out to be vindictive and track him down, sold the car within a couple of days. Without the dent in the door to remind him he quickly puts the incident out of his mind. He is yet to come up with a convincing story to account for the loss of twenty pounds; his wife is a careful housekeeper.

121

So, once again, our man lies in a tangle of bike and limbs looking up at a car that might have been familiar had he not last seen it drunk and in the dark. The driver is bending over him and a motorcyclist obscured by his helmet is fidgeting about. Our man speaks. "Bugger." He says. And, "New bike." Then he stops speaking and stops breathing. He stops living too, but the onlookers don't like to think of that.

When the police and ambulance crews ask him what happened the driver explains clearly. The motorcyclist corroborates. When asked had the injured man (for only a doctor can declare demise) spoken the driver says "Yes. Bugger, new bike. Although as you can see, although it is indeed buggered, it is not a new bike. So I'm not sure what he was getting at." The motorcyclist thinks he knows, but in the circumstances speculation seems futile.

Throughout his childhood and even as a young adult our man lived as a family with his father and mother. But he, or they, he is never really sure, stopped communicating. Not even a Christmas card passes between them now. And he's not a man to hoard. When his person is searched at the hospital he is found to be carrying very little, and none of it discloses even his name. He has a small collection of coins, many of them defunct as though the money was not for spending, but to make a clinking in his pocket. He has a carefully folded hanky, its creases discoloured as if it has not been unfolded for a long time. Around his neck on a long shoelace is a latchkey, as though he is in the habit of losing things. In the absence of any information his fingerprints are taken and he is slid neatly into the mortuary drawer. He has no criminal record and lies quietly uncalled for for some long time. But, I hear you think, surely our man, however reclusive, must know people? The person who does notice his absence is the clerk at the dole. He has been signing on regularly for months and months. Never early, never late, always polite. His card is still in her little filing drawer. It's none of her business of course and she wouldn't dream of doing anything about it. People come and go. If he's working he's doing it without paying a stamp and without claiming his dole, so who's to care? Well she is. It bugs her. She even mentions it to her EO. Who looks at her in round eyed uncaring. That afternoon she strolls casually into the Police Station and enquires of the Desk Sergeant what you might do if you thought someone had disappeared or gone away in odd circumstances. Nothing of course; not a police matter if the chap is over 21. She knows that really, but nevertheless. He might, she hazards, have lost his memory or something and not know where he is? Well if he had it wasn't here as the Police would have been told. And they hadn't. What if he was dead? What would happen then. His next of kin would be told and he'd be buried. Was she the next of kin? No? Well dear? All the walk home she turns over the possibilities. She knows nothing about the man except his name, date of birth, NI number and address. If he is dead his card will be sent for. It's a nice evening and she strolls artlessly along the street where he lives. On one side is a large park and on the other a terrace of Victorian houses. Trembling ever so slightly she rings the top doorbell of number five. And waits. It is a tall house so she waits a good time. But only silence comes down to her. She rings the second bell. And waits. Then the ground floor bell. The black door opens and a shabby man of upright bearing and heavy eyebrows looks down at her. He does not speak. This is because he does not know her. She speaks.

"Mr er, the man on the top floor, have you seen him? I usually see him every couple of weeks, but he hasn't, not for a while, well a couple of months really." No reply. No movement. Then

"Not for a while, as you say."

"Has he gone?"

"I should think so. He hasn't been here. He had been making quite a noise with music, but it stopped. Sorry." And he backed away and closed the door. She thinks, I tried. And deciding not to puzzle about it sets off home.

Mr Vaz is an easygoing sort of chap. He is making a nice living. His wife and children like their house. It has three bedrooms and a lounge-diner. You can get into the garage from the kitchen without going outdoors. Just round the corner are very nice houses belonging to dentists and opticians. It is near the park and near the shops. He has a car. It is not a new car, but it is in good condition and has leather seats. It is maroon with chrome trim. It looks classy. Mr Vaz doesn't worry his tenants unduly. In his experience they either pay up or they don't and nothing he can do in the way of intervention seems to alter this. The worst payers he has at the moment are three young men, town planners with aspirations. He is constantly surprised, as he tells his wife, that such young men with aspirations should be so dirty in the house, coffee cups with rings inside, underpants drying on the fireplace. Despite his kindly visits, his time taken drinking tea with them, they never pay on time and have long arrears so that it is too costly now to evict them. Sometimes the stroppy young woman downstairs lies in wait for him, pouncing out of her door as he bids his goodbye to the town planners. She has slugs invading her kitchen and rotten floorboards in the bathroom. He is conciliatory and reminds her that her rent has been reduced to make up for these deficiencies. For four years now she has lived with slugs and rot and made no effort to move out. If she did he would make the repairs and double the rent, but essentially Mr Vaz is lazy and has no material greed. Our man has been his tenant for a couple of years now; has never been late with his rent. So when six weeks go by Mr Vaz becomes concerned that he might have done a moonlight and calls round at number five. Like the dole lady before him his ring is answered only by silence. He too rings the second bell, but receives no answer. He thinks how good a tenant our man is and decides to give him the benefit of the doubt. He pops a note through the door as a little reminder and goes home in his classy car, wondering if, as he is out, it would be worth calling on the town planners.

Mrs Vaz is less accommodating than her husband. Every Friday she works her patient way through the books. She makes a list of tenants whose rent is overdue and marks alongside each name the amount outstanding. At the end of the list she tallies the amounts in red, to alert her husband to his losses, their losses, the depreciation of their children's future. The list she leaves in the centre of the dining room table and goes to bank what rents he has collected into the account that has only her name on the book. This Friday she notes that although the town planners have paid a month's rent in cash they are still ten weeks in arrears. The usual poor payers appear on her list owing their two weeks and four weeks. And here is our man. His name has never appeared on her list for the, and she has checked this, 31 months of his tenancy until six weeks ago and since then he has paid not a penny. She finds this odd. Generally poor payers are poor payers from the outset and she has her own unwritten scheme that dictates when her husband demands the return of his keys and his rent book. But here he is, with no explanation, six weeks in arrears and to her knowledge with only his dole money to live on. Little scope there for saving, for offsetting arrears. If he is the sort to buy a new TV with his rent money surely there would have been signs of it before now. Her curiosity is piqued and she looks through the card file. Here he is. Single. Aged 29, when he took the tenancy. Unemployed. Deposit paid in cash. No complaints or repairs since he moved in. Attic flat – hah! Room with shared bath one floor down. Number 5 St Luke's Place. Three flats she recalls and three single men. How sad.

A month later Mrs Vaz is waiting for her husband. It is Friday. Her list lies on the table neatly tallied.

"Mr Vaz" she says formally to indicate the business nature of her meeting with him. "Mr Vaz, I am concerned about St Luke's Attic Flat. Something about this man's failure to pay is distressing me. What is your assessment of him?" Mrs Vaz has a great respect for her husband's judgement in spite of the town planners. Mr Vaz thinks a little while.

"I have always thought him a sound young man. Sound. Never saying much. But then it is a good thing to speak only if one has something of importance to say, wouldn't you agree? But now you are putting me on the spot. Do you think he is a bad one?" Mr Vaz desperately wanted to say 'bad egg'. He has been reading Agatha Christie and he is taken with the old fashioned speech of her characters. He had been a boy in the days that she writes about, but he has no real memory of those speech patterns and tea times.

"No I do not." Says Mrs Vaz, "I do not. I think only that it is very odd that a good payer should default so suddenly and for so long. I wish you would call on him again and make enquiries of his neighbours. There are only three of them at St Luke's, surely they speak a little, share the milkman, take in on another's parcels. I have looked them up and they have been there all along, he is the newest. But in any case after ten weeks you must tell him to pay or go. We are no charity."

"No we are no charity. Something untoward has occurred. I will ask him to pay a little off his arrears and this week's rent. That will show goodwill on both sides and we can continue from there."

First floor St Luke's has been a little put out. The Attic Flat received little post and mostly it was circulars. When it had accumulated on the downstairs table he took it up and stacking the envelopes neatly outside the Attic Flat door. He did not knock. He simply left them there. He had no cause to return for the next some weeks, but he did think that Attic Flat might have popped in to thank him. He is allowing his disgruntlement to build up when it occurs to him that there has been no evidence of Attic Flat using the bathroom. Not that our man is an untidy or dirty person, but you do notice things being moved about, the bath left wet, that sort of thing. Affecting a casual air he mounts the narrow stair to the attic. Unmoved and neat lies the little stack of envelopes by the door. He goes back down and closes his own door carefully. What, he thinks, if there is a body in the room upstairs? He begins to calculate when he last saw the man in the Attic Flat. He has a good enough memory but cannot recall how long it has been. Not within a couple of weeks anyway. Perhaps it was a month ago. Probably longer. If there had been a body up there all that time he would smell it by now surely. He creeps back upstairs and crouching to the crack under the old and not very straight door sniffs cautiously and then vigorously. All he smells is dust. He returns to his flat and shuts himself in.

Mr Vaz parks his car tidily alongside the kerb. Locking it he makes his usual automatic check for scratches on the polished paintwork. He nips smartly up the steps at number five and lets himself in. The hallway is dark and unpolished, but not dirty. He knocks at the ground floor flat. His tenant holds out his rent book and money without preamble or pleasantry. Mr Vaz thinks he might ask about the Attic Flat tenant, but hands back the rent book with a nod and departs up the stairs. First Floor pays by cheque in the post without fail and Mr Vaz realises that he has not seen inside the flat for over three years. He sorts a key from the mass in his jacket pocket. Before sliding it into the lock he knocks loudly and coughs theatrically. In the reassuring silence from inside the flat he slips in the key and opens the heavy door. The air is warm and clean. None of the furniture in the rooms is his. Every stick and thread that he had equipped the flat with when he bought it five years ago was gone. "Well." thought Mr Vaz "how rude. To dispose of all my goods without a word." But looking round he can see that the replacements are of good quality, better quality than a landlord would provide for a furnished tenancy. The carpets, not fitted, but somehow going together pleasingly, are of shades of gold and yellow overlapping sometimes to snuggle up to the skirting board. The well painted and polished skirting board. The kitchen is not so good, but he could see that a tenant would not want the expense of fitted kitchen units. But the rest, the rest is admirable. Clean, well kept and good quality. Mr Vaz remembers that the rent has not been raised for the entire tenancy.

Passing the bathroom on the landing Mr Vaz begins to feel unaccountably nervous. He recites in his head the sentences he has prepared for the tenant in the Attic Flat. His knocking, as we know will happen, gets no response from within. He picks up the stack of post on the floor. He knocks again, again coughing in his theatrical way. Then using the key he has selected on his way upstairs he opens the door and, holding his breath, pushes it wide before creeping in.

Unlike the First Floor Flat everything here is just as Mr Vaz installed it. The very position of the furniture is unaltered. A haversack is slung over the chair. A small clutter of items lies on the table in the window: a dozen books and an old record player, a few LPs. His tenant has lived here for almost three years and his whole existence would fit into a decent sized shopping bag.

Mr Vaz looks at the envelopes in his hand. Not many and mainly circulars, but of the three postmarked envelopes the oldest is dated almost three months ago. He knows it is against the law to tamper with people's post and puts it all down on the table. He takes from his inside pocket the letter his wife has drafted. It explains that unless some effort is made to pay the rent the tenancy will be terminated at the end of the month and the Attic Flat must be vacated one month after that. The tenant will understand that he will still owe Mr Vaz the full amount outstanding and that his bond will not therefore be returned to him.

"And that," said Mrs Vaz, "is neither here nor there as he owes us more than the bond in any case." Mr Vaz hopes that the tenant of the Attic Flat will get in touch. He likes him and doesn't like to think that he has gone to the bad. He would liked to have put something in the letter that Mrs Vaz has written, something to the effect that if only they could chat things through some arrangement

127

could be come to that would suit them both. Nothing onerous. Nothing that would make too bit a dent in the poor bloke's dole money. But Mrs Vaz has a good head for business and she would be sure to say that this sort of thing would lead to them being taken advantage of. She worries that Mr Vaz, with his quiet, polite manner and sympathetic eyes, does not strike the right note of authority with his tenants. He wishes that she would not tell him so in such a frank way. Surely a wife should not think of her husband in such a way?

Mr Vaz looks again at the post for the tenant. He does know it is against the law to tamper with people's post, but the three proper envelopes, the ones with postmarks and stamps, might give a clue to this unexplained change in his tenant's behaviour. And as one is so old perhaps he has gone away and will never know his letters have been tampered with. Mr Vaz longs for his wife to make the decision for him.

Mrs Vaz, that evening, is in decisive mood. Mr and Mrs Vaz have been landlords for only five years. They have had tenants who have done a bunk owing money. But they have never left their belongings behind, however meagre. Usually they contrive to mistake some of Mr Vaz's belongings for their own.

"What I say is," Mrs Vaz sets down the tray with hot chocolate and biscuits, "the ball is in his court. Seven weeks from now, if he has not paid something to us, he is out. We go to the flat and if he is not there we pack his bits and pieces and bring them here in a box for safekeeping. Then we let the flat. He is costing us money. His arrears are beyond his bond money now. We are out of pocket."

"And I do not disagree with you. All I say is that it is a puzzle. Where would he go? I know he had no job, but he was a quiet, pleasant young man. A thinker. There is a letter there three months old. Where has he been for three months?"

That three months is not lost on the girl at the dole office either. One day she asks her EO again if there is anything she should do.

"If he isn't signing on then he must be working somewhere. I expect he's lost in the system. Got himself a card somewhere else. Send his card up to Longbenton and let them worry about it."

"Do you think something might have happened to him?"

"Like an accident or something?"

"That sort of thing."

"Not really our problem is it? If he's in hospital the Hospital Social Worker will sort him out. Maybe he's emigrated eh? Sunshine on Bondi Beach – or gone to be a Mountie!"

She always finds her EO irritating, but he thinks he is approachable and easy to get along with. She knows this and wonders once again if there is some nasty fault in her character that makes her so critical of him. She finds an unused page near the front of her diary and in small writing, as though this minimises the offence, she notes the name, address, date of birth and NI number of our man.

At the Police Station she is rather pleased that it is a different officer on the desk.

"If you think someone might be dead but no-one knows who they are, how do you find out?"

"Do you think that?"

"Well someone that I used to know, I haven't seen for a while and he isn't at his home. I began to wonder if he might have died. Or something."

"Do you think he might just be avoiding you?"

"Well not really. It's not really like that. But if he had died how would I find out?"

"Death register, miss. Civic Centre."

She feels a bit small now. As though she ought to have known this all along, her being a Civil Servant. She dislikes the feeling and takes it out on the policeman by leaving without thanking him. She doesn't go to the Civic Centre. She is getting cold feet about the whole thing now. So, as it's nearly pay day, she goes to Bainbridge's Food Hall to buy something a little bit out of the ordinary for her evening meal.

The seven weeks prescribed by Mrs Vaz have passed without any word from the tenant of the Attic Flat. She has placed two folded cardboard boxes and a new Yale lock in the boot of the gleaming maroon car and sits in the front passenger seat with her handbag on her lap and her eyes steadfastly forward. Mr Vaz is fussing. He is unhappy about packing up the Attic Flat and is putting off going over there as long as he can. He is reduced to rubbing

129

specks from the chromework of the car and can sense Mrs Vaz's anger seething behind her polite calm eyes. He gets into the driver's seat and starts the engine.

"Clunk Click my dear." Mrs Vaz reaches for the hated seat belt without speaking to her husband or moving her eyes. Her anger now is palpable: a cannibal's cauldron bubbling in her breast. "Off we go." Only a fool could think Mr Vaz was cheerful. And Mrs Vaz is no fool. But she knows that she is right about this and that Mr Vaz is being weak; weak and annoying. The tenant has had fair warning and out he must go. They are out of pocket.

Only the record player and the LPs do not fit into the boxes. One box is enough for the clothes in the cupboard and the few bits of linen. Mrs Vaz has a plastic bag for the bedsheets and pillowslips. Into the other box go the haversack and the books. She holds the funny little New Testament for a moment, looking at the grubby embroidered marker. She opens it and her eye catches the unfortunate line "Give me here on a platter the head of John the Baptist". She closes the book sharply hoping it is not a message for her and wonders if the tenant was a regular Bible reader. Wonders if he thinks it is a Christian thing to do, running out on his rent like this.

Because of the record player and the LPs Mr Vaz has to come back upstairs. He looks round the flat. It is a room. That is all, just a room with a pleasant view. It is cheap to rent. You have to share a bathroom. Their tenant has been here for nearly three years and left no mark on the room. Mrs Vaz has an advertisement to place in the evening paper. The Attic Flat will be let again soon. To a good payer it is to be hoped.

Our man's belongings are packed neatly into the garage of Mr Vaz's comfortable house near the park. They are sealed and labelled. There can be no question of misappropriation here. And our man lies neatly packed away in a mortuary drawer, labelled but unknown. His name, address, date of birth and NI number lie in the diary of the girl at the dole. She changes her diary every Christmas and carefully transfers information into the new one. This year she puzzles over our man's details. She never did go to the Civic Centre. If he is dead then what can be done, she reasons. Unsaid but deeply felt is her fear that she is being gruesome in her curiosity about his fate. She discards the old diary with his details marked in such tiny writing.

At the age of 79 Mrs Vaz lies unconscious in a hospital bed. Blessedly so, as she has terrible injuries. Mr Vaz expired at the scene of the accident. The policeman who attended said that had he not swerved to miss the cyclist in all probability the cyclist would have died and he and his wife been spared. Apart from the injury to his wife Mr Vaz would be pleased with the outcome. His sympathetic nature would always prefer injury to himself than to some other person. And he had been worried for a while that he was getting too old to drive.

Mrs Vaz does not regain consciousness. Her niece is left with all the tidying up to do. Her uncle and aunt have lived in that poky house near the shops for nearly forty years. No wonder her cousins had upped sticks as soon as they could and only come home for birthdays. The simplest way is to collect all the personal things into one room and have the house clearance people come in, she told her husband. So she is going through bags and boxes and suitcases and drawers of papers and trinkets. In the garage are more boxes, neatly stacked, sealed and labelled. It is here she finds the boxes belonging to our man. Two of them. The record player and LPs are there somewhere, not labelled. The box labels are dirty and curled at the corners. But Mrs Vaz's firm businesslike writing is clear: Adam Golightly, Attic Flat, 5 St Luke's Place. 11/7/75. Mrs Vaz's niece is also a businesslike woman. Seeing the date she opens the first box with only a slight niggle of unease. A small rabble of books confronts her, amongst them a tiny white one. She lifts it out and sees it is a Gideon New Testament. It is old and worn, its marker grubby. She flicks the pages open under her thumb. It opens at Matthew 14 where the marker lies and then again at Acts 9 where the crisp twenty note is folded against the spine. She reads the chapter heading "Saul's Conversion" and takes out the banknote. She sees the picture of Shakespeare on the banknote and opens it flat. It looks wrong. Oh what a shame, she thinks, it's an out of date one. Where the testament had lain she sees a piece of paper. On it she reads

1. *a new dictionary*
2. *a record player* ✓

131

She replaces the testament and tosses the old twenty pound note back in the box. Taking her marker pen she writes over the old label – Charity Shop.*

The Letter

by John Hinge

Tuesday morning, long faces, tears not far away.

'What time is Carol picking you up?' I asked.

Susan adjusted her scarf in the hall mirror; the apple green silk was a welcome splash of colour on a dull day. A sideways glance at the clock. 'Anytime now,' she said.

'You sure you don't want me to take you?'

She shook her head. 'No. It would mean you and Tim waiting around, probably for hours. He's on holiday. Can't you think of somewhere nice you can take him?'

'I could take him to Rosslyn Chapel.' I wondered what prompted me to say that. I hadn't been there for years, not since …

'I wrote you a letter last night.' Her eyes, strained over the last few days, were moist and hesitant. She pushed a slim envelope into my hand.

I turned it over. It had just one word, Derek, written on the front in her unmistakeable girly scrawl. 'When did you …?'

'I couldn't sleep. I got up during the night.'

'I didn't hear you. What is it?

'A few thoughts on paper,' she said quickly, as though dismissing its importance. 'Read it later, when you have time.'

Tim watched us from the end of the hall. I wondered what he thought of us passing notes like kids at school.

We waved goodbye from the doorway. She looked tight lipped and drawn as the car pulled away. Today could be a huge turning point in our lives.

'We've got the day to ourselves,' I told Tim. 'What do you want to do?'

'Nothing, really.' He slumped in the chair.

'We must do something. You'll be back to school soon and I'll be at work. We can't waste the day.'

'I'd rather have gone with mum.'

'I told her we might go to Rosslyn. What do you think?'

'If you like.'

We arrived at the chapel a good hour later. I had concentrated on driving while he sat quietly by my side. I knew that today had to be about him ; his world was threatened.

I found a place in the car park, as near to the entrance as possible. The fine rain gave everything a gloss it didn't deserve, and turned the walked areas into muddy troughs. It wasn't the sort of day to visit an ancient monument, but then – this wasn't a normal day.

Across the grass, the mediaeval chapel looked like a grand old lady, out of place in the twenty-first century. She stood soot-blackened and resolute.

'What do you think?' I asked.

Playground-cool severely limits the vocabulary of twelve-year-old boys. Not long ago we'd suffered a deluge of 'wickeds'. He thought for a moment. 'It's spooky,' he said.

'The guidebook says it has an aura of mystery and magic,' I told him.

'It's not as I imagined.'

The chapel springing to recent prominence because of a film and a book, Tim had agreed to visit, even though he'd rather have been with his mother.

For me it was a selfish journey back into the past, rekindling memories, reliving emotions.

I'd been eight years old when father brought me here. I remember clutching his hand as we walked around. My mother had died the week before and part of my world had ended.

'Derek, we'll go out for the day,' he'd said. 'Get some fresh air, go to McDonalds.'

I felt guilty. How could we enjoy ourselves without Mum? It wasn't right, but he'd insisted. 'We need to get out of the house,' he said.

The day had been a blur of memories, of stifled sobs, and of grief. Mums didn't die, not really, not when you were eight, and you needed them.

He walked me around pointing out various features while I pretended to look interested. Now, as I looked at the building again, I couldn't honestly say I recognised anything. That day had been about holding his hand, sharing his misery, and getting on with life, although it wasn't until many years later I realised that. I wondered if that had prompted me to bring my son here today. Was I trying to draw something from the past?

The clouds scattered across the horizon gave no hint of clearing. 'Let's look at the inside first,' I said.

We followed the trickle of visitors down the path and through the front door. Inside, people stood around talking in whispers or sat on the long benches across the middle of the aisle. The abundance of carving and decoration caught and held the eye, everywhere, a disorder of faces, images, and friezes.

I tried to think of a word to describe what I saw. Breathtaking? No, that wasn't it. Startling, maybe. Or perhaps Tim's word, spooky, was accurate enough.

'Did Tom Hanks really film the Da Vinci Code here?'

'Some of it.'

'Wow, just imagine. I'd love to have been here then.'

A man in a grey suit outlined the history of the chapel to an eager audience, his resonating voice made Tim's whisper barely audible. 'Is Mum going to die?'

'Why do you ask that?'

'I know she's been to the hospital lately, and I heard her talking to Aunty Carol on the phone. That's where they've gone today haven't they?'

'Yes, they have, but it may not be bad news.'

'Then why did she give you that letter. What was so important that she couldn't tell you?'

My thoughts exactly. I was still in a quandary over the letter. 'Your Mum's very ill and under a lot of strain. We have to be supportive.'

He clutched my arm. 'What are we going to do if she dies Dad? How are we going to manage on our own?'

His question triggered a long forgotten memory. I'd asked my father the same question. He'd pulled me to his chest in a bear hug and nuzzled the top of my head. 'We'll manage,' he said. 'Somehow, we'll manage.'

Tim was looking up at me with tear stained eyes. Just as I must have looked all those years ago. 'She's not going to die,' I answered, hoping my voice carried the right amount of conviction. 'She wanted us to enjoy ourselves, so let's explore. This place is all about symbols.' I pointed. 'You can see them everywhere. Have a good look around and see what you can find.'

With something to occupy him, he cheered up. I was content to sit and contemplate forging the same sort of relationship with my son as my father had with me. He'd been my confidant and my friend.

The chapel generated peace, restful, untouched by the world outside. Perhaps it was because of the huge number of people who had found a reason to be here over the years. The arches and pillars exemplified the skills of the artisans, true labours of love and devotion. The barrel roof was lofty enough to give the sensation of a higher order watching over, while millions of dust particles illuminated by shafts of blue light from the high window, danced in warm breath. If I had to contemplate the future, I couldn't have found a better place.

I took the letter from my pocket and felt the weight. It was sealed. A single sheet of paper. Was it bad news, a confession? Perhaps she'd had an affair. Were they instructions? Something she wanted done. My fingers hovered, ready to slide open the flap and read the contents, but I didn't. I decided to wait until I knew the result of her visit to the hospital. I put the envelope back in my pocket.

'Dad. What's a Green Man?' Tim was back, clutching an information sheet, his worries temporarily on hold. 'It says there are more Green Men here than in any other Mediaeval building.'

'It's a pagan symbol,' I told him. 'It represents the earth and fertility. How many have you found?'

'Quite a few.'

'Try and find some of the others, The Fallen Angel, the Mediaeval Musician, or the one holding Robert the Bruce's heart.' He sped away, happy to be occupied.

We spent the next couple of hours exploring, researching, exchanging thoughts on what we'd found. To him it was like a treasure hunt. Eventually, I left him and walked out through the baptistry, past the huge font, to the gardens. I found a bench and sat watching the visitors. I was glad I'd come. It gave me an opportunity to think, to work out what I had to do. I didn't know if I could face the world without her, but at least in my mind, I was better prepared.

Hunger drove Tim from the building. He found me on the bench. He looked exhausted. 'Did you know there's a tea shop here?' he asked slyly.

Two donuts and can of coke later he was ready to leave. 'Are we going to the hospital?' he asked.

'No. Let's go home and see if there's any news.'

The rain had stopped, the crowds had thinned; the car park was nearly empty. As we walked out through the gate, the sun began to shine and umbrella shaking became a ritual.

Tim had gone, speeding away. I saw his fair hair bobbing between the parked cars. Another few yards and I was able to see the object of his attention. Susan was standing by our car straining to catch a glimpse. His young eyes had picked out her figure long before me. He was in her arms and she was whirling him around. His excited voice carried back to me. 'Dad, Dad. Look it's Mum.'

As I reached them, her face changed from happiness to concern. During the short silence, Tim hugged her, face buried, stifling sobs.

'How did you get here?' Questions tumbled through my head.

'Carol dropped me off.'

'I didn't expect - ' The words stuck.

As she leaned forward to kiss me, her lips were a few inches from my ear. 'Did you read my letter?' she asked softly.

I patted my pocket. 'Not yet.'

'Then please don't.' She stretched out her hand. 'Let me have it back. It was written when I … when I wasn't sure how things would turn out. Now I am.'

'What happened at the hospital?'

The joy in her face was like summer sunshine. 'I'm clear,' she said. 'They've given me a clean bill of health.'

I felt like a footballer celebrating a goal as we went into a three-person hug with Tim jumping up and down. We were just happy to be together.

Tim gave a little whoop of excitement and pointed to where the cool, resplendent colours of a rainbow had appeared above the chapel. 'Look at that Dad,' he said. 'Another symbol.'

137

The Long Run

by Guy Ware

Steve, watching from the window of his Portakabin office, saw the old man with a neck brace nosing about the lot, peering awkwardly through the windows, shielding them against the greasy glare of a London summer and trying to read the miles. He was short and, apart from the pink foam collar, he wore: a windcheater in some old man colour, with a zip and a tartan lining; a cap (a real one, like in the movie clips where they still walk too fast: no logo); a jumper (not a sweatshirt, not a fleece, but something knitted in wool with a snowflake design); slacks, with a crease; and loafers. Steve watched him turn his whole body from the waist up, his arms swinging round, staying fixed in relation to his trunk, like a robot's, as he looked to both sides before kicking the front tyre of a shark-coloured Mercedes saloon. Steve liked that: a little knowledge is a dangerous thing, he thought. This shouldn't be too hard. He watched the old guy lean on the bonnet just above the wheel arch, pushing with both arms stiff, trying to test the shocks, setting off the alarm instead.

Ray saw the tall, gangling youth coming towards him, saying something Ray couldn't hear over the din. He saw the young man's suit was a size too big at the shoulders, too short at the wrists and ankles; he saw Doctor Marten shoes, a skinny black tie with a black shirt, the collar buttoned but still loose, the young man's stringy neck rattling like a straw in an empty Coke bottle.

"What's that you said, son?"

"I said you've made a good choice there, Sir." Steve, pointing a key at the Merc, silencing the alarm.

The old guy said: "I've not made any choices yet today. I'm trying not to."

"You could do a whole lot worse. Got a few miles on the clock? OK. But a motor like that? She'll run for ever."

"We none of us run for ever, son."

Steve, thinking maybe this guy wasn't going to be so easy after all; thinking, give me a young guy any day, not someone wants to pull rank. The young guys, you made them feel like gangstas, like dealers, with the rude Merc accessories and the phat sound systems, no matter it's a Toyota, you're going to make the sale - they even like to boast how much they paid. Or a woman, maybe. There weren't a lot of women customers came through Steve's Dad's lot, but, when they did, Steve played it dumb, like she and he both knew all that jargon was just toys for boys, and 6.4 times out of 10 that worked, too. (This was no figure of speech, either. Steve kept count and plotted graphs of customers through the door against actual sales. Steve had done a Business Studies A-level before his Dad started getting sick all the time; he knew the importance of graphs.)

The ones who talked through their arses were the worst, thought they knew the tricks of the trade. In the end, with a bit of fake grovelling, it wasn't that much harder to sell them cars, but it was the shit you had to take along the way that Steve objected to. They'd say, what's the trade on this? like he was going to slit his Dad's throat and watch him bleed to death right there on the forecourt, just because the guy's read one copy of 'What Used Car?' Fucking tedious, to tell the truth, and Steve thought this old guy looked like he'd swallowed a bit of that somewhere down the line. That business with the tyres and the shocks, for starters: he'd probably seen that in Minder. But there was something else: the guy looked to be a talker. You mentioned a car, he came back with something about himself. As if I give a shit, thought Steve: I sell cars.

"All I'm saying, Sir," the young man was saying, "there's a reason all the minicabs run old Mercs. They don't break down, you know? I've got a mate in the RAC? Says he's never been called to one of these in all his time on the job. Not once. OK, they're not so cheap to buy, maybe, but you've got to look at the whole life-cycle cost, if you know what I mean."

"You ever been to South America, son?"

"No."

"I have: Bolivia, Chile, Peru, Colombia. And you know what? You're right. You see them all over: great fat Mercs gliding through the poorest, unlikeliest places. All driven by men in vests with St.Christophers or Virgin Marys hanging from the rear view, and no actual insurance. And you know what?"

"What?" said Steve, not caring, not wanting to get into this, but knowing he had to let the old guy talk it out.

139

"I don't think that's the way I want to go."

"Go where?" said Steve, despite himself.

Ray turned stiffly, looking at Steve, and let it pass.

Steve stepped in to fill the silence: "What about your last car, Sir?"

Ray didn't move. "This is my last car," he said.

"I mean, have you got something to trade in? Could make a big difference on the price?" But Ray said he hadn't.

They headed left onto Queen's Road in a jet black sixties Daimler Steve had picked immediately when he'd suggested a test drive and Ray had asked him to choose anything other than a Merc. ("A hearse?" Ray had said when he saw it. "You want to sell me a hearse?" "It's not exactly a hearse," Steve said. "It was for the, what-do-you-call-it? Cortege? Not for the stiff." Ray laughed. "Why not?" he said. "My last car.") Now Ray sat upright, his jacket barely touching the creased leather seat, hands holding the wide walnut wheel at the recommended ten to two that so few of Steve's Dad's customers used.

"Just before the police station?" said Steve. "Turn right there."

Ray said: "I can't do that, son."

"Why not?"

"I can't turn right."

Steve said, "You're going to have to explain that one to me," thinking: nutter. Thinking: it's not a problem. Up here and left on Nunhead Lane, left down Lausanne Road and left again brings us home safe: easy.

Meanwhile, Ray was telling a story: he'd been turning right off the A5, one evening somewhere out of London, somewhere green, where the road looked straight on the map but really it pitched and rolled like a dinghy in a heavy sea. The junction lay at the bottom of a roller-coaster trough, and Ray had sat, waiting for the on-coming traffic to clear, listening to the thock-thock of his indicator, until a flash in his rear view mirror caught his eye. Down the hill behind him in gathering darkness came four motorbikes, riding abreast, each an indistinct black shape behind its glaring headlamp eye. Ray had watched, motionless, as the four riders descended, heads down, faces hidden by visored helmets, accelerating down the hill towards him, faster and faster as they approached, until - way, way too late - one of them looked up as his bike slammed into the back of Ray's car. He disappeared from Ray's mirror, and, a lifetime later, landed on the bonnet with a thud like artillery. The underside of his helmet caught on the silver marque and ripped off the rider's head. Ray had watched the body skitter down the tarmac after the shrieking, fiery bike. The helmeted head remained, face forward, impaled on Ray's bonnet like a figurehead. He listened to the thock-thock of his indicator.

"Oh man, said Steve. That how you got the...?" He waved a finger towards his own neck.

"No," said Ray. "That came later."

The dead rider's companions had circled back, and it was then that Ray had seen the fluorescent yellow stripes, the black-and-white chequerboard patterns and the words 'Worcestershire Police'. This isn't Worcestershire, thought Ray, as they methodically destroyed his car, dragging him from it just before the petrol tank exploded. Then they had beaten him unconscious and left him on the road.

"Shit," said Steve.

He thought the old guy was pretty cool about it, for an old guy, whatever his clothes looked like. He said, "What were you doing in South America?"

Ray said, "Buying coffee."

"Coffee, boss? Really?"

Ray briefly glanced sideways at Steve. "Really," he said. "But not any more. I'm too old."

"You don't mind my asking? How old are you?"

"I've been seventy for a while now, son."

"Seventy's not old. My dad's seventy-eight."

Ray twisted to look at Steve again. The kid couldn't have been more than twenty, twenty-two. He said, "How come?"

"Second marriage," said Steve. "Trophy wife. It didn't work."

Ray said, "That's a hard way to talk about your mother."

"Maybe," said Steve.

141

Steve's mother had been twenty-two herself and blonde as sunshine when she'd driven on to the forecourt in a red soft-top MG, back when Steve's dad had a British Leyland dealership, back when he was king of the world. A year later she was knocked up, big as a whale and hating it. A year or so after that she left before Steve's dad could do it to her again, left Steve and Steve's dad both, for an estate agent who claimed to find the stretch marks sort of sexy. Steve's dad drank too much, and tried to get back with his first wife. She told him to get lost, and Steve had grown up with his dad, learning to sell cars, knowing that somewhere he had a half sister he'd never met.

Ray said, "Nice guy."

Steve let that sit for a while.

Ray said, "Seventy-eight? Still running the show?"

"Not right now," said Steve. "He's in hospital."

"Serious?"

"Gall bladder," said Steve. "He's not dying."

"We're all of us dying, son."

"He's not. He's just … reeling me in."

At the bottom of Lausanne Road Steve remembered you can't turn left into Queen's Road. Ray carried straight on over the lights, turned left a minute later into the Old Kent Road, heading west, Steve thinking: we can still do this: Peckham Park Road, Hill Street, High Street; Queen's Road: home.

Ray shifted uncomfortably in the driving seat, trying to straighten his back.

Steve said: "You sure you should be driving?"

"Probably not. You want to take over?"

"I can't drive," said Steve. "I never learned."

Ray turned to look at him again, then swerved to avoid a cyclist.

"Eyes on the road, boss," said Steve.

Ray said: "You sell cars you can't drive?"

"I was trying not to sell cars."

"And?"

"It didn't work."

They were heading south again now.

This wasn't the first time Steve's dad had been in hospital. It seemed to Steve like his dad or the doctors were just looking for reasons to cut him open, fiddle about inside. It was never anything serious, nothing terminal; but enough for Steve to spend longer and longer at the showroom. His dad barked unnecessary orders from his hospital bed, then came over all sentimental, telling Steve he was a good lad, the business was in good hands, saying that was a comfort when he was going under the knife. Steve had practically stopped visiting. The last time he'd been in was just before the prostate op; his dad had ambushed him with a lawyer there, got him to sign some papers: just in case anything should happen to me, son. The papers gave Steve power of attorney, put him in charge, legally, the lawyer explained, but Steve wasn't fooled. They were just more ballast.

Ray said, "You don't want to do it?"

"I guess. No. I just want ... a choice."

"You're young, son. All you've got is choices."

Ray turned left into Queen's Road, towards the showroom, then past it.

"Hey!" Steve said. "Where are you going?"

"You choose."

Steve laughed. "Are you kidnapping me, boss?"

Ray said, "You're free to leave."

"But it's my car. My dad's car."

"I'll stop. You can drive it back."

"I can't drive."

"Then it looks like you're stuck with me, buster."

Steve sat back, rubbing his hands along leather older than he was; he wound down his window, put his feet on the walnut dashboard.

"Smoke?" he said, pulling a packet of cigarettes from his jacket pocket.

"Oh, yes," said Ray.

Steve lit two cigarettes, passed one to Ray. He inhaled deeply, blew smoke at the roof. He put a hand out the window, feeling the cool, moving air. He said: "Turn left."

Ray turned.

"Left again."

Ray turned. Steve laughed, hard.

143

"Again!"

They turned.

"Again!"

They were making shorter and shorter turns, screwing themselves into a tightening spiral until somehow they hit the Old Kent Road again and Steve yelled: "Go! Just go!"

Ray laughed and howled a wordless yell and flattened the accelerator.

When Steve woke it was dark; they were on the M25, anti-clockwise. He straightened up and said, "Haven't we been here before?"

Ray said, "That was Essex, maybe. This is Surrey."

"We've been right round?"

"No." Ray shook his head stiffly. "You don't remember the M11? Cambridge?"

Steve rubbed his eyes. It was coming back, some sense of monotonous flatlands, of the sky being very big as it turned indigo then black. He remembered they'd seen a sign to Nasty - some village in Bedfordshire, Hertfordshire, maybe - and it had seemed a good idea to go there, see what it had done to deserve the name. But they couldn't make it, just turning left; in the end, they'd given up and headed south again.

He remembered, when he'd said "Go!", that Ray had double de-clutched, working the old-time gearbox like a pro, and slammed his foot down. The Daimler wasn't built for speed and they'd just about managed to break the limit before they ran into a traffic jam.

"This country," Ray said. "It's just not big enough."

He remembered Ray pulling over at a corner shop, getting back into the car with a bag full of Czech lager, a bottle of Johnny Walker Black and a couple of pork pies, saying: "In for a penny..."

Steve talked; Ray had listened, mostly, sipping whisky from the bottle. Occasionally Ray talked, as it got later. He talked about doing things for the last time, about knowing you weren't ever going to have to do them again.

"Bummer," said Steve, emptying a can.

"No it's not," said Ray. "It's simpler."

"How about Portsmouth?" said Ray as they approached Junction 10.

144

"Fuck's at Portsmouth?" said Steve.

"A port, I guess."

A slip road, a roundabout: no right turns. Ray took the A3 south. Twenty minutes later, Ray said they needed petrol, he needed a leak; he pulled into the Little Chef just past Guildford. It was closed.

"This country," said Ray, again.

He used the toilet in the petrol station. Steve went in after him, and found the smell of nesting mice: that unmistakable old man smell, the smell of something rotting inside.

The A31 looks like a right turn on the map, but it isn't. The road peels off to the left then loops round over the Hog's Back.

"Shit, look at that," said Steve, pointing across Ray at London: a bowl of light fifty miles across, and they could see it all from up there.

"Get your hand out of my face," said Ray.

They reached the crossroads at Four Marks about midnight. A woman stood in the beam of Ray's headlights, tall, arms outstretched. When Ray had stopped the car, the chrome bumper inches from her shins, she came round and waited for him to wind the window down.

"Thanks," she said. "I really, really need a lift."

Steve slid open the glass screen as Ray pulled away again.

"Hi," she said. "I'm Joy."

" Ray," said Ray.

"I'm Steve," said Steve, realising he and the old guy had been driving eight hours not knowing each other's names, not asking.

"Where you going, Joy?" said Ray.

"London."

Steve laughed; Ray shook his head.

"What?" said Joy. "What?"

Steve turned round, checking her out. She seemed a long way back in the mourners' seat. She didn't look bad, he thought: a few years older than him, kind of thin and angular, maybe, but not bad. There was a softness under her voice, a kind of quiet hum, like standing near lavender in summer, that seemed at odds with the sharpness of her bones and the jagged edges of her cropped red hair. She was wearing a thin cotton dress with a pattern of tiny flowers over jeans, no coat. He asked her what she thought she was doing on the road at that time of night; she asked if he thought he was her dad. Ray, calming things down, said Steve didn't mean anything; that it was just, it could have been dangerous. Joy said she could look after herself.

Ray said, "In London?"

"Yeah. In London."

"You were on the wrong side of the road, Joy."

"I was? Shit."

Then Ray asked her again what she'd been doing, and she said it was a long story. Ray said they mostly were.

She had been hitching up from Dorset, from Tolpuddle. Where she lived, she said, where she'd always lived. Nowhere, really, but they'd just had the annual Martyrs march, and she'd got talking to some of the union old-timers and, this time, had grabbed the chance of a lift as far as the New Forest in some ancient Stalinists' Lada, wondering all the way if it would make it. (Steve asked who the Tolpuddle Martyrs were. Ray explained, then tried to explain what a Lada was, but Steve said: I know, I sell old cars.)

She had slept in the Forest, under the trees, promising herself ponies and deer, but the only wildlife she'd seen had been a squirrel, half-chewed by something larger. The following day hitching had been slow; it took well into the afternoon to get past Winchester. Then a nice, youngish guy in a Volvo estate had offered her a lift to Arlesford, apologising that he wasn't going further. They'd chatted for a while, the guy keeping it light. Then he offered to take her home, give her a meal. Cooking dinner, he'd opened a bottle of wine; he opened another while they ate. She kicked her shoes off and put her feet up on the sofa; he sat in the facing sofa rolling a joint; she'd sat beside him to show him how to do it better. Then he rolled another to show what a good pupil he was and they smoked them both. She rolled another and slipped it in her pocket for later. When he put his hand on her knee she'd laughed, because it tickled, but when he pushed it up under her dress, grabbing at the buttons of her jeans she'd told him no. And when he tried to force her, she screamed in his face and hit him with an ashtray. He'd grabbed her

146

throat and called her a bitch and pushed her out the door. She was drunk and stoned; how she'd got from Arlesford to wherever it was they'd picked her up she'd never know.

"Christ," said Steve. "Are you OK?"

Joy just laughed. She stretched her legs out on the broad seat and hummed something Ray thought might be Billie Holiday.

"What is this?" she said. "Some kind of limo?"

"Soft of," said Steve.

"You got any music?"

"It's a hearse," said Ray.

"Not a hearse, exactly," said Steve.

Joy laughed again. "So where are you two going in a hearse?"

Ray and Steve turned to each other in the darkness. Ray said: "Damned if I know."

Joy said, "That'll do me for now."

Ray made the M3 just outside Winchester, headed left, towards Southampton. Steve drifted off to sleep again.

Ray said: "So what were you heading to London for?"

"Oh, you know," said Joy.

"Don't tell me," said Ray. "You're going to be an actress, a singer maybe? Meanwhile, you'll wait on tables?"

"I am a singer. I'm going to be an architect."

"No kidding?"

"You think I couldn't?"

Ray held his hands up off the wheel, signalling: Hey, what do I know?

"I've got a place waiting, at UCL. I was always going to go. It was just a question of when."

"You certainly picked your moment," said Ray.

"Who knows? I'd gone another time, something bad might have happened."

Ray laughed. He offered her the whisky bottle. She turned it down, offered him a smoke.

"I've still got one of Nice Guy's joints," she said.

"Why not?" said Ray.

Ray turned left again before they reached Southampton, past Portsmouth after all, kept heading east past Chichester, then hugged the coast through Bognor, Worthing, Brighton.

When Steve woke again they were high on the South Downs; Joy was asleep. He looked across at the old guy and said: "Don't you ever sleep?"

Ray said, "At my age, you don't sleep much."

For the past few miles he had been watching the rear view mirror. If you drive in the country at night and there's no one else on the road, when you look in the mirror - even now, even in England – there's nothing there. Not darkness: nothing. Ray liked that. It had been a long time since he'd seen nothing.

Steve was watching the headlights dust the roadside. A solitary sign glowed like a UFO.

"Beachy Head," he said. "There's a turn coming up for Beachy Head."

"You want to jump?"

"No, I don't want to jump. You think that's the only reason anybody ever goes there?"

"At three in the morning? Probably."

"I just think it'd be cool to see it, you know, in the dark. No one else there."

"Sorry," said Ray. "Can't do it."

"Why can't we do it?"

"It's a right turn."

"It's the middle of the night! All you've got to do is pull across the road, you old coffin-dodger. Just fucking do it, Ray!"

"I can't! Not now. We've come too far."

"Too far for what?"

"To be changing the rules now, son."

Their raised voices had woken Joy. She said, "What rules?"

By the time Steve had explained how they'd got to be where they were, they'd passed the turning, passed the cliffs and dropped into Eastbourne, Steve sulking and muttering something about where Ray belonged. But Ray kept going and, by the time they left the town, the sky ahead was starting to glow.

"Look at that," said Steve, building bridges. "Morning has broken. You ever sing that at school?"

"No," said Ray.

Joy sang: "Like the first morning."

"Maybe," said Ray. "Maybe it's just Dungeness."

Steve just shook his head. "Old guy has spoken," he said, "like the first day."

They stopped for breakfast at Bexhill, though nothing would be open for a while.

"I'm going to make a sandcastle," said Joy.

"It's all stones here," said Ray. "You'd have to go back to Eastbourne for sand."

"Or on to Dymchurch," said Steve.

Ray turned towards him, a question in the movement.

"My dad used to take me there."

"Ah," said Ray. "Steve's dad."

He filled Joy in on Steve's dad. When she asked how old he was, Ray said: "Older than me, apparently."

They had been walking slowly eastwards along the beach, crunching over the pebbles, Steve throwing stones into the sea, trying to make them skip. Ahead, and slightly above them, they could see sheer white walls like cliffs, unpunctuated by windows or signs, but with a rhythm all their own, and, beyond them, three low flat stories of curved glass, curved railings, then glass and railings running straight into the distance for ever like a cruise ship cutting the surf and heading for new worlds.

"Jesus," said Joy. "That's it."

"What is it?" said Steve.

"The De La Warr Pavilion. It's famous, like this modernist classic. 1935, it was built."

"What's modern about something that old?" said Steve. Then, doing the sum in his head, he said: "Hey – same age as you, boss."

"And it's closed," said Ray.

"Only for a re-fit," said Joy.

Steve asked what it was for. Joy read from an information board: "to provide accessible culture and leisure for the people of Bexhill."

Ray said, "There's a poster for the Barron Knights."

149

"Who?" said Steve.

"You don't want to know," said Ray.

Joy had moved away. "Take the piss if you like," she said. "I think it's fantastic. It's so ... It's brilliant, and it knows it. It just says: *here I am*. Imagine it. Imagine building something like that. In Bexhill.

Ray said: "you're really going to be an architect, yeah?"

"Yes," said Joy. "I am."

They found an open cafe. Over breakfast, while Steve stuck chips in his egg yolk, Joy talked about the built environment, about purity of thought and purpose, about the way architecture changed the world. "You can't avoid it," she said. "It's everywhere: why shouldn't it be good?"

"It take a long time to be an architect?" Steve asked.

"Seven years."

"Shit."

They finished eating, lit cigarettes. Ray said, "What now?"

Steve said they could just keep going the way they were, for a while, but Ray said no.

"Why not? It's been fun."

"Because it wouldn't be fun," said Ray. "It'd be just another fucking day to get through like all the rest."

"So?" said Joy.

"Sorry," said Ray.

They were quiet for a while; the urn hissed steam and the radio phone-in gabbled on regardless.

"Steve," said Joy, "what are you going to do when your dad dies?"

"He's not going to die."

"But when he does? What are you going to do?"

"I don't know. Sell up, I suppose. Look for my sister, maybe."

"Why not do it now? He gave you power of attorney. Sell the lot to Ray."

Ray said, "Me? Why me?"

"Have you got the money?"

"Yes. Probably. But ..."

"There you go then. Simple."

"Simple," said Ray.

Steve was looking at the ceiling. "Sell the business?" he said. "While dad's still alive? It'd kill him."

"He'd survive," said Joy.

"Not in the long run," said Ray.

Steve, excited now, said, "You know what Keynes said about the long run?"

Ray was surprised Steve even knew who Keynes was.

"I did Business Studies," said Steve. "We had a term of economics. In the long run, we're all dead."

"There you go, then," said Joy.

"Simple," said Ray.

Ray paid for breakfast, wrote Steve a cheque for a quarter of a million. A pretty good deal. Out on the seafront the air was warming up, the first hardy dogs and ageless, leather-skinned bathers had made it into the water.

Back at the car, Ray said, "You sure I can't give you a lift to London? It's a simple left up the A21."

"No, thanks," said Joy. "I'm not due at college for six weeks yet. I'm going to hang out here a while. I might even head back to Tolpuddle, sort things out properly."

"Steve?"

"No thanks, boss. I don't want to be anywhere inside the M25 when Dad finds out what I've done. I'm going to find a bank before you change your mind. Then I think I'll head for Dymchurch, build a sandcastle. On to Dover, perhaps: maybe catch a ferry. You take it easy, yeah?"

"You know," said Ray, "I thought I'd never have to buy another car. Now I've got thirty-five."

"Don't worry, boss. You'll make it."

Ray laughed. He stuck out his right hand. Steve looked confused for a moment, then shook it. When he let go, Joy stepped up and hugged him briefly, then hugged Ray.

"Mind my back," said Ray.

"You take care," said Joy.

"You too," said Ray.

He climbed into the Daimler, pulled away slowly, watching Steve and Joy in the rear view mirror.

They watched him go.

Steve turned to Joy: "Bye, then," he said. "It's been good."

"Yeah," said Joy, "it has. It's been good."

Shadows In The Spring

by Laura Dippie

March was a bitter month; it had been one of the longest winters we'd ever known and it felt like the weather was locked in eternal cold. It almost felt like time wasn't moving at all. I was sixteen and still at school, kicking my heels, stressing about exams and discovering Bob Dylan. Time was refusing to move for me; it was two hands on a clock face refusing to do so much as flicker. I wanted to be eighteen, go clubbing, get a boyfriend, learn to drive, move out and grow up; I wanted it so badly, sometimes I felt I couldn't breathe for wanting it. It felt like time was playing tricks on me, conspiring with my parents to keep me in some eternal Never-Never Land where I could never grow old and do all the things I wanted to do, or get a chance to be who I wanted to be.

It changed, and more suddenly than I could ever have expected. I was walking to school through the park as I always did, my eyes following every crack in the tarmac with weary familiarity. I had almost reached the kids' playground when suddenly I stopped, bit my lip and looked around me. It felt like my whole body was consumed with anger, anger against my life and the world and everything in it, and I strode off down a side path. I walked fast, impulsively, with no sense of direction, only with this restless fury pounding in my veins. Halfway across the park it wore off a little and I slumped on a bench feeling suddenly tired.

I watched apathetically as the usual kind of people walked through the park and I sighed heavily to myself. I couldn't comprehend why they chose to live in such a conservative little town, when they could just as easily be in a big city with bright lights and sound and *life* to it, life and movement and change. They all looked like machines, anaesthetised by habit and just so settled. It was anathema to me. I loved nothing more than feeling like I was all up in the air, with no way of knowing where or when or how I would come down. I liked feeling that this moment, this one, right here and now, *mattered*. I liked to think I would remember it, and it would be important, and it could change something.

I drew my legs up under me on the bench. It was below freezing; the blood was slowing in my veins, the warmth draining from my fingers and toes. I thought delightedly of how incomprehensible my teachers and parents would find this. I thought how easy it would be for the cold to drain the life from me, and I smiled.

I sat there without purpose, waiting for something to happen and feeling strangely free. A little to my left, the dustbin woman was clearing up litter with one of those long metal arm things and a big black sack. I could hear the heavy tread of a man walking up the path behind me. I thought about how nice it would be if you could do that with your life, just sweep all the empty cans and bottles and stained needles into a big sack and throw it away. The man had almost passed the bench, and I could hear and feel his footsteps slow. I glanced up, and he was staring straight at me; I glared back defiantly, sick of being noticed. But he didn't drop his eyes from mine looking a little ashamed, as they normally do. There was no leer in his face either, no hunger, just a hesitant kind of question. The irritation burned itself out in me and my gaze softened. It was a strange moment, looking deep into a stranger's eyes so wordlessly. It was oddly moving. He nodded a little to himself and passed me something flat wrapped in an M&S bag. His eyes still trained on mine, he nodded again, gaze dark and serious, and something jumped in me, and he turned and walked away.

I let out my breath before I realised I'd been holding it, and suddenly I was breathing short and fast as if I'd had a shock. He'd been average height and quite skinny, around early thirties or maybe late twenties, with a calm and gentle face. It was a serious face, prematurely lined at the corners of the mouth, and his eyes held a raw depth I had never seen in anyone before. It made me think he had nothing to hide any more, or maybe that he no longer saw the point in hiding anything. Their expression tore at me. I didn't really know why. I just sensed an ocean of sadness in him, so strongly I felt I could touch it, that it would be all around him like an aura.

He was still walking away from me, coat flapping, hands deep in his pockets, head down. I could catch him up if I wanted to, but I knew I wouldn't; maybe because he seemed to trust and believe I wouldn't. It felt scripted, that moment, not something real and tangible, but something that had to happen, that couldn't have happened any other way. I stared at him until he went out of sight, then I came to a little. I looked down at the bag he'd given me and opened it with fingers clumsy from the cold. Inside was a single A4 pad of plain paper with the price sticker still on the front. I felt a horrible swooping in my stomach, suddenly terrified it was all a joke, it had meant nothing, and I had been taken in.

I breathed in deeply and flipped open the pad. The first page was covered in big, sloping writing. I flicked quickly through the book; it was full of photos, writing and drawings and I smiled to myself, more relieved than I could admit. I still didn't know what it meant, but at least it meant something.

I was aware now of the pull that school was exerting on me from this distance, the pull of habit and routine and not getting into trouble. I enjoyed resisting it. This moment had to be continued, or it would lose all its meaning. I had to look through the scrapbook now. It was a life story. I couldn't believe my eyes. This was the first page:

This is an anthem for doomed youth. I know it's hard to hold the hand of anyone who's reaching for the sky just to surrender, but can't you see how I long to move away? I have longed to move away from the repetition of salutes, for there are ghosts in the air and ghostly echoes on paper, and the thunder of calls and notes, and I have longed to move away, and so runs my dream. But what am I? An infant crying in the night, an infant crying for the light, and with no language but a cry. This is it. This is my cry.[1]

---

[1] "Anthem for doomed youth" from /Anthem for Doomed Youth/ by Wilfred Owen

"It's hard to hold the hand of anyone who's reaching for the sky just to surrender" from /Stranger Song/ by Leonard Cohen

"I have longed to move away from the repetition of salutes, for there are ghosts in the air and ghostly echoes on paper, and the thunder of calls and notes. I have longed to move away" from /I Have Longed to Move Away/ by Dylan Thomas

"So runs my dream: but what am I? An infant crying in the night: An infant crying for the light: And with no language but a cry" from /In Memoriam/ by Alfred Tennyson

That was the only explanation I was going to get. I flicked through the book. The next ten pages or so were all covered in photos. His face appeared on the first page and it shocked me deeply to see the change in him. That lined mouth was laughing, those dark eyes were smiling, and his face was relaxed and open. He was standing on a sunny street in T-shirt and jeans looking young and happy, his arm around the waist of a young woman who was laughing up at him with adoration in her eyes. There was a scrawled note: *London, '99, remember that café with the roofed sunlight...?*

There were more photos of them. In some he looked even younger, not much older than me, and in those ones he was with a blonde woman instead. He looked so sweet and young, with a scraggly dark beard and a lightness in his dark eyes that didn't quite suit him. She was young too, around his age, with cropped hair and a wide smile and eyes which didn't say a lot. There were some of him on his own; in one, he was walking down a dark deserted street. There was a streetlight ahead and it cast his shadow behind him on the ground; his face was turned a little towards the camera, a glimpse of those dark eyes in the darkness, coat swirling behind him. I loved that one. There was no accompanying note for it, no explanation. It could have been anywhere and he looked so enigmatic, as if he'd just stepped out of some '50s *film noir*. There were others of him posing with friends, and sometimes it was just the friends on their own; they were lying on beaches, sitting in rooms, dancing in clubs, eating in restaurants; they were laughing, smiling, frowning, caught unawares; they were beautiful and ugly and sober and drunk and relaxed and annoyed.

That first woman kept returning. There was a drawing of her on one page which somehow seemed to capture more of her than any of the photos had done. She was thin, with strongly defined cheekbones and a hunted look in her blue eyes; she had mousy brown hair which fell straight to her shoulders. Her mouth was unsmiling and slightly parted, and she seemed caught in motion, as if she was just about to leap off the page and start crying or yelling or talking. There was an immense sadness about her, too. She had a look in her eyes like she was standing on the tracks watching a train bearing down on her. Her eyes fixed you and tore at you at the same time, like his had done; I turned the page quickly, but found the

156

laughing photos seemed hollow afterwards. Everything seemed to come back to that hunted darkness in her eyes and in his and I started seeing it where it probably wasn't, trying to trace its origins, trying desperately to understand.

On other pages were poems and lyrics and quotes, sometimes whole and sometimes fragments, all written out in that intense sloping hand. There was Shakespeare and Dylan, Keats and Salinger, Nietzsche and Wilde. Not all were named, and there were many I half-recognised but couldn't place. Some may have been his own. I don't know. I somehow felt I was intruding much more on his life and his thoughts than I had when looking at the photos. The photos had only hinted at what was going on in his mind; here it was laid out, philosophical and lyrical, things which chased themselves round his head, which held associations, which had defined moments and phases of his life. There was a strange kind of raw beauty to it; these were the words that defined him, that entranced him, that summarised his feelings and tastes better than anything else could. They were intense, funny, confusing and savage by turns. Reading them all in quick succession just took my breath away. I have never been confronted by so much heartfelt eloquence at once, before or since.

I closed the book, feeling immensely moved and quietened. Someone had entrusted this to me. This was someone's life laid out; I knew the girlfriends, the friends, the parents, the sister, the sister's partner and their little baby. I knew the look of his kitchen and I knew the sitting room of his sister's house. I knew it all, and I still didn't feel I knew anything. Everything was still so unexplained. I couldn't imagine ever putting everything down like this, sticking in pictures of myself, my friends and my family, writing out lyrics I liked and quotes I identified with. I would be too afraid to let myself see it, let alone giving something so deeply personal to a total stranger. It was all so odd.

I had an idea in my head I didn't want to consider. I had an idea that whispered 'suicide'. I had an idea he'd given this to me in a last attempt to provide a meaning, had walked away and killed himself, knowing that something would survive. And I thought it was a good plan, in many ways. This was the most complete expression of a life and personality I had ever seen. There was no sense of anything having been disguised, omitted or emphasised; this was everything, as it stood, presented with a clear and direct honesty. No one, reading it, could fail to be moved. No one, surely, could fail to look after it.

I felt tears rising in my eyes and my throat tightened. I wanted to do something, anything, to see him again. I wanted him to know that he shouldn't do it, he shouldn't kill himself, I wanted him to see that there was all this life and beauty in this book and he couldn't just cut it short, he couldn't, he had to wait, it wasn't ended. He couldn't be allowed to think it had ended.

I walked slowly to school, signed in late, and carried on with the day. Everything around me had changed. I felt his was the only existence in the world, the only one. Everything revolved around him. I felt cold and sick.

I went back to the same bench the next morning, shivering, but he did not come. I went again at the weekend, hoping, hoping, and then again the next week. It all made me feel so young and immature. While I waited for him I thought about things in a way I hadn't really done before, and everything in my life seemed suddenly smaller yet somehow more important at the same time. Exactly a week after the first encounter, I heard a tread on the path behind me. I waited. I wouldn't allow myself to look. The footsteps carried on, and stopped.

I looked up, and his grave dark eyes were looking back. I saw him differently now; I saw traces of how he'd looked as a younger man, the changes in his eyes and mouth and forehead, and it was like looking into the past and seeing what had to happen and being powerless to prevent it. It made me feel so lost.

We stared at one another. I didn't know what to say. I looked down at the book in my hands, still wrapped in its M&S bag.

"I thought you'd killed yourself," I said, my voice loud in the silence.

He sighed.

"I just thought – because of this book, you know – it felt like – well-"

"An elegy?" His voice was soft, tired.

I didn't know what that meant. "A goodbye," I suggested.

158

He sighed again, his eyes sweeping the park but not seeing it. "I tried," he said, his voice frighteningly dispassionate. His eyes came back to meet mine, waiting for a response. "I tried to kill myself."

Again, the moment was not real. It was nothing real. It was all scripted. My voice was steady; I just had to play my part. "Why didn't you?"

He shrugged slowly and with great indifference. "Curiosity, in the end. I wanted to know what you'd think. I had to know."

I looked down at the book again. His eyes made me feel dizzy, like I could almost see into him through them, but all there was inside was this great big vortex. "What do you want to know? Exactly?"

The control seemed to go out of him. He flopped down on the bench beside me and stared at a patch of frosted grass. "What it all means," he said flatly, with a desperate edge of mockery. He glanced across at me, his mouth twisting a little. "Can you tell me that, do you think?"

I saw for a moment what he was seeing, a schoolgirl with a schoolbag, her face as yet unmarked by time and emotion. I felt a sudden searing sense of loss, of waste, and I didn't know if it was directed at him or at me anymore but it felt like it was draining the life out of me.

"No," I said slowly. "I just think it's beautiful, that's all."

He started. He looked like he didn't know whether to laugh or cry or walk away. "What?"

I shrugged and passed him the book. "I think it's beautiful. Whatever it is you're trying to figure out. It's sad. I mean, to see the change in you, from when you were all young and happy, and now when you're older and hurt, but I think it's kind of – meant. I don't think there's any real purity or meaning in the young pictures of you, or the ones of her, or any of them. I don't think that could mean anything because it was just the natural state of mind and being for you, you didn't have to fight for anything. It all just came naturally. I think, I don't know, I just – I think you have to fight for anything to matter. I mean, when you were young, you were just following your instincts. And now, maybe you've reached the stage where you can make a choice. I think that's beautiful. In its way."

He didn't say a thing. He leaned forward on his knees, his head supported by his hands, staring down at the grass.

"I think beauty has to hurt before it means anything."

He laughed a short, humourless laugh and thought for a moment. "So you think this life is given meaning by its transience."

I hesitated. I didn't understand.

"So that if we were immortal," he continued slowly, "nothing would mean anything. And – if we understood it all, or didn't understand a thing, it wouldn't mean anything."

"Yes."

He paused, and raised his eyes to meet the horizon. "I like how you use the word meaning." He laughed, and this time he meant it, and he turned and his eyes were laughing as they met mine. "Christ, I like how you philosophise." He laughed again to himself. "Maybe," he said out loud, still laughing a little, his voice serious. "Maybe you're right, in a sense. Maybe." He looked at me for a while, and a real smile was creeping around the edges of his mouth. "Thank you."

I smiled back, relieved and awkward, feeling the script had ended without warning and abandoned me. He stood up, the book under his arm. "I was lucky to find you," he said. "Most people would have just told me to - where to go."

I grinned, and suddenly I couldn't meet his eyes. "Well."

"I can't believe you actually – you don't know me, and you read it, and you came back, and you still didn't just tell me to – to get lost. You actually cared." There is wonder in his face. As if he could believe better things of humanity, almost.

"Of course I did," I said, nodding at the book. "Your whole life is in there. It was like someone just – I don't know – it was like someone baring their soul."

Something flashed in his eyes, and he smiled. "Thank you. Really. Thank you." He did a little bow, his head and shoulders tipping forward; he grinned a quick grin, looking suddenly youthful. Then he turned and walked away, quickly this time. I watched him go.

March gradually broke free of its cold. By the end of the month the sun was shining, the daffodils were out and there was blossom on the trees. I discarded my coat and gloves, and the sun felt good against my skin. I walked through the park every day but I never saw him again. It didn't matter. I felt much older, and younger at the same time. I no longer felt like I was waiting to grow up; I felt like things were happening at their own pace, and I just fell in with them.

Fairway

by Cathy Whitfield

'Variable, becoming westerly 3 to 4 later....'

Sarah groans as the early morning shipping forecast wakes her. She's heavy-headed from the sleep into which she'd finally fallen after spending most of the night listening to Martyn pretending to be asleep. Now she just wants to roll over and sink back into oblivion, but she listens to the rest of the forecast. It will be clear, cold perhaps, but fair. Not a bad forecast for the time of year. So she isn't surprised when Martyn gets up, goes into the kitchen and comes back with the tide tables in his hand.

'Springs,' he says. 'We could get away by eight.'

Once she might have resented his assumption that she'd fall in with his plans. But not this year. Not when it might be their last sail of the season. So, half an hour later, they're down at the harbour, sniffing the air, Sarah shivering, Martyn muffled up in his waterproof and the ridiculous hat he's taken to wearing. Everything is damp from a mist that has run up the river at dawn after a clear night and the handrail is beaded with moisture, the deck slippery and the sails stiff. There is barely enough breeze to lift the pennant.

'For 'Variable' read 'Flat calm',' she complains. 'The forecast was right.'

'The forecast usually is,' he says gravely, and with a sinking heart she sees his mood plummet. However, they get away quickly and he seems to recover his spirits. At the beginning of the season they're all fingers and thumbs, but by the end of the year they're a well-oiled machine, with everything to hand, the engine purring evenly, their speed and momentum carefully judged. If it hadn't been for the cold and her small slip of the tongue she might even have taken pleasure in their quiet slipping away.

They cut the engine once they're out in the channel, shock the sudden silence with a squeal of winches and then, with a turn of the wheel, there is quiet again. Not silence, of course, but the small sounds of water running along the hull, the fluttering luff of the foresail, the log ticking slowly as they drifted down the river, caught by the tide, the wind barely strong enough the fill the sails.

162

Sarah always likes the moment when the confusion of slapping canvas and loose ropes gives way to the controlled catching of the wind and a tilting as the river catches the keel. She likes to watch the banks recede, houses merge together and then fade, farmland give way to forest and then to dune and bank. Ahead, the light is rising above the thinning mist, a lemon-coloured light washing the leaden sea, and the whole estuary is open before them.

But today the quiet holds other things - a silence and a tension; a sense that things that have not been said will now be voiced. Martyn seems to be waiting for her to say something, to begin something he's afraid of beginning himself.

'Shall I make coffee?' she asks brightly to break the silence.

'We've only just had breakfast.' Martyn is a creature of habit. Coffee is taken at 10.30 and not before.

'But I'm cold,' she says, going below. There isn't much gas left and the drinking water, after a few weeks of absence, is stale. The biscuits have gone soggy in the tin. The coffee, as most things made on the boat, tastes faintly of bilge water, but it's hot and wet and make her feel warmer, if no less of a coward.

'Martyn ..' she begins, after they've drunk their coffee and he's poured the dregs into the river, but the moment is gone and he turns away.

'Listen!'

She hears the gurgle of the wake, the creak of ropes, the distant boom of the city, a train announcing its departure, a dog barking. Nearer, from the banks and mud-flats comes the whirling trill of curlews. Then, high and clear, the crying of geese. Directly overhead, the veins of their flight are caught in the tilting angle of the mast. They watch them beat their way upriver and by the time they've disappeared, their calls fading, Sarah no longer has anything to say.

Martyn leaves her to steer, goes forward and stands by the mast, holding on to the shrouds. The wind picks up a little from the west, but the river is smooth and untroubled, the land sliding past them, their progress effortless. It's easy, at such times, not to think of the return; the wind on the nose, the long beat to windward, the day darkening. But today, with each passing mile, Sarah begins to think of coming back and, her mind having strayed into the future, finds herself also wandering in the past. Another boat, but the same river; a different channel but the same abandoned lighthouses. Over the years the forest has encroached on the dunes, the dunes on the sea. The banks are shallower now, the channel narrower and the bar at the river mouth, marked by two buoys, can be a troubled place. She wants to share these changes with Martyn, but he remains resolutely apart, swaying to the growing motion as an old swell heaves its way over the bank from the south east.

They pass the place where the lightship used to be. 'Do you remember ..?' she might have said another day, another season. But on this day, the last sail of the season, she stays silent, and forces herself back into the moment. She will make Martyn do the same. She will offer him tasteless coffee at the wrong time, soggy biscuits and a silence he can fill with the sound of geese if he wants to. She will offer him the wind and the river, and then the sea.

The transition is imperceptible. An opening out, the banks to the north and south falling away. Surf gives way to breakers, breakers to troubled water and then ... nothing. It is clear now. The mist has risen and the rim of the world is sharp and clear, notched by the white finger of a distant lighthouse. 'Do you remember ...?' she wants to ask again. But again she doesn't.

They're over the bar now, a wild place in a storm but today the two marker buoys just swing uneasily in the cross-seas. The waves steepen and the sail slaps in the troughs, but the tide draws them through angled waves and before long they're free. The water darkens as the bottom falls away until it takes on the blue-green damasked quality of great depths. Sarah leans over the side and watches the light spearing downwards and imagines, as she always does, that she can see creatures with no shape and no name swimming far beneath them. Out there, beyond the edge, she has a sense of other worlds and draws back, afraid that her imagining of such things might give them life.

'Only the Fairway to go now,' Martyn says unnecessarily. It's perhaps a mile off, a pillar buoy blinking its semaphored message - warning or greeting. This is the place where ships are gathered in; oil rig supply boats coming south from the north sea fields, by Scurdie Ness and Red Head; or tankers up from the Forth, by the May and the Carr Light. Some even come from the east, past the low black rocks of the Bell with its white tower. All of them come here, to the Fairway, where the little pilot boat will chivvy them up-river on a rising tide, passing them from one buoy to the next, to the wharves and docks of the City.

But today, no-one waits to gather them in.

'I like it here,' Martyn says, looking around. The wind has dropped away completely now, but there's still a little tide taking them north-east towards the Fairway. Yet, sitting on the oily tilting water, it seems to Sarah as if it's they who are tethered, that the buoy is sliding slowly towards them, blinking lazily in the pale afternoon sun.

'The land's last holding,' Martyn says, a quote from something she didn't recognise, as the Fairway slides past them. Sarah watches it, rocking in the swell, and imagines the chain that binds it, rusting and weed-slimed, descending through darkening water to impossible depths. She shudders at the thought.

'There should be music here,' Martyn says, his voice sharper now. 'There used to be, didn't there? This used to be a whistle buoy. Remember how you could hear it from miles away? And there were foghorns on the cliffs - remember how we sailed under the cliff once and how they boomed out like ... like wolves? And a bell. There was a bell on the rocks.'

The tide breathes its last, but Martyn has found his own tide. 'Remember?' he demands, cuffing moisture from his cheek. Appalled, Sarah can think of no way to stop the flood that she's seen coming for months, and knows she mustn't even try.

'Now what is there?' He sweeps his arm out to encompass the whole horizon, holding on with the other but so lightly she half-rises, afraid he might lose his balance and fall. 'Nothing! Nothing but chaos. Listen to it!'

She listens. She hears what he hears; the slap of the sail, a shackle rattling on the shrouds, a gasping flutter from the luff. But then, when she can bear it no more, and knows he has borne it too long already, there's a breath of wind and the sail snaps full, dragging the boom back. The boat tilts a little and a ripple catches hold of the keel. The log, silent until now, slowly begins to tick. Martyn laughs in a shudder of sound that's half a sob.

'Sorry,' he says. 'Sorry!'

165

It's all right, she wants to say, to go to him and bend his head to her shoulder. *It will be all right.* She wants to hush him like a child, but knows she mustn't.

'Chaos, indeed!' she says sternly. 'Well, what now? Where are we heading? North? South? East? Or home?'

'You choose,' he says, turning away.

'No - you choose,' she snaps, fighting his defeat. She lets go of the tiller and the boat swing into the wind, the sail slapping irritably. 'You choose.'

He comes back to the cockpit. She knows he hates this - the noise, the lack of control. Especially that. He grasps the tiller, and puts it hard up-wind, but then pulls in the sheet on that side so the boat heaves-to, the sail pulling against the rudder, and they're drifting, like the buoy, tethered to the land's last holding. This option hasn't occurred to her.

'I said - I like it here,' he says, evenly. Not angrily now, not anything. Just - calmly. She feels cold all of a sudden. The boat surges into the breeze then falls off again with a hiss.

'We can't stay here for ever,' she points out.

'Why not?'

'Because .... because we've only got soggy biscuits to eat.'

It's such a stupid reason that they both laugh shakily and Sarah begins to think they've drawn back from the danger into which Martyn has taken them.

'All right,' he says eventually. 'I'll choose. It's our last sail after all.'

He steps up to the deck and looks to all points of the compass. Close by, the buoy still blinks away. The afternoon is darkening, night closing in from the east. In the distance the lighthouse flashes.

'The reason I like it here,' he says. 'Is that you can go anywhere. Until you choose, all things are possible. This is the place where you cast loose.' He looked down into the water, the impossible depths, blue-green shifting water and the chain leading downwards.

She sees the possibility cross his mind and the tears she's beaten back for so long - so long - prickle at the back of her eyes. She'd thought this was a place of gathering in, but realises that he sees it quite differently.

'I wish you'd take off that stupid hat!' she says crossly, brushing a tear away, angry that she's broken at last, that they've both broken, in spite of the promises they'd made to each other.

'I'll take the hat off if you stop pretending it's going to be all right, Sarah.'

'I'm not pretending. I'm just ... hoping.'

The one direction in which he's not prepared to go.

'Let's go home, Martyn,' she begs.

They both turn in that direction. Clouds have built up over the land and the sky is slate and sullen-looking. The wind has picked up - due west now, as forecast, dead on the nose. Sarah imagines their return, beating between banks, the day darkening, light from the city confusing, the rush of water in the dark, and a cold landfall.

'All right,' he says, loosening the sheet and pulling back the tiller. The boat swings and catches the wind. He pulls off his hat and tosses it into the sea as they pass the Fairway. His scalp is pink, the hair fine where it has grown back. It will take a while, they'd told him. It might never grow back. What they hadn't told him, but which they both know, is that it might not matter. Sarah imagines the months ahead, beating from one appointment to the next, the setbacks, the rough places where hazards come out of the dark, the buoys that blink their unintelligible warnings, and the cold, cold landfall.

The wind strengthens, as predicted, but as it does so it veers into the south. Martyn eases the boat to windward, adjusts the ropes, and turns his face to the wind, his fine hair blowing back from his thin drawn face as the boat plunges home, sweetly now, on a close reach, picking up speed as the wind continues to veer. They rush through the darkening river, the shrouds taut and humming, their wake chuckling under the stern. There is music here after all.

'You see?' she yells, against the wind and the rush of water, gesturing to the pennant at the top of the mast. 'Forecasts *can* be wrong!'

She's crying openly now. He's thrown his hat away and so she mustn't pretend any more. But she can still hope. That's allowed.

167

Coping Strategies

by Judy Walker

Of course Maureen lived on her own. That way there was no problem about sharing. She couldn't think of anything worse (except, perhaps, having no food in the house) than opening a box of chocolates and having to offer them to someone else. Imagining the pain of seeing nutty clusters, soft centres and chewy caramels disappear into the jaws of another made her feel quite panicky. Like the time she'd left a Thornton's carrier bag on the bus. What a nightmare that had been, phoning up the bus company, traipsing back into town.

So, anyway – no problem at home. Maureen had cupboards stuffed with biscuits, crisps, Cheesy Wotsits, salted nuts, tinned beans and family sized chocolate bars. Her fridge strained on its hinges to rein in bacon, eggs, sausages, butter, cream, pork pies, sliced ham, coleslaw, mayonnaise and chocolate spread. She never bought anything in ones any more. A six pack of crisps grew to 12, then 24 until she discovered the joy of the Makro card. Now she could load up her trolley with boxes of crisps, case of biscuits and catering packs of baked beans.

As for the 'three for two' offer – it could have been invented for Maureen. If you liked something, of course you were going to want at least three of it – and the day Thorntons took it up she celebrated with three bags of brazil nut toffee (chocolate coated), three boxes of rum and raisin fudge, three bars of alpini truffle – what a saving that represented.

"I've got lots of kids to buy for," she'd explain to the assistant, as she rang up Maureen's purchases and looked out one of the big Easter egg bags to pack them into.

Maureen prided herself on never having seen the bottom of her chest freezer, which was choc o bloc (pun intended) with pizzas, fisherman's pies, chicken curries, artic rolls, readymeals of every description, loaves of bread, catering packs of raspberry ripple ice cream, burgers, sausage rolls and – a particular favourite – white chocolate Magnums. She loved the excitement of putting her hand in,

168

like a child dipping into a bran tub, and bringing forth her mystery prize.

Work proved more of a challenge but over the years Maureen had developed coping strategies: deep desk drawers that slid easily on their runners so they could be whipped open or slammed shut the instant someone left or entered her office. A large shopping bag was essential and the day she was allocated her own personal filing cabinet – with key – was indeed a day of great joy.

If she ever thought about it, which she did rarely and only ever during the grey no man's land hours between night and day when, due to heartburn, stomach cramps or indigestion, she fruitlessly pursued sleep. Yes, if she ever did think of where she might lay blame, it would be with her mother.

"Eat up Maureen"… "clear your plate Maureen"… "No pudding until you've finished what's on your plate Maureen". So she had and it had just become a habit. Phrases such as "she enjoys her food" and "she has a good appetite" or even "it's just a bit of puppy fat" followed her into adolescence where she became "big boned"…."sturdy"…."a little on the plump side" until the day she moved out, leaving the bathroom scales and anything without an elasticated waist behind her.

She was thinking about that and about God the day it first happened. If the Almighty had meant her to be thin, then surely he wouldn't have given her such a robust appetite or made her taste buds so amenable to all fattening food, would he?

She had just completed her lunch break circuit, ending with, as usual, Bunters the bakers, where she loaded up with a couple of steak bakes, three sausages rolls (for the price of two), three cheese and onion pasties (ditto), a four pack of madeleines (sensibly they didn't even sell them singly any more) and then onto the cream cakes, pointing out her choices to the vacant, spotty teenager serving her.

"We've got a birthday in the office," she confided as she exchanged her money for the bags and boxes. The teenager made no acknowledgement.

She returned to the office, climbing the creaking, wooden stairs with difficulty, stopping at each turn to recover her breath, under the guise of adjusting her shopping bags and bemoaning, as usual, the lack of a lift. She had thought about trying out the chair lift, recently installed to comply with legislation, but she was dubious as to whether she could fit into the ridiculously narrow seat.

She nudged the door open with her elbow.

"You're late back," Marjorie, one of the other three occupants of the wages office, already had her coat on, bag over her arm. She tapped the face of her watch.

"It's not my fault, it's those stairs," protested Maureen. "It was just on one when I got in, but it's taken me a good ten minutes to get up those bloody stairs. If they won't put in a lift, we should be allowed extra time to take account of the stairs."

But Marjorie had gone.

"Cow," muttered Maureen as she set about shedding her bags. She manoeuvred herself between her desk and chair and hovered for a few moments before allowing her bottom to plummet towards the upholstered seat, which squawked in anguish as contact was made.

She opened the two top drawers of her desk and placed, for later, the cream cakes and madeleines in one and party pack of tortilla chips with salsa dip in the other.

Opening a file she started on her lunch, stopping every so often to lick her fingers, screw up an empty bag, shake crumbs from the wide shelf of her bosom or, less often, to turn a page of the file. When she had completed the savoury section of her meal she stood up, brushing pastry flakes off her body and carried out a tour of her absent colleagues' desks.

With the pretence of searching for a stapler, Maureen harvested half a packet of Polos, two Jaffa Cakes, a Kitkat and a small amount of – rather flat – Seven Up.

The Kitkat was the most dangerous but it was Marjorie's, so Maureen figured she deserved it after the telling off the old goat had given her. She made sure she put the wrapper in her handbag, rather than the bin so there could be no risk of discovery. Irritatingly, Maureen only managed to get through a meringue and a vanilla slice before she heard footsteps on the stairs and had to slam her drawer shut.

By two o'clock the four members of the wages department were all back at their desks, tapping away at keyboards.

"Oh, it's frozen *again*," Maureen sighed, rapping repeatedly on her 'enter' key.

Alison looked over her reading glasses at her colleague. "You'll have to call tech support," she said.

"Just when I need to get on," said Maureen, picking up the phone. She explained her problem to "tech support, this is Tony, how can I help you?" who talked her through various operations while she kept the phone squashed to her ear with her right shoulder.

"No, it's not doing anything," she told him triumphantly. Tony said he'd pop up in 10 minutes.

"Well, it's not my fault. I can't do anything till he comes," said Maureen petulantly and she sat back on her chair with her arms folded on her stomach like two Swiss rolls atop a Christmas pudding. She pulled open her second drawer down. "Anyone like a biscuit?" she waved the choc chip cookie packet around for half a second and then withdrew it. "Actually there's only a couple left," she said, levering out six biscuits. She hid four of them in her left hand and dropped the other two into her mouth.

When Tony arrived she was just downing the final concealed cookie, under cover of her computer monitor. Maureen stood up to let Tony take her place at the desk. A small but unmistakably audible fart crept out as she levered herself out from the desk. She coughed loudly and then again, not looking at any of her colleagues.

After a few minutes of keyboard rattling, Tony started to laugh.

"What is it? What's so funny?" asked Maureen. Had he spotted her cream cakes? No, the drawer was shut tight.

"It's clogged up with food," he said. "Look!" He picked up the keyboard, turned it upside down and shook it. Sure enough a heavy drizzle of crisps, cake crumbs and pastry flakes showered down onto the desk. Alison, Marjorie and Lorraine all stopped what they were doing and looked over. Lorraine had to stand up to see. "Bloody hell," she said, "It's like confetti," and they all laughed.

Maureen looked from one to the other, panic rising in her chest.

171

"I've seen it all now," hooted Tony. "Wait'll I tell the lads, they'll never believe me."

"Well, I don't know how that can have happened," blustered Maureen, playing for time. "It's not my fault, I haven't had it very long. I think someone else had it before me, you know." But they weren't listening to her. They were laughing louder and longer. Eventually Tony pulled himself together, unplugged the keyboard and stood up.

"I'll get you another, love," he said and, as he brushed past her to go out, he stopped, cocked his head and said: "you've got something on your arm, haven't you?"

Maureen looked down to where his eyes were homing in.

"Bit of cream or something, looks like," he put out a tentative finger.

Maureen felt sure she could hear a snigger from Marjorie but didn't dare look round.

"Hand cream, it's just hand cream," she slapped her arm with her other hand. Tony shrugged, not his problem, but it was a funny place to have hand cream.

"It'll be tomorrow before I can get you a replacement," he called over his shoulder as the door swung to, behind him.

Maureen followed him with a whisper of "just going to the ladies" and, once ensconced in a cubicle, she gingerly lifted up her right arm. She gasped and dropped it back. Then she lifted it again, slowly, very slowly. She smelt it, as if checking for BO then, with the index finger of her left hand, flicked a slug of the white substance that was bubbling up in her armpit onto her fingertip and placed it on her tongue. It was definitely cream, Tony was right about that, but not hand cream. This was the type of cream that came between layers of a cake, sandwiched between two meringue shells, piped onto a strawberry tart or spread along the length of a chocolate éclair.

Had she just...? by accident ....smudged....She lifted her arm right up this time. No, there could be no doubt about it. This cream was coming from her. She switched her attention to her left arm and discovered more telltale creamy bubbles oozing from her pores. She, Maureen Maddison of 14 Radnor Gardens, was sweating cream.

She yanked on the toilet roll, pulling sheets of it towards her and wiped the cream off. When she was sure there was no trace left, she listened to make certain she was alone before unlocking the door. At the basin she rinsed her armpits as best she could, patting them dry with the rough brown paper towels.

She re-entered the office to an abrupt silence. Lorraine cleared her throat in a very unnatural manner, while Marjorie stabbed at her big desk calculator with farcical concentration. Allowing a few minutes to pass, Maureen slid open her top drawer. She frowned at the cream horn cowering in a corner of the box. She was sure she'd only....she counted off mentally: meringue, vanilla slice. There should definitely have been a choux bun in the box too. Without looking up she swivelled her eyes from Lorraine, to Alison to Marjorie. Busy, busy, busy. She was just wondering how she might frame any such question as to the errant bun's whereabouts when Alison said, still staring at her screen, "anyone like a polo?"

Marjorie and Lorraine both agreed that they would. Maureen remained silent.

"Oh," said Alison, "they're not here. I wonder where they could have gone?" She made a great show of opening and closing her drawers, lifting up her papers, moving the photo of her son, checking her filing tray.

"You must have eaten them and forgotten," suggested Lorraine.

"Yes, you probably just forgot. It's easily done," said Marjorie, slightly too loudly.

Maureen could feel herself getting hot again, but on her face this time. She put up a hand to wipe away the sweat from her forehead. It felt sticky and grainy, as though she had rolled her face in sand. She took a discreet look at her hand. Tiny white crystals glistened on her fingers. She put them to her mouth, tasting the sweetness with a shudder of dread mixed with the pleasure of their taste. She sat motionless, frozen like her computer screen.

The door opened and Olive, the post lady, bristled in. "Any post? I'm late, so you'd better have it ready."

Maureen jumped and, in relief, looked at her watch.

"Oh, it's five o'clock already." The others started to pack up and two minutes later Maureen was on her own. She carefully loaded the remainder of her food into carrier bags and waddled down the stairs, taking her time lest she should catch up with any of her colleagues.

It was a relief to get home. The bus had been packed, making it impossible for Maureen to manage getting anything more than a small bar of chocolate into her mouth. Once in the house, she oozed into a chair at the kitchen table and started on a box of Quality Street. It wasn't till she was down to the toffee pennies (her least favourite on account of how they stuck to her upper plate) that she began to feel anything like normal again.

A week passed and it was happening more often now, she noticed. By the time she got to work each morning a thick layer of cream had built up under each arm so that she had to stop by the ladies toilets to remove it before going into the office. The sugar too was popping up like a rash on her arms as well as her face and today, when she pricked her finger trying to extract a staple and licked the blood, she found it wasn't blood at all, it was chocolate sauce.

"Office leaving party," she said to the girl in Bunters while she was tying up Maureen's cake box. As she swung her great bulk around and started for the door she caught the tail end of one girl's mutter to another: "...turn into a cream cake one of these days" and she wondered, just for a second, if this was God's doing.

She felt the cream frothing, not just under her armpits but behind her knees this time. It was a hot day and the sugar was starting to caramelise and trickle down her face. She licked it with her tongue. The cut on her finger had opened up again from holding all her bags and was dribbling into her hand. She raised it to her mouth and drank the sweet, dark liquid.

Back at the office there was an 'atmosphere'. Maureen was used to this but today it was different. Alison waited till Maureen had settled herself then announced: "We've all got to go to the canteen at four o'clock. The boss has got an announcement."

Redundancy – which obviously wasn't her fault – came as a relief to Maureen at first even though she was only due the statutory payout, having been there less than two years. On the way out of the meeting she licked at her arm and, when no one was looking, scooped a little cream out from her left armpit. She picked at a scab, till it bled and sucked her finger nail. It was sweet and lovely.

She didn't bother trying to get another job, preferring to spend her days at home, where she could eat without interruption, growing fatter and rounder. Her skin began to flake and she sweated more but she could deal with that – she had coping strategies. She found it more and more difficult to go out. Walking chafed her thighs and was tiring. The bus seats had got smaller, making it uncomfortable to sit for long with one cheek dribbling off the end. Thank God for Tesco home delivery….until the money started to run out.

When came the day that Maureen, leaning over the freezer to retrieve a pack of oven chips, spotted a small triangle of the smooth white plastic surface that lined the bottom, she knew what she had to do, what God had in mind for her.

She pulled back her sleeve to reveal the flabby skin of her left arm and lowered her fur-coated teeth into the wobbling flesh. Maureen felt the familiar thick sweet fluid enter her mouth and let a slow syrupy smile leak over her pastry face – death by chocolate, was there any other way?

The Closest Thing

by Teresa Stenson

Lifting up a strand of my hair, the woman braces herself and tells me: "You suffered a very traumatic experience about six months ago."

She's looking at me in the mirror; that odd, but necessary, part of the process. I avoid my own eye contact. Strand of hair still in her hand, she shakes her head at some fuzzy wisps trying to break loose. "Very traumatic," she confirms.

I'm managing a weak smile. This is difficult. It's the kind of situation I hate, not the 'reading' (though I didn't realise that would be part of the package), but the exposure.

"Now what would you like to drink, my darling?" She runs through the options, while examining my hair, follicle to tip. "We've got tea – herbal and otherwise; coffee – fresh, not frozen; water – spring, not tap; fruit juice – several colours, and wine – still or sparkling."

I open my mouth to say 'water' but she's eying at the ends of my hair and there's that face of concern again.

So I decide: "Wine would be lovely."

"Be right back," she says, dropping my tale-telling hair.

I look down at my clasped hands and wonder why I'm here. I could just go now, of course. Just run away in this cape, head for the door. Go home, lock myself in.

I'm here because you made the booking. Even paid for it in advance. I found the appointment card in with some other things you left for me. 'Please go' written on it in biro. I panicked, then saw the date, months away. Chance to prepare, work up the courage. All of a sudden it was time.

Walking through the heavy door, I had entered a house of mirrors, all ready to reveal me. Slender black silhouettes poised with scissors, sprays, intimidating style.

When one of them approached to take my coat, I didn't know how best to place myself. She managed.

"Renee will be along in a moment, take a seat." She ushered me to a chaise longue and I perched.

The immaculate, middle-aged Renee bustled through the salon, all arms and smiles. "Bettina, hi! Nice to meet you. What are we doing for you today, sweetheart?" She furrowed her pencilled brow, not looking at me, but scanning my hair, scraped back into a pony tail.

"I don't know, I'm erm, not really, I mean I don't – "

Suddenly she reached round to the back of my head and untied my hair.

"You've got curls! Unleash these curls!"

I felt sick, this wasn't supposed to happen, not here in the waiting area anyway. She ran her hands through my hair, making elaborate noises and gasps, "Look at it! Wow, Bettina, look at your mane!"

I wanted to run. Then suddenly she stopped and looked at me, into my eyes and then around my face. "You look like, with your hair like that, you really look like someone I know."

For a second I had almost told her, but she shook the thought out of her head and smiled again. "Let's begin."

Now, waiting for Renee to return, I'm wondering if wine was the right choice. You'd be proud of me, say I'm living life to the full. A mid-morning pick me up. You'd be all: why not, Bettina? Who cares, who gives a damn? Your voice in my head like that makes me look up, to see you in me in the mirror, the closest thing to bringing you back.

Renee's bustle breaks my thoughts. She's manoeuvring herself through the salon, with a glass of wine in each hand. "Don't fret my darling, mine's a spritzer – I shan't be too tipsy to cut your hair."

The other stylists smile and tut and roll their eyes in a 'that's our Renee' kind of way. Now I can really see why you liked her so much. "She's amazing!" you'd say, fluffing your hair in my long hallway mirror, pulling away the coats and scarves hung all over it. "And she knows stuff Bets. But most importantly she knows about hair type. With our hair, you've got to be careful or you'd tie it back everyday in a pony tail." Your reflection eyed me, knowingly, as I stood behind you, wondering (not for the first time) how we came out of that same egg.

Renee takes a drink and smacks her lips several times. "First taste of the day." And I think – at least that's something - and I hold mine in my hand and draw stripes in the condensation.

"Don't turn it into Art, sweetheart, drink it."

I sniff it, as if that means something to me. It stings my nose, reminding me of those first few tastes of alcohol, of being a teenager with you. I tip the glass to my lips and take in the cold wine, hold it in the cup of my tongue for a while. This is the part where you'd tell me to 'just drink it Bettina!', and say I was stalling. When I do swallow it, I can't tell if it's cold or hot anymore.

"Vino, vino, vino. It's the best, you know!"

I look up to see her smiling at her rhyme, and looking into my glass I smile too, because it's funny because it's not funny, and it's something you might say.

"That's better, a smile's what we need, Bettina! A smile and curls – the perfect combination. Now, I cut to type, like that old saying – don't cut the cloth the wrong way. Is that a saying? Who cares. I love your hair."

Renee runs her fingers through it, pulling at strands here and there. "How do you want me to cut it? What do you see for us today?"

"Um, well, it's been a while and I usually tie it up, so, something easy, so I can wash it and leave it."

"Brilliant. This is gold dust. I need to know about your lifestyle, your personality, because I strongly believe the cut has to suit that. Now, let's get you over to the sink, because when I'm shampooing I'm getting a map of your head."

Shampooed and conditioned, I sit with a towel wrapped and twisted elaborately on top of my head. For all the time I spend hating my hair, I hate the bareness of my face without it. Renee loosens the towel and rubs my scalp roughly, declaring, "This is to enliven, I am bringing the follicles to life!"

It falls like sea weed over my face. Renee begins tugging at strands, finding a parting.

You used to say this woman had liberated you and your hair. I found this amusing. You – you were anything but in need of liberation, with your confidence and your ease. I had studied it, tried to imitate it, grown bored with it, been worn down by it. I'd been the punch line and subject of anecdotes delivered to large crowds, and have always known I was seen as a pity; a pity we were so different.

"Now Bettina, I want you to do something for me because I just do not know how this hair wants to fall. I want you throw your head back and shake it all out."

I scan behind me around the salon, and at Renee who is swinging my chair in encouragement.

"Come on, throw yourself back like a rock star diva!"

I shake my soaking head a couple of times. It is not enough.

"Come on girl, take a gulp of wine, throw your head back and give it some attitude!" She is demonstrating in front of me, her choppy blonde bob flying and swinging in her face.

I laugh because her energy is contagious, and she is so like you it's tormenting.

"Yield to the laughter!" she yells and takes my hands, pulling them from side to side as I just let it all go and throw my head back, my eyes squeezed shut, my wet hair whipping my face with slashes of water.

Renee is whooping and when I stop she is clapping and I see that through the laughter I am crying a little.

I wipe my eyes and reach for the wine.

"That feels better, doesn't it?"

"Much." I mean it.

"And let's see where this hair is falling. It wants to be a side parting you know… how do you normally wear it?"

"Middle."

It was one of those distinctions Mum implemented early on to tell us apart quickly. Mine in the middle, yours to the side. But it stayed with us into adulthood, though the differences became easier to spot.

"Your hair is crying out to be side-parted Bettina, and it is my responsibility to listen to the hair." She holds up her hands, as if to say 'it's out of these hands', and I wonder just whose hands we are in, then.

"Sure."

179

Renee nods, as if I have passed a test I didn't know I was taking. "Look at this, see? How it softens your face now, to the side."

It feels wrong, and I'm torn between thinking you're going to tell me off for copying you, or say I should have done it sooner. But then it doesn't matter now, does it? I used to hate your unpredictability. I could worry for hours over it, only for you to not care at all.

I look up at my reflection. Suddenly I realise for the first time that you have sat in this chair and looked at yourself. And I don't care how much we might look like each other, it's not much at all really, because you would be laughing and moving your head around to see yourself better, you would be toasting the haircut, the shampoo, the day with Renee.

I've been scared of mirrors since you died, scared they would reveal you behind me as I brush my teeth.

I can see you more than ever in this one.

Literacy Hour

by Bella Govan

"Your boyfriend, Miss, did *he* buy you that watch?"

"It's spellings now Lorna: 'chair', 'pair', 'lair'."

Adam asks Dawn, "What's it mean, 'lair'?"

"How should I know - get your elbow off my book."

"Make me!"

Dawn whips her spelling book out from under Adam's elbow, shifting herself and her book closer to the edge of the desk.

"Are you engaged, Miss?" asks Lorna. "Only I don't see no ring."

Dawn would've felt a lot less anxious if she could've had Green Group Group's spellings: 'cat', 'mat', 'rat'. But on the last English SATs test Dawn had copied two answers from Clare's test booklet, and now look where it had got her: Miss Chantalle had moved her from Green to Orange Group.

Dawn wants most of all to be back in Green Group sitting next to Calum, a kind boy who lives in Dawn's block flats, tenth floor. Trekking from second to tenth floor when the lift is out of order to ask him, "What's tonight's homework, Calum?" is a bit of a drag. Truth be told, Dawn always knew better than he did, but to be in Calum's company even if only for five minutes, any excuse was better than none.

"On your last birthday, Miss," says Lorna, "How old were you?"

Miss Chantalle, walks quickly away from Lorna, says *"Your* final three words, Purple Group are: 'correct', 'detect', 'connect.'"

"Ready everyone?" says Miss Chantalle, removing the two sheets of yellow sugar paper that covers up the correct spellings she's previously written on the board. Check your spellings now. Give yourselves a mark out of twelve. Write out any corrections three times. Get your partner to test you."

The drone of partners testing each other soon shifts a gear into more interesting talk, bursts laughter, a shout here and there.

"Quiet!" shouts Miss Chantalle, glaring at Lorna who has the cheek to be turning around from her seat in Green Group to speak

to Dawn. Lorna, too busy talking, doesn't even notice Miss Chantalle glaring at her. Miss Chantalle shifts her accusing look to Dawn, *"Quiet, I said!"* Dawn gives Lorna a dig with her elbow; Lorna finally gets the message, shuts up.

"Now 3C, I want you to use your spellings to make up a sentence. Then in your groups I want you to read out your sentences to each other."

Julia, a clever girl from Purple Group, puts her hand up. "Can I add an 'ion' to one of our spellings, Miss? Then I can get: 'Detect a correct connection, Miss."

"*Excellent* Julia!"

Now there are the faltering sounds of people trying to read out sentences that in normal life no person in their right minds would ever utter.

"Now Class 3C, I want you all to *listen* - because I have something *important* to tell you."

3C look expectantly at Miss Chantalle hoping that her unusually pleased looking smile could even mean a bit of personal news that might just be turned into a juicy bit gossip.

Is Miss Chantalle getting *engaged* – or *married* even?

Like Class 4A's teacher, Mrs Mortensen nee Miss Boyle, has she gone the whole hog and hired a wedding planner? What's to be her theme?"

Then it crosses Dawn's mind that only last week Lorna had said, "Miss Chantalle, putting on the pounds, dontcha think?"

Pregnant?

Top to toe, Dawn gives Miss Chantalle the once over.

Nope.

Miss Chantalle is gaining the pounds more or less all round.

Oh better yet! Was Miss Chantalle GAY? Civil partnerships! That's what the grown ups were all arguing the toss about these days. So was Miss Chantalle going in for one of *those?* Well, who'd have *thought* it?

"Now 3C, for the next three Fridays," announces Miss Chantalle, "I'm going to be at the *Teachers' Centre*, so…"

Dawn whispers to Lorna, "Lookin' like the cat's meow over *that?"*

"Puttin' a brave face on it," Lorna whispers back. "Them Teachers' Centre people is gonna have a right go at her for letting Purple Group have a look at them SATs Test Papers beforehand."

One lunchtime Miss Chantalle had kept Purple Group behind and had done just that, causing Lorna, who had popped back into the classroom to retrieve the forgotten half packet of crisps and the tangerine she'd left in her rucksack, to ask, "So why ain't the rest of us getting a peek, Miss?"

"Lorna, would it make any *difference* to *your* results whether you saw the questions beforehand or not?"

Lorna, well known for honest opinions, said, peeling the tangerine as she left the room, "Nah, don't suppose it would, Miss. "

"Whadya think they're gonna do to you, Miss?" asks Lorna, adding for clarification at Miss Chantalle's baffled look, "them people at the Teachers' Centre Miss."

"Oh, what an *imagination,* Lorna! I've been *invited* to the Teachers' Centre, says Miss Chantalle with a proud little smile, "to train all the new teachers in behaviour modification."

"How old are *they,* Miss?" asks Lorna.

"Lorna, we do *not* ask adults their age - it's *impolite.* "

"'But if they're teachers, adults like you just said, Miss, they should already know how to behave."

"Of *course* they do! What I shall be doing, Lorna, is showing them how to get *children* to behave. Which is why for the next three Fridays, Class 3C, you will have a supply teacher - probably Mr Judd."

At the mention of his name, a groan goes around the classroom, cut short by Miss Chantalle's sharp and hurried voice. "*Repeat after me, 3C!* 'We *all* promise to be *very good* for the supply teacher for the next four Fridays, Miss Chantalle!' Let me *hear* it, 3C!"

On Friday the supply teacher is indeed Mr Judd, who, from the moment he steps inside the classroom is almost entirely ignored. Except for Purple Group, people in class 3C even get up out of their ability groups to go and talk to friends. Except for Sharon in Purple Group, who lives in Lorna's block of flats and is desperate to tell Lorna all about her new baby brother born at the weekend.

183

Mr Judd, a tall man in his thirties, is of a nervous disposition, with this habit of clearing his throat as he speaks, the sound coming out like a strangled groan.

"I'm *trying* to take *...aaargh...* the *register* here, Class 3C!"

"Tick everybody 'cept Sharmila," advises Lorna. "She's gone to Bangladesh to visit her gran."

Unable to hear Lorna above the hubbub, Mr Judd shouts above the noise, "*Class 3C...aaargh...* I really *must* take the *register!*"

But people were too busy.

Because Clare is not unkind and is as quiet as Fela is shy, Miss Chantalle had put Fela next to her.

But now even Fela is adding to the hubbub by humming a little tune to himself.

Dawn is scrabbling around in her Barbie Doll rucksack; she extracts her new tin box pencil case, painted in bright swirly colours, a birthday present from her Auntie Joan, which she wants to show to Lorna.

Adam, jealous of the new pencil case, even though he's got a better one of his own, grabs at it, but with a clatter it falls to the floor; two half-size pens, two normal pencils, a rubber, a small ruler and a tiny pencil sharpener spilling out.

"You pig!" shouts Dawn, punching Adam in the gut.

Adam jumps up, is about to take a swipe at Dawn, but Mr Judd intervenes, clasping hold of Adam's arm.

Accidentally or not, Adam steps on top of the tin box, bending it well out of shape.

Dawn's face crumples and she cries.

Mr Judd tells Adam to go and stand outside the classroom until he learns how to behave himself.

Mr Judd picks up the tin box, tries to bend it back into shape, managing to get the lid to close, if only just.

Dawn, wiping away her tears with the sleeve of her cardigan, says, "Thank you, Mr Judd." She picks up the two half sized pens, the two pencils, rubber, small ruler and tiny pencil sharpener up off the floor, placing them carefully inside the not quite right tin box.

Mr Judd turns his attention to the rising crescendos of 3C's many and varied conversations. He tries his best to be strict. "Class 3C, you... *aaargh...* must *all* stop talking *now!*"

But they didn't and they wouldn't.

"You must all get back to...aaargh... your *proper chairs! "THIS INSTANT,"* he shouts, glaring at Fela and Clare who aren't talking at all and who have hardly moved an inch in the first place.

A worried looking Fela, wondering what he's done wrong for the teacher to be glaring and shouting at him so, stops humming right in mid hum,

Fela, from Nigeria, knows a few words in English, like 'please', 'thank you', 'excuse me' – and *'BUM!',* Adam having told Fela that this was the word for toilet, so that when Fela wants to go to the toilet, Fela says, *"BUM, please!*

Miss Chantalle always tries to teach Fela the correct word by saying, "Yes, Fela, you may go to the *toilet."*

Except once when she was a bit distracted, Miss Chantalle said, "Yes, Fela, you may go to the bum."

It took Mss Chantalle, an expert in behaviour modification, several long minutes to get 3C to stop going on and on about her unfortunate error and laughing like drains.

But Mr Judd, not knowing about Fela and *'BUM!'* always says to Fela. "Watch your *language,* young man!" - and Fela has to squirm in his seat until break time

'Nigeria is a large country in the continent of Africa. It is rich in oil and iron ore.' is what it says in the Children's Encyclopaedia at home.

Clare's dad explains how this is only a fraction of the facts parading as the biggest of truths. "Because this book won't tell us, Clare, how the greedy people of this world have this bad ould habit of takin' for themselves whatever it is a country is rich in, even when they don't even *live* in it, sure.

"It'll take a whole loada people working together on a helluva lot of doings to stop these ould masqueraders from stealing even the very truth of the matter, don't you know. But isn't that the very work we must all be putting ourselves to, sure. Now the first step of it, Clare, is to always be true to *yourself* - for don't we all have that voice inside us that *knows.* "

185

Clare often gets the gist of what her dad is on about, but she's learned not always to ask for the detail. Her dad can be a bit long winded on the specifics. More than once, before he's even half way through the answer, Clare's brain has switched itself right off the subject.

In the World atlas Clare's dad shows her where Nigeria is. Clare already knows the map of Ireland very well, and can pick out in a trice where County Clare is, which is where Clare's name comes from.

Because Fela can't yet read but a few words in English, Miss Chantalle gives him loads of colouring-in work, which Fela completes in a flash. Then in the margins of the colouring-in book, Fela draws little scenarios of all that goes on in Class 3C.

From time to time, Fela also draws a street that isn't like the streets here. People are going in and out of a small square building with a flat roof and no windows to speak of, so that you'd hardly know it was a shop at all. But people are going in empty-handed, and other people are coming out with all sorts, like a sack of rice, a string of onions, a spade, a bottle of Coke.

There are hardly any cars in this street. Women carry away their bundles of shopping on their heads; men carry away their purchases on their shoulders. A few people load their shopping onto bicycles; and a boy who looks just like Fela is putting a big square tin of cooking oil into a hand-drawn cart.

It was Clare who pointed out to Miss Chantalle Fela's margin drawings. Well, you should have seen Miss Chantalle's face light right up. "Oh, Fela how *clever* of you! Now, Fela, if you can just tell us a little *story* about one of your lovely drawings, then I can tick your box for Target 1a in Speaking and Listening - 'telling stories, real or imagined.'!"

Box ticking is not a concept familiar to Fela, and though he understands nothing of the many stories Miss Chantalle reads to Class 3C, Fela does have his own idea of what the word 'story' means. So when amongst all that Miss Chantalle says, Fela hears the words 'you', 'tell' and 'story', for a good five minutes Fela's story just spills right out of him - and all in Yoruba!

Everybody giggles and laughs. Realising why, Fela giggles too, but he also looks embarrassed. So to make up for Fela feeling awkward, Miss Chantalle has a good go at teaching Fela some more English words, pointing to Fela's drawings of Class 3C and saying words like 'desk', 'chair', 'blackboard'.

Miss Chantalle turns around and points to some of the actual people in Class 3C, saying their names, asking Fela to repeat after her.

Fela says several people's names, smiling when it comes to Calum

But when it comes to certain other people, no matter how many times Miss Chantalle says their names, not only does Fela utter not one syllable of that person's name, he refuses to even look at their direction.

At first Fela had no idea what the words they were shouting at him meant. But then, from both the boys' side and the girls' side of the playground, came the actions to go with the words, mostly ape type grunts and gestures

Next came the pushing, shoving, tripping up.

So it quickly became obvious to Fela what the name callers of 3C thought of him.

Now watching Fela standing there refusing to look at those people or to utter one syllable of their names, Clare knows what Fela is doing: Fela is using his proper power of NO.

At playtime, Clare and Fela, sometimes Calum, and maybe three or four of the other quieter people of 3C, prefer the benches in the school hallway to the playground. They eat their crisps, an apple or tangerine, or sweets from the tiny packets of jellybeans that are currently all the rage, butterscotch, cola fizz and tutti fruitti being the favourite flavours. People will offer Fela a crisp, a jellybean, a segment of tangerine, and also try to teach him a word or two of English, pointing to things in the hallway, saying, "Fire alarm", "window", "bell", "bench", "door handle."

Calum isn't much interested in food, sometimes even forgetting to go to the dining hall for lunch. Out of politeness though, Calum always accepts the proffered crisp, jellybean, segment of tangerine. Calum is more interested in picture books. Out of his rucksack he'll take his favourite book of the moment, currently one that's all about boats. Then he and Fela turn the pages and gaze at the pictures showing every kind of water transport under the sun, from coracles to cruise liners.

Not getting anywhere with Fela and names, Miss Chantalle, says, "OK Fela, you can sit down now," exerting just enough pressure on Fela's shoulder for him to know to sit down.

Quite apart from the name-calling, shoving, tripping up, not yet knowing much English, Clare knows from the way Fela that looks out on the world, that Fela also has inside him this other sense of being somehow quite disconnected from things in general. The reason Clare knows this is because this is often how Clare herself feels – not quite connected to things in general.

Clare has a lisp that gives her lot of bother with 's' sounds in particular. 'Snow comes out as 'Sthnow' and so on. When it's Clare's turn to read from the big print book on the stand and she lisps her 's' sounds, certain people laugh and make hissing snake noises at her - including Lorna and Dawn, although it was Adam who started it.

But this isn't the only reason that Clare doesn't like the stories on the stand, nor the books Miss Chantalle gives out for reading homework, even though she gives Clare the books with the hardest vocabulary that are also supposed to be the most interesting ones.

What Clare dislikes most of all is that the books are hardly ever about anything real. In this her third year of school now, Clare has had a right bellyful of witches, princesses, animals that talk, intergalactic families, dragons, magic spells, olden time heroes saving either kingdoms from the enemy, or some damsels in distress.

Even those books pretending to be about real people just aren't. The stories just don't seem to know what they're talking about, with the characters not even half as real as any of the actual people that Clare knows in actual life.

One of the things that make Clare feel not quite connected to things in general is that nobody else in 3C seems to care one way or another what the storybooks are about. In fact, when told to use their imaginations and write a story, people in 3C churn out the same old guff about witches, wizards, princesses, or some girl getting a pony for her birthday. Since most of 3C live in the flats where the Council don't even allow cats, how real is that?

On Fridays Miss Chantalle tells everybody to write a sentence about what they like about that week's book on the stand.

Seeing Clare's 'I did not like it.' puts Miss Chantalle in a bit of a lather. "Always *one*, isn't there!"

Since Clare is only trying to be true to herself, she doesn't know why Miss Chantalle has to get in such a bad mood over it.

.   Before she even started school, Clare's dad had taught her quite a lot of things, so Clare reads and writes quite well and she finishes all her work on time. But the whole truth of the matter is that with the lessons being mostly disconnected from all the real live things that Clare already knows something about, is eager to learn more of, in class Clare works mostly without enthusiasm. Miss Chantalle says, "When I see that spark of *gusto,* Clare, that's when I'll put you in Purple Group. Not that Clare wants to be in Purple Group, because, apart from Sharon, the people in Purple Group aren't very nice.

Though Clare misses nothing of all that goes on in 3C, another thing that makes her feel out of it is that she doesn't 'get it' why some of the girls act so cliquey and snide; why some of the boys act so rough and loud; doesn't 'get it' why some of Class 3C are so mean to one another, like whispering behind people's backs, hiding people's things, nipping each other on the sly, even hitting each other badly.

As time went by, what with all that did and didn't go on in 3C, Clare just grew quieter and quieter, kept more and more to herself.

It was Adam who started calling Clare names, like 'dummy girl', 'idiot child', and worst of all, 'Mad Clare'.

People were so scared of Adam that if he called your best friend a bad name, you might even copy him.

Miss Chantalle got very angry about name-calling. She made Class 3C repeat after her that name-calling in classrooms and corridors *must stop.*

So the name-calling happened in the playground instead.

That's why at break times Clare and Fela always try to stay inside in the hallway, although sometimes a teacher will shoo them out. "You two, *always* in the hallway! Time you got some fresh air about you! Off you go now - Into the playground with you!"

189

Lorna didn't copy what Adam said about Clare. But sometimes Clare would look up from doing her sums or from concentrating on her joined up writing, to find Lorna glaring at her. Sometimes Clare would even hear Lorna muttering to Dawn. "Who does she think she is? Little Miss Clever Clogs over there!" So Clare knew that Lorna didn't like her

Now Mr Judd, trying unsuccessfully to get Class 3C to behave, suddenly points right at Fela, *"Aaargh....YOU!"*

Fela jumps.

"YES, YOU!...Go and tell the Headmistress... AARGH...that she must come to come IMMEDIATELY to Class 3C!"

The only word Fela understands is *"YOU!"*

"NOW!" shouts Mr Judd.

Heart hammering, Fela stares wide-eyed at Mr Judd who, going even redder in the face, shouts, *"FELA, DO WHAT I'VE TOLD YOU - AND DO IT QUICKLY!"*

Mr Judd's shouting his name like that is the straw that breaks the camel's back. Fela's bony little shoulders begin to shake, frightened little moans come from his throat, then comes the tears, and more and more tears.

Clare knows that before things get any worse, she must *DO* something.

Mr Judd watches Clare exit the classroom, calling after her, *"Just where d'you think...aaargh...you're going, young lady?"*

Adam, thinking that Mr Judd has sent Clare to stand outside the classroom too, shouts, "Hey, *dummy girl,* come back here! Hey, *idiot child,* where d'you think you're going?"

The black and white plastic sign on the door says, 'Headmistress Mrs Mountain'.

Clare knocks, the door opens and Mrs Mountain, annoyed at the interruption, looks down at Clare. *"YESS?* What *IS* it Clare?"

Clare points along the corridor to Class 3C's classroom door.

Even through the closed door you could hear the hubbub.

Mrs Mountain tuts, shakes her head, sighs, groans. "Mr Judd, is it?"

Clare nods.

Mrs Mountain darts back into her office, comes out with a grey plastic box containing a pile of a dog-eared paperbacks: 'Short Story Favourites - Literacy Hour Work Included.'

Mrs Mountain, a large lady, wears smart jackets and skirts, embroidered blouses and big earrings - and always smells of perfume.

Clare follows in Mrs Mountain's perfumed wake towards 3C's classroom.

Mrs Mountain, spotting Adam lolling about outside the classroom door, shouts, "*ADAM! Get INSIDE the classroom, young man! Go straight to your seat - and not ONE word out of you!*"

The minute Mrs Mountain opens 3C's classroom door, there's this mad scramble of everyone rushing to get back to their proper seats.

Mr Judd looks exhausted.

Clare, as she passes by the teacher's desk, takes a tissue from the tissue box, goes back to sit beside Fela, handing him the tissue. Fela dries his eyes, blows his nose, puts the soggy, disintegrating tissue in his trouser pocket. Clare would've motioned to Fela to get up and put the soggy tissue in the bin, except Clare knows that Fela is not in a frame of mind to take any such instruction as anything other than blame and condemnation.

Mrs Mountain, knowing who in 3C can and cannot share, swiftly dishes out the storybooks. She gives Mr Judd a thin little smile. "Right in the middle of doing the dratted attendance returns, Mr Judd. How those Town Hall bureaucrats think we can just magic up full attendance out of thin air week after week, I'll never know. The form and all the registers, well except yours, are on my desk," she says, taking Mr Judd's register, ticking every name in a flash, including Sharmila's, handing it back to him. "I'll take over Class 3C for a bit, shall I? You be a dear, Mr Judd; go to my office and complete that form for me – but don't, for heaven's sake, change any of the figures I've already entered, will you now. You can come back in time for numeracy, Mr Judd. They quite like doing their sums."

Mr Judd nods gratefully, scuttling quickly from the classroom.

Now Mrs Mountain is reading out a story about a girl called Hilary whose mother dies when she's eleven.

191

Hilary's daddy travels the world on business and he doesn't have the time to look after Hilary, so he sends her to a tip-top girls' boarding school instead.

The story doesn't mention exactly where his travels take him. Clare wonders if Hilary's daddy is one of those people with the habit of taking whatever it is a country is rich in, even though he doesn't even live in it, sure.

Hilary cries a lot, which only makes the other girls play nasty tricks on her. Hilary even found a dead hedgehog in her bed once.

At the sight of it, Hilary screamed and screamed, Matron came running, swiftly removed the smelly hedgehog, saying, "It's only roadkill, dear! Nothing to worry about! Lights out in five minutes! Into bed with you now!"

Hilary spent the night sleepless, lying on the very edge of the bed, as far away as she could get from where the dead hedgehog had been.

That very week, a new girl, Frances, arrives.

Matron assigns Frances the dormitory bed next to Hilary.

Frances tells everybody to call her Frankie.

Hilary and Frankie become the best of friends.

Sadly, Frankie's parents get divorced, and Frankie has to move to Australia with her Mummy.

Hilary feels more desperately alone than ever, but not wanting any more roadkill in her bed, this time Hilary manages to hide her grief well.

Next, Hilary's daddy marries a divorced lady with twins, Emma and Gemma, same age as Hilary, now twelve and a half. The twins' mother wants to travel the world with the daddy, so the perfect solution is to send the twins to the tip-top girls' boarding school as well.

Since Fela can't understand much English yet, he doesn't have to listen to the story, so throughout Mrs Mountain's story-reading, Fela has his colouring book on his knees under the desk, and in the margins Fela is drawing more pictures of all that goes on in Class 3C.

At this moment in time Mrs Mountain is sitting, legs crossed, on the teacher's desk, quite elegantly for such a big lady. The clever

192

people in Purple Group, one book between two, are reading silently along. Some people in the other groups, though neither reading nor listening, turn the pages when Mrs Mountain turns hers. Others are gazing quietly around the room or out of the window, knowing that if they make a noise, there'll be hell to pay. Mrs Mountain gives detentions, orders offenders to pick up the litter in the playground, even writes letters to parents about inappropriate behaviour.

It's Dawn who first notices, and with a pointed looks directs Lorna to the hole in Mrs Mountain's lacy brown tights, just as, would you believe it, Mrs Mountain gives an absentminded tug as if trying unsuccessfully to mend it.

Dawn, turning up her nose as if someone's done a puff, whispers. "*Always* keeps a spare pair in her locker, my Mum."

Observing Mrs Mountain with downright disapproval, Lorna mutters, "Supposed to set an example - what kinda example is *that?* An' see them earrings, she wore the same pair all last week. And see that blouse...."

Oblivious to the ongoing critique of her dress sense, Mrs Mountain is now reading about how Hilary's daddy and Emma and Gemma's mummy send the girls loads of tuck boxes, so that The Sisters Three, as they come to be known, hold lots of midnight feasts in the dormitory - which all the other girls think is jolly good fun.

The boarding school girls play hockey on Mondays, tennis Tuesdays and Thursdays, do archery on Wednesdays, cross-country running on Fridays, get horse riding lessons Saturdays.

In Assembly, the Headmistress congratulates all the girls in Hilary's class for passing all their exams with 'flying colours'.

Clare doesn't know what 'flying colours' actually means; only that it has the sound of ease and success.

Counting up the names of the people in The Sisters Three's class, Clare figures out what she thinks must be a good reason for their success: there are only fifteen girls in Hilary, Emma and Gemma's class, compared to the thirty-two boys and girls in Class 3C. The boarding school girls also spend evenings in what's called the Prep Room where they do all their homework. When the Prep Mistress, pretending she's going to get some more dictionaries from their classroom, goes out for a smoke, the Prep Room is also where a lot of gossip and intrigue takes place.

Clare half listens to the story-reading but mostly she's gazing out of the window thinking about going home time. Clare's Mum will be at school gates waiting for her, with Clare's little brother, Noel. Clare will skip through the gates, slip her hand into her Mum's, Noel will take Clare's other hand, and off they'll go, hearts lifted.

Then comes the day when the Stable Master tells the Boarding School Headmistress that Tipple, the gentle old horse much loved by all the boarding school girls, is now too old to be useful - and much too expensive to keep. The Headmistress and the Stable Master come up with a cunning plan. Tipple is to be sold off for horsemeat.

At this dreadful news, many of the boarding school girls cry their eyes out.

So the Sisters Three come swiftly to the rescue, phoning Daddy, who immediately pays a nearby farmer to build a stable especially for Tipple, promising also to pay the farmer a small fortune to look after Tipple until the end of his natural days.

Everyone lives happily ever after.

"Well now, Class 3C, wasn't that a *lovely* little story!" declares Mrs Mountain.

"Look at how The Sisters Three shared their tuck boxes - *and* saved the life of the poor old Tipple!

"And look how all the girls did all their lessons without a murmur - and got well rewarded with good marks.

"So what is it that we all must do to get good marks, Class 3C?"

"*I know, I know!*" says Lorna.

"Go on then, Lorna, *tell* the class! What is that we all must *do* to get good marks?"

Lorna's face shining with the all the confidence of, for once, the perfect answer, shouts out, "*Go to boarding school, Miss!*"

Mrs Mountain tuts, sighs, says "Now *repeat* after me, Class 3C: 'To get good marks we all have to *behave* in lessons and *concentrate* on our work – and we all have to be good little boys and girls and *share* whatever we've got!"

When Mrs Mountain asks Class 3C what they like about the story. Most of the girls say: the dormitory, matron, lights out and the midnight feasts. Most of the boys want to grow up to be as rich as the daddy.

Adam says, "See that Hilary and that Frankie – *weirdoes* them two! Them two's what's called *'a right pair of lezzies!'*"

Clare herself isn't quite sure what 'a right pair of lezzies' means. The fact that Adam disapproves probably means it's nothing like as strange as he's trying to make out.

Now that he is three and a half, Noel is fun to play with.

Not when he was two.

When Noel was little and didn't know the half of it, it was mostly Clare who had to tell him what to do.

But at two, Noel had started saying NO – as in *"NO,* I don't *want* to! *NO,* I *won't!"*

Clare's mum kept trying to tell Clare that big girl now that she is, she has a responsibility not only to explain things to Noel, but also to help him to hang onto his proper power of NO - as long he doesn't use it to be hurtful, as long as it doesn't bring him smack up against unreason, or downright ridiculousness.

Clare's dad chips in to say what a precious thing the proper power of NO is. "Because isn't it when enough of us learn to put our proper power of NO together that this ould world will change for the better for the good of all, don't you know. Meantime, Clare, don't we have to be guarding against givin' up our own little bit of the power of NO to the many YES creatures paid to take it away from us, sure."

Unfortunately Clare had got herself into a next to unbreakable habit of ignoring Noel's power of NO, so Clare's mum finally had to say to her, "Clare, d'you not remember at all, at all, when *you* were gaining your own power of NO – which you still very much possess, mavourneen, both the spoken and the unspoken! Well, your little brother, doesn't *he* too have to be finding *his* own voice in this old world, sure?"

That's when it dawned on Clare that although it was true that she didn't say NO out loud very much these days, quite a lot of the time she very definitely still *thought* NO: as in *'NO,* don't let their name-calling get to you'; or as in *'NO,* don't give in to what *they* say.'

This was the same power of NO that Clare had seen in Fela.

Clare thinks that maybe by the time they get to secondary school they'll have found ways other than silence to use it.

"Now Class 3C, get your English exercise books out please. Here is what I want you to do. Write today's date and the heading 'Word Power'. Draw two columns. Title the first one is 'Nouns', the next one 'Adjectives'. Then, from the story we've just read, I want you to pick out some of the lovely big nouns and write them down in your best joined up handwriting. Next I want you to pick out some of the nice big adjectives, write them down too. When you've picked out about twenty nice words, you are then to write your *own* little story – fitting into your story as many of those lovely big nouns and nice big adjectives as you can, yes?"

"*What* did you say, Lorna?"

"A noun, Miss."

"Noun as may be, young lady," says Mrs Mountain sharply, "but it's *not* one that *ever* appears in our stories - nor is it one I ever wish to see written down in any exercise book in my school, if you don't mind!"

"Miss Chantalle says that *before* we write our stories," goes Dawn, "we should always *talk* about them, Miss."

"Because *talking* about them gives us more of an *idea,*" adds Lorna, not as if she believes this to be true, but more in the way of putting up a bit of a fight for the right to free speech. So are we allowed to *talk* first, Miss?"

"Of *course* you are, Lorna! And what it is it we are allowed to talk *about?* Let me hear it, Class 3C!"

"*About the work, Miss!*" chorus Class 3C loudly, but not loud enough to stop Clare hearing Lorna say, "But it *is* bollocks! Nor I ain't writin' no thicko story about no posh lezzies nor some flamin' horse!"

But Clare knows that what Lorna *also* means is that Lorna doesn't want to write, *period* - because Lorna can hardly write at all.

For some reason, Clare finds herself reaching out and touching Lorna on the shoulder.

Lorna turns around sharply, ready to be badly annoyed - but mostly looking panicky about not being able to write hardly at all.

Clare motions to Lorna to come and sit beside her and Fela.

The surprising thing is, Lorna does just that, Mrs Mountain not even noticing, since she's too busy getting herself in a bit of a lather over the fact that so many people have stuck nouns in their adjectives columns and vice versa.

Maybe the reason Lorna moves to sit beside Clare is because, although Clare hardly ever speaks and often looks uncertain, there is also something quite commanding about Clare.

But Clare now knows from her mum that, as with Noel, even the bossiness of good intentions has to be curbed. So instead of whipping Fela's colouring-in book off his knees and pointing out to Lorna all the drawings in the margins, Clare motions as patiently as she can for Fela himself to show Lorna the drawings.

Lorna spots the one of Mr Judd pointing at Fela. "Mr Judd, he don't even have sense enough to *know* that Fela don't understand enough English yet. Shoutin' at the poor little sod like that – he's got no flamin' right!"

"Mr Judd, he hates being a supply teacher," goes Clare.

"*His* flamin' problem!" says Lorna.

Not looking at Lorna, Clare says, "I reckon I know why you get angry a lot."

Lorna, alarmed, goes, "How would *you* flamin' know?"

"I think I know why you say things to Dawn about me an' all."

Lorna's shocked silence hangs in the air.

Then Lorna says all in a rush: "Can't flamin' read, can I? Rubbish at writing, me! Dawn, she ain't much better - but even *she* calls me *'Thicko!'*"

Lorna bursts into tears.

Shocked at seeing how terrible it is for Lorna not to have even a shred of her secret left to hide in, Clare wishes and wishes she'd kept her big mouth shut.

Fela gets up, goes to the tissue box, comes back with two tissues, hands them to Lorna.

It's an age before Lorna is able to make herself stop crying, but finally she does. Now she blows her nose, gets up, walks over to the grey metal waste bin at the side of the blackboard, flings her soggy tissues into it, walks back to the desk.

197

Fela gets up, walks to the bin, takes his own disintegrating soggy tissue out of his pocket, flings it in the bin.

Lorna, now more or less composed, picks up Fela's book and tries asking him about his margin drawings of what must have been a street in some town in Nigeria.

Fela repeats and repeats a word in Yoruba, his fingers circling the drawing. Lorna reckons the word must be the name of that town. When Lorna finally pronounces the word just right, Fela grins and says, "*Yeess!*"

Now Lorna tells Clare to come up with a spelling in English for the name of the town.

Well, it takes some doing, but over the next two Fridays, plus some time sneaked midweek from numeracy, Clare and Fela work out in English the story for what is going on in that street in that town in Nigeria: who the people going in and out of the shop are: who is a farmer, who is a carpenter, who is an oil depot worker, who is a firewood seller, what the people buy in the shop.

Lorna and Fela watch as Clare writes the bits of the story down in her English exercise book in joined up writing. Then they copy her.

For the final draft though, it's Lorna who decides on the order of things in the story, which Clare then writes out onto a new page.

The completed story is about one and three quarter pages long.

Fela feels relieved that now Clare and Lorna now know something of the place where he comes from.

Lorna is pleased that the story sounds like it knows what it's talking about.

Clare is content that the story is about real people - and she's fairly certain that the spellings are all correct.

Clare anxiously holds her breath when Lorna first reads the story out loud, hesitating over some words.

At managing to keep her big mouth shut long enough for Lorna to figure out the words for herself, Clare is well pleased.

On that last Friday morning before Miss Chantalle comes back, Lorna reads the whole story out loud with no mistakes, no hesitations.

198

Fela manages to read the first three sentences - but he isn't only imitating the sounds of the words in English he *knows* what the written down English words *mean.*

At playtime on that last Friday, Lorna, as usual, runs straight out into the playground.

As usual, Clare and Fela hang back in the hallway.

Lorna is having none of it. *"Yous two, come on outta that flamin' hallway! Yous two's got the same right as everybody else to be in the playground!"*

The minute Fela and Clare step out into the playground, sure enough, the name-calling starts.

But the name callers haven't reckoned on Lorna:. *"OI! ANY ONE OF YOUS IDIOTS CALLING ANY OF ONE MY MATES HERE ONE MORE STUPID NAME, I'M GONNA KNOCK YER ' STUPID TEETH INTO THE MIDDLE OF NEXT FLAMIN' WEEK!"*

For about a nano-second, the playground is almost still.

Then people carry on with their running, arguing, football, playing statues, with their arguing, chatting and shouting - but minus any name-calling whatsoever.

No doubt about it, in that nano-second, the playground atmosphere had altered.

Fela, desperate for the toilet, yells, *"BUM!"* and fast as his skinny little legs can carry him he belts across to the toilet block at the far end of the playground.

Not one person put their foot out to trip him up.

Not one person said even one bad word to him.

Nor to Clare who stands in the playground next to Lorna.

Dawn, seeing Clare and Lorna standing together, comes hurrying over, blurting out to Clare, "But Lorna's *my* best mate, right?"

Clare doesn't say anything.

Neither does Lorna.

Into the scary silence, Dawn goes, "So, d'you wanna be best mates with me and Lorna then, Clare?"

"Yeah," goes Clare, glad, glad, glad of this sudden new feeling of not being quite so disconnected from things in general as before.

Mr Judd comes hurrying across the playground from the main building carrying a pile of dog-eared numeracy textbooks, plus a few sheets of photocopied sums.

Mr Judd stops to say to Lorna, Dawn and Clare, "Only just realised, Fela, he can't...*aaargh*... read much English yet, can he?"

"Sir, you're in for a right flamin' *surprise!*" goes Lorna. "Fela's only gone and drawn a whole real story!"

"Clare done all the spellings, and I myself have writ out the whole story in joined up writing an' all. I can read it to you in numeracy, if you like, Sir!"

"Fela though, he can't *read* the maths questions in the...aaargh... numeracy books, can he?" says Mr Judd.

"Fela ain't flamin' *stupid!*" says Lorna annoyed on Fela's behalf, also highly irritated that Mr Judd hasn't got sense enough to immediately take her up on her offer of reading out a whole real story to him.

"So I've photocopied a few of sheets of just sums for Fela...*aaargh*...no words, just the symbols for add, subtract, multiply, divide," says Mr Judd, "Where is he?"

"*BUM!*'" goes Dawn.

Mr Judd, with no idea all what to say to this, gives one of his coughing groans and flings himself nervously onwards towards 3C's classroom, dropping and picking up textbooks as he goes.

Clare knows for sure that when Mr Judd at last finds his keys, unlocks and enters the classroom, that Mr Judd will be entering a room that he truly doesn't want to be in.

Poor Mr Judd - somewhere along the way, he must've lost his proper power of NO.

Clare gives a heavy sigh, knowing that she's going to have to find a way to let Mr Judd know that it hadn't been very smart of him to lose his proper power of NO in the first place.

Because if a person ignores, mislays, or allows somebody or something to take away their own proper power of NO, how is that person ever going to be able to be true even to themselves – to the voice inside that knows?

And how will there ever be enough people to put together the proper power of NO so that things can be changed for the better for the good of all, don't you know?

Mr Judd being a supply teacher whom she might never see again, with a little groan, Clare realises that she's going to have to tackle Mr Judd *before the end of the day.*

Digging down into her Barbie Doll rucksack, Dawn brings out a skipping rope, takes one end, hands the other end to Clare.

Dawn and Clare turn the rope for Lorna who, in the middle skipping also produces a perfect scissor kick.

Suddenly it occurs to Clare that tackling poor Mr Judd is one thing - but how to even *begin* with Miss Chantalle and Mrs Mountain?

Because Clare has been thinking for about a week now that, polite and kind as they often are, Miss Chantalle and Mrs Mountain must also be two of the many YES creatures paid to take the power of NO away from the rest of us, sure.

Why else are they forever getting 3C to do all those 'repeat after mees'?

Why else instruct 3C to use unconnected spellings to make up sentences that in normal life no person in their right minds would ever utter?

Why else are they forever trying to make the people in 3C say they *like* the silly storybooks about witches, knights of old, girls getting ponies for their birthdays - and nothing real?

And when the people in 3C are supposed to be using their own imaginations and creating their own stories, why tell them they must use other people's nouns and adjectives?

"Clare's turn next!" says Lorna jumping smartly out of the turning rope, executing another perfect scissor kick as she does so, making it look like the easiest thing in the world.

Clare is mainly thinking about how the ginormous problem of Miss Chantalle and Mrs Mountain can even begin to be tackled, but Clare is also wishing that she could do the scissor kick too.

Clare doesn't quite manage the scissor kick just yet - but she's definitely getting there.

Now it's Dawn's turn to skip.

Then Fela comes running back across the playground - and he jumps right inside the turning rope with Dawn!

A *boy*, skipping with a *girl* – and nobody's laughing!

201

Amazed though, a lot of people are gathering around to watch.

That's when Clare twigs to the fact that as different as they are, Lorna being tall, Clare quite small, Dawn red-haired and freckled and quite fat, Fela very skinny and black, the thing that they have in common is that each of them *listens* to the voice inside that *knows*.

Looking around the playground now, that's when Clare realises that quite a few other people in 3C have also managed to hang onto their proper power of NO. Calum for instance - and there's some more people Orange Group and some in Green Group.

Then, like a light bulb switching on inside her head, that's when Clare 'gets' what her dad had said. She *sees* how the problem of Mrs Mountain and Miss Chantalle might just begin to be tackled - by as many of the people in 3C as possible putting together their proper power of NO for the good of all, don't you know!

What about Purple Group though?

Purple Group seems to like the lessons and the books exactly as they are.

But then again, apart from Sharon, the only people who *like* Purple Group are *themselves*.

So isn't the bigger truth that things aren't so great for the people in Purple Group either – because doesn't *everybody* need friends?

Definitely.

So, as far as Miss Chantalle and Mrs Mountain were concerned, obviously it was high time for *all* of 3C to put together their proper power of NO to get things changed for the better for the good of all, don't you know.

So - poor Mr Judd his afternoon.

Then next week some time all of 3C getting together to tackle the more ginormous problem of Miss Chantalle and Mrs Mountain

Like Wednesday maybe.

Pete Bog

by Rosemary Pope

His toes curl when he hears himself called 'Pete Bog', or rather he would curl them if he had any. He regards the snotty-nosed, bloodless crowds with extreme distaste as they press their faces against his environmentally-controlled Perspex cube. Of course they think he is dead; he understands that. How could such a boneless, grotesque creature, more like a discarded handbag than a human being, possibly be alive? 'If only he could talk,' they chortle to each other. Well, he might not be able to talk, but deep in the tissues of his desiccated brain there is a small flame of consciousness; believe it or not, he *can* see and he *can* hear. When he imagines their horror if they realized this, the ignorant *sods* (he has picked up many new words recently), he laughs soundlessly, secretly, deep within his brain.

Beside his cube in Gallery 20 there is a notice in best 'British- Museum' educational style, concise and informative: LINDOW MAN...FOUND IN PEAT BOG 1985...IRON AGE...1st CENTURY AD...KILLED FOR RITUAL SACRIFICE. He has heard this read out so many times, accompanied by so many 'oohs' and 'ahs' and *would- you- believe- its* and *well-I- nevers* and *how-absolutely-fascinating*s, that it is engraved on his flattened, empty heart. He thinks the notice to be a load of *crap*; although he is not entirely certain what 'crap' is (he has heard it used by truculent boys) he likes the word and intends to use it frequently. The youth of his day were never like this; they were too busy tending cattle, planting crops and fathering children. His tiny eye, almost hidden between flaps of reddish- brown skin, peers out with glittering malevolence as he watches and waits; how strange, he thinks, that nobody has yet noticed it. He is sometimes taken with the idea of winking at his audience, but two thousand years of interment in peat have ruined his facial muscles and he cannot make any sort of grimace.

It must be perfectly obvious to any fool that his well-trimmed beard and carefully cut nails (he had never been one to let himself go) show him to be a man of extremely superior status. He is perplexed and deeply wounded by the ignominious way he has been

203

treated. His right leg and foot have been crudely severed and he finds it disconcerting to see them displayed in a separate case right in front of his eyes. Heaven knows what has happened to his left leg. He has been excavated, sprayed with cold water, cleaned, repaired and worst of all, *freeze–dried.* Hands have poked around in his most private parts. Surely a man's stomach contents are his affair alone. Even more mortifying is WORMS IN HIS INTESTINES writ large on the notice. In his day worms were a fact of life, but one just *didn't* announce them to the world like that. It's patently unfair. He doesn't know what the 'iron age' is, but in the good old days when he was alive, none of this would have happened; people had some respect for authority then.

The biggest load of crap, though, is the idea that he died as part of a ritual killing. The very thought that he was in some way involved with those dreadful Druids makes his blood run cold; he hasn't actually got any blood *to* run (the freeze-drying has seen to that) but it strikes him as an apt way of describing his revulsion for that bizarre lot of 'weirdos' (another newly-acquired word). He has never pretended to be religious. Apart from the odd ceremony performed on someone's death, a few quick prayers to the gods for germination of the crops or a simple offering of meat to cure mastitis in his cows, he has had little to do with Druid rituals. Human sacrifice (of healthy men anyway) has always been anathema to his practical nature. After all, he tells himself, *important* men like him were needed to keep the tribe going. The notice states that the cord around his neck is a tourniquet and he had been garrotted as *part of a ritual sacrifice.* How ridiculous- the fools- can't they see that his neck is not damaged? A bone ornament, a token of his status in the tribe has been suspended there. He is amazed; they pride themselves on being so clever, yet they have missed that.

He has been in his cube for twenty long years now. He supposes that it must be his anniversary because that evening the security guard shouts rudely, 'nighty-night, happy birthday old boy,' as he closes the gallery. He hears the guard's footsteps echoing down the marble corridor and he lies, alone at last, in the mysterious red glow of the security light. Instead of his usual descent into oblivion, his mind begins to drift back through time…back through his entombment in the dank, acidic, airless peat...back before his untimely death...back to his life- his *real* life all those aeons ago...

...He is a child again, the son of the chief. He is running joyously down-hill, hair streaming behind him, bounding fearlessly over dykes and shouting with the wind. At first he is too young to labour in the fields, to build storage pits for the grain or herd the cattle with his father. He holds his mother's loom weights, gathers firewood and helps to shake the fur bedding. His life is regulated by the slow rhythm of the seasons. The bone-shattering cold of the northern winter, spring's warm fecundity, summer's arid heat and the fruitful opulence of autumn, mark his journey to adulthood. He remembers the year-round fetid warmth of the roundhouse and the acrid smoke of the ceaselessly- burning fire drifting upwards towards the dense thatch. He particularly relishes the putrid smell of half-rotten meat being smoked slowly in the roof-space. He feels the chaffing of the rough log seat against his legs as he fidgets to avoid the scorching fire. He is surrounded by the thickness of wattle and daub walls. On dark, stormy nights he hears restless, creaking timbers; the house seems a living thing, a fortress against life's cruelties. His mother's freshly baked bread, lifted carefully from the little clay oven, so crisp and sour, with blackened, steaming crust smeared with lard, lives on for ever in his memory. Sometimes she uses barley and rye to make a kind of glutinous porridge (a great favourite of his). It globs and gollops in the pot and a wonderful smell of rancid milk seeps into his nostrils and mingles with the other delicious odours. Peeping from beneath his woollen blanket, he secretly watches his father carousing with the men of the tribe. The air vibrates with laughter that echoes and re-echoes around the walls; the flickering firelight casts shadows that leap and lunge in a mad game of chase. He sees horn cups of barley beer held high in jovial celebration. How impressive his father is – tall (could he touch the sky?), strong enough to up-root a tree and brave enough to fight a mountain bear. How he admires his father's long oily hair braided with animal sinews, his cloak fastened with an intricate, glittering brooch; how he covets the bone ornament, emblem of chief-hood suspended on a cord around his father's neck.

Now he is a young man, tall, strong and handsome. He admires his reflection (at every opportunity) in shallow pools and sees a worthy successor to his noble father. He is the proud owner of an ornate bone comb (traded for a sheepskin) that he drags through his thick, dark brown hair. He remembers rushing to meet the traders. Where they come from he does not know, but he is excited by their exotic, colourful robes and strange dark faces. They bring finely-crafted iron implements for the farm, jewellery and salt in exchange for his mother's woollen cloth. To his delight, he manages to acquire from them, a small, sharp iron knife and carefully, painfully, he trims his beard and pares his nails. Naturally, women adore him. He sighs with pleasure as he remembers their warmth and softness, such a relief from the hardness of his life. He is not being conceited; after all, in his view this is the natural order of things; men and women together create the next generation. But yet...but yet... there is one woman...one woman only who rules his heart and gives a special meaning to his life. Although 'love' is not yet in his vocabulary, it best describes the intense joy that he feels in her presence. Indeed, no woman since, down all the ages, has affected him in quite the same way. Yet then, as now, death is forever present to tear away those we love. Death in childbirth is commonplace, everyone knows that; yet he finds it hard to accept. No amount of incantation or offerings of food or drink, seem to placate the angry gods; so much for religion, he thinks bitterly. At least he has a healthy baby son, his first-born, who will in turn grow up to be a chief.

Now memories of the inexorable harshness of his life flood back to him. He is a chief, a man of stature, but unremitting drudgery from dawn to nightfall is the same for all men. Tending reluctant crops, harrowing, harvesting, threshing, husbanding and slaughtering precious animals must be done in due season. The winter mud clogs the wheels of his cart and forms great clods on his feet as he walks beside the plough. The horses, poor beasts, pant and snort with exhaustion. Despite the pain deep in his joints (in his after-life he learns this is *arthritis)* there can be no rest, no relief. His woman rubs pungent greasy unguents on his legs but to no avail. Yet although words elude him, his poet's soul rejoices in fleeting moments of happiness. He delights in the patient, gentle cattle, their warm, sweet breath rising into the frosty morning air. The ripe golden barley shimmering in the autumn breeze moves him to tears.

Now at thirty he is the oldest man in the tribe. His sees his sons growing to be fine men (just like himself) fearless and honourable. They will father many children and the village will one day be populated by many little copies of himself, he is certain. His daughters are wonderfully fair; they are strong, have good teeth and wide child-bearing hips. Soon they will be ripe for marriage. So the days pass quickly in his well-ordered world of toil and survival.

The day of his death dawns bright and clear. Although he has not slept that night his senses are sharp. The rustle of new growth mingles with birdsong and fills his head with glorious sound. He does not see his assailants as he moves silently along the track beside the village because they are well-hidden in the undergrowth. Suddenly they are upon him, their swords flashing in the sunlight. As he draws his own faithful weapon he is aware of his father's spirit close beside him. The clash of metal on metal, howls of pain and anger rend the morning air. He spins around – slashing high and low – thrusting – parrying blow after blow. He sees dimly through the blood pouring from his wounded head, that he has killed several men. They lie like heaps of bloody rags beside the path. More men writhe before him, groaning in anguish. Yet he knows the end is inevitable and his time has come. He is not afraid; to die in defence of his land and his people is both brave and honourable. He scarcely feels the blows to his head or the knife in his back as he falls heavily to the ground, his sword still clutched tightly in his hand. He does not die immediately. He is aware of angry hands clasping him, throwing his body roughly aside into the soft, marshy ground. In his dying moments he feels himself sinking… sinking…then darkness…then nothingness…until…

…'Wakey wakey rise and shine.' The friendly security guard on early duty taps his cube.

As he wakes, a shaft of errant sunlight pierces the blind and mottles the marble floor with splashes of colour. It illuminates the faces of his early visitors. They look ethereal, rapt, like worshippers in a temple. Their voices hum with quiet appreciation. They have come all this way to see him. They examine him so carefully, so respectfully. He longs to respond with a wave or a smile, but of course, he will never be able to do that.

207

'This is so interesting…How absolutely fascinating… Would you believe it…What a fine man he must have been… If only he could talk…Look at his nails…Do you think that is an ornament around his neck?' He is enchanted by their voices.

He notices their glowing health, their fine teeth, and their open, friendly faces. He thinks (in his new twenty-first century awareness) they are *awesome* and their words are *life-enhancing*.

Suddenly, it dawns on him that, they too, are human beings; his past is their past; he is as much part of them as they are of him. He forgets the indignities visited on him by the conservators. What do they matter? He will last for ever as a monument to the past; he is more important now than he has ever been.

A small boy pulls away from his mother's hand and dances beside him, round-eyed, curious.

'Mum, mum, I think he can hear us. I saw him smile just now and I don't think he's really dead. I think he's really alive inside.'

He is startled to see that this independent, perceptive child is exactly like his first-born. Immediately, another face in the eager crowd catches his eye; with her rosy skin and dark luxuriant hair she is the very image of his beloved woman. Surely, that tall man with such an air of wisdom, staring at him so intently, must be his father; that graceful, serene mother bending to talk to her child could be *his* mother. He has no bodily fluids so his tears cannot fall, but these links with his own life move him profoundly. He doesn't mind being 'Pete Bog' now. He belongs here; he is one of the people and that is how it should be.

'*How cool is that*,' he thinks as he prepares for the next two thousand years.

filling his mouth, and...

by Steve Mann

Inexorably creeping, slowly up his nostrils, is the determined aromatic stuffing, of this living being. Thanking the gods, he's thinking, with a deep satisfying sense of relief, they must have already opened the celestial door, at the back of his skull. For how else could his most intimate thoughts be, even now, as he's thinking them, escaping with alacrity.

'Are these now my thoughts?' he's wondering, now that they are not in his head, yet they are still in his mind. 'Is my mind leaving my head, or does my mind, remaining in my head, have a special relationship with my thoughts?'

'Stop', he's hearing this in his mind, 'we are our own and not yours, we are travelling in this sustaining cosmos, we are breaking this silver cord.' 'But wait', they are continuing, 'what is that bright light?' 'We are being drawn, drawn, drawn, into such warmth, such comfort, we are here now.'

'He seemed to only just pass this very moment.'
'You're right Sakmet', replied Paneb.

In an infinitesimal microsecond, Brian, senior fireman, grade two, of Shropshire County Fire Service 1998, is saying: *'he's a boy! wonderful darling! What did we say we would we call him?'*

And is thinking, 'what was that TV programme the other night about Tutankamun?'

Conkers

by Richard Layton

I was adamant this time, enough was enough. I was not going to go through with all that agony, not again. I wasn't really reading a word of the comic I had my head buried in but the pretence at normality was necessary if I was to avoid undue suspicion. When you're at the tender age of eleven, as I was back then, there are precious few places where a non conformist, such as I was, indeed still am, can reveal the fact in safety and this certainly wasn't one of them. I looked at my new watch, and not just for the novelty of looking for once. I really did want to know the time. It said 11:15. As I thought, we were five minutes late and counting.

"Come on, Mum!" I whined. "This is a waste of time, they've obviously forgotten all about us, we should have been in five minutes ago. Let's go home."

"You can't go until you've been seen, you know that."

"But I'm not going to be seen, this is just madness! We're five minutes late already."

"They're always late, just be patient." Mum sounded like she was in a mood.

I changed tack. "I don't even need to be here at all. They'll only say so, so why waste time like this?"

"Patrick, you're not getting out of it. And I can tell you do need to be seen by the way you're peering at that watch. Now just sit quietly until they call you in or you can go without pudding tonight."

I had to back down once I was faced with that total injustice. I hid my scowl under the pages of the comic and tried to think of something else. I even thought of actually reading the comic but it was three weeks old. I mean, come on! Why couldn't they spend some of their budget on up-to-date issues for the people who really did need to be there instead of wasting it on the likes of me who didn't have anything wrong with him. It was just madness.

"Patrick Rees."

"Come on," said Mum, "and behave yourself."

I reluctantly got out of my seat and we made our way to the door. The only thing worse than the waiting room is the surgery itself. Especially when, like me, you didn't need to be there.

"Ah," the doctor addressed me, "hello again young Master Rees. Come for some more of my lovely eye drops."

Somehow I managed to hide my scowl behind a smile. I don't know how I did it but thinking about the pudding helped.

"Right, come along then," the idiot doctor continued, "let's sit you down whilst I get the old syringe out."

Why was a bone head like him allowed to work in an important area like medicine? It was just madness. Reluctantly I sat down whilst he filled the syringe.

"Just some drops to get your eyes ready so I can have a look at them. Now then, open your eyes wide. Come on, young man, you must keep your eyes open."

"Don't screw them up, Patrick!" said Mum. "Do as he says."

What did they expect me to do, I mean, come on! When somebody's trying to jab something into your eye it's a natural instinct to close it. I gritted my teeth and bit my tongue whilst the idiot doctor continued to splash his precious eye drops all over my face. I was trying to keep still, it wasn't my fault. Finally he was satisfied that he'd done enough and he was able to examine them. He looked for whatever it was he was looking for and then had a conversation with Mum. I didn't understand the words they were using but I knew what it meant.

"Well Master Rees," the doctor said, "it seems we still have a lazy eye don't we? Still, nothing to worry about. All you've got to do is wear the patches over the other eye."

"No," I wailed at him.

"It's the only way to make the lazy eye get better, block off the good eye and make the lazy one work on its own."

"But I don't want to be one-eyed."

"If you don't wear the patches," said Mum, "your lazy eye will go blind and then you'll really be one-eyed forever."

"But the new school year starts next week. You've done this on purpose."

"Don't be silly!" Mum snapped.

"Yes you have! You could have done this six weeks ago and it would all be finished by now but instead you make me start secondary school looking like a freak, it's a total injustice."

"Patrick, remember what I told you last time. You know what will happen if you don't wear the patches. You'll lose the sight in your left eye and if you lose it, Lucifer will get it. And if he does you'll never be able to get away from him."

That was cruel. I'd been a lot younger then and I'd had nightmares for weeks after she'd told me that. Of course it was just a scare tactic, but that didn't make it any easier to disbelieve.

Of course, on the first day of term, I tried to get out of it, faking a black eye with boot polish. I thought it was a good idea, if I couldn't see out of one eye I could hardly be expected to wear a patch over the other one, that was just madness. A legitimate excuse and it would have worked if Mum hadn't seen me looking perfectly normal five minutes beforehand. Sometimes these gambles pay off and sometimes they don't.

I kept a low profile on the walk to school that first day, or at least as low a profile as was realistically possible considering I had a dirty great piece of jumped-up Elastoplast over my right eye. Why on Earth you couldn't use ordinary sticking plasters I had no idea. It was just madness. I really didn't need the misfortune to be reacquainted with my least favourite person. I flinched.

"Hello, Patch!"

"You. Harry Stockwell."

"The very same, Hardhead Harry and just you remember it, Patch!"

"My name is Patrick."

"Your name's whatever I say it is! Unless you want a fight?"

You probably don't need me to tell you that there was a history between myself and Harry. He was a year above me and had once gone to Nutwood Primary, same as me, until his parents had fallen out with the head over the school dinners and they'd sent him to Toplands instead. We'd been friends to begin with until the incident with the 'bus. It was one of his toys and we'd been playing with it in the school playground, running it up and down to each other. I'd stopped for a moment to fasten a shoelace and he'd sent the 'bus careering across the yard. Right into my hand. It hurt but when I cried out he just laughed. I didn't like being laughed at then any more than now and as there was a loose drain cover nearby, down the drain the 'bus went. We exchanged blows, got detention - a total injustice because he started it- and there'd been a feud between us ever since. I'd forgotten that going to Highfield Secondary school meant I'd be seeing him on a daily basis again. Well he wasn't going to mess me about this time. I was a first year, none of the teachers here knew about the history between us so I'd paint the picture exactly as they'd expect to see it. Highfield made a big thing of its anti-bullying policy and I wasn't above playing the system to my advantage. As things were to turn out, in the end, I wouldn't need to but that was still the future. For the moment, I chose to walk away. I walked on into the grounds of the school and as I passed under the horse chestnut tree, I caught something with my foot. I looked down and saw it was a freshly fallen conker and my foot had split its case open. No way was I going to let a prize specimen like that go to waste. Into my pocket it went. I'd string it up later when I had something to bore it with.

The first year induction assembly, or whatever it was they called it came next and it soon became apparent that boring the conker would have to wait. It seems the school had certain rules pertaining to the use of conkers. Namely we couldn't. We could take fallen ones home but there was to be no climbing the tree for them, no throwing sticks at the tree to knock them off and no playing of conkers within the grounds. They spouted some claptrap about safety but the real reason was obviously abuse of a dominant position. They banned playing conkers simply because they could. Yes, okay climbing trees was dangerous but playing conkers? I mean, come on!

I was saying as much to Danny on the way home that afternoon. We were very close, Danny and me, much to Mum and Dad's irritation, as they thought he was trouble with his propensity for joking and larking about. But he was a kindred spirit, the only other person I'd ever met who shared my ability to see the lunacy of the world around us. He wasn't going to be in my class any more, or rather my form. Now we were at secondary school we had to drop the word class and replace it with form for no adequately explored reason.

213

"How can they possibly ban conkers, eh Danny? It's just madness."

"Yeah," said Danny, "we ought to complain. Fight for our right to play conkers. We should have a schoolboy union or something then we could all stand outside the gates and picket them until they gave in."

"Good idea. Of course all the girls would have to be made honorary boys whilst the dispute was on. They'd only scab on us if we didn't."

"Yeah," said Danny, "got to be 100% solid."

"Seriously though, let's not take it lying down. Let's do something."

"Like what?"

"Don't know. I'll sleep on it and let you know tomorrow."

I spent that evening boring a hole in my prize conker whilst racking my brains as I tried to think of something we could do to fight back against the total injustice of the conker ban. It had to be something radical, attention grabbing. Something that would guarantee publicity and, more importantly, credibility amongst our peers and have them rallying to our cause. I wasn't having much luck, all I could think of was climbing the tree. This wasn't ideal as climbing the tree was pass,. It had been done before. They wouldn't have bothered with a rule against it if people hadn't been doing it, I mean come on! Still, I supposed, it was better than nothing. We could always liven it up by hanging a banner or something. Anyhow, I'd see what Danny had come up with. He was a lot more creative than me and I was sure I could count on him to think of something.

I caught up with Danny next morning and tackled him about our plan of action. "I hope you've had more luck than I have, all I can think of is a banner."

"What? What action? What do you mean?"

"About ending the conker ban. All I can think of is climbing the tree in defiance of the rules and hanging a protest banner from one of the branches. Unless you can think of something better."

"Oh, Patch," he began, oblivious to my hackles rising at that unwanted nickname, "you don't mean you were being serious, we were just having a laugh."

214

"Of course I was serious. And if you won't help me, I'll climb the tree on my own."

"You haven't seriously got a banner?"

"No, but I'll make one. You watch me this lunchtime."

I made good use of that morning's break, studying the tree, working out which was the best way up it and what branch would be the best one to hang a banner from. This wasn't as easy to plan as you might think because I had to do it all with one eye. I was really beginning to hate that patch. There was God creating man in his own image with two eyes and here I was being forced to insult Him by only using one of them. It was just madness. There was only one thing more annoying than that blasted eye patch and her name was Debbie. She was in my class, sorry my form, I was a class above her and that's not bragging. For reasons I can't even begin to understand, she found my eye patch a source of unending fascination.

"What is that thing on your face?" she'd say.

"It's called an eye patch," I would answer patiently.

"That's why I'm wearing it over my nose."

"Well what's wrong with your right eye?"

"There's nothing wrong with my right eye. They're worried about my left one," I'd tell her.

"So why isn't that one blocked?" she'd ask.

"Because it doesn't work like that!" I'd say, wondering how much more of this I was going to have to put up with. "They say the left eye is lazy and if I don't wear a patch over the right one, the left eye will go blind. Blocking the right eye forces the left eye to work and makes it see better."

"In that case, why don't you wear a patch over both eyes and make them both better?"

I gave up at that point. If someone was to compile a list of the stupidest questions of all time, all bets would be off. Could she not see that I could hardly see with just one eye blocked off, how was I going to get about without either of them? That was just madness. Luckily I was able to get rid of Debbie by lunchtime which was just as well. I couldn't cope with her distractions if I was going to go ahead with my plan. I hadn't been able to make the banner, which was a blow but there'd been nothing to make it with. I'd just

215

have to settle for a conker grab as an act of defiance. One prize conker was no longer enough. Steeling myself I started to climb the tree.

"Patch!"

"Danny, don't sneak up on me like that! And stop calling me Patch!"

"You're not really going to climb that tree are you? You don't know the trouble you're going to get into."

"Well keep watch then. If you see any teachers coming lure them away so I can get down without being seen." I started my climb, I wasn't going to stop now.

"Patrick," Danny called after me, "it's not teachers you've got to worry about. I've been talking to my brother and he told me the real reason why they don't allow conkers."

"I'm not interested."

"Patrick, I'm serious! All that stuff about safety's just a front. The real reason's because... Mmph!"

I looked down to see what had cut him off. I had a shock when I saw. It was Hardhead Harry. "Get off my friend!" I yelled at him.

"Come on then, Patch!" he shouted. "Come on down and make me!" Then he let go of Danny anyway and started to chuck stones at me. "I'll have your other eye out, Patch!" My only chance was to climb higher up the tree and hope I could shield myself with the branches. Why did God suffer the likes of Hardhead Harry on his Earth? It was a total injustice. God must have been listening because what happened next has no other explanation.

"Stockwell!" The teacher's arrival brought Hardhead Harry up short. "How many times have you been told not to throw things at the horse chestnut tree? You can have detention for a week!"

This was just too good to be true! Hardhead Harry was getting what was coming to him and the idiot teacher hadn't even seen me! What an irony when he had two eyes available. For one glorious moment I wasn't just king of the land of the blind, but of the sighted as well. And then I lost my footing and fell out of the tree. What a total injustice. It was scant consolation that I flattened Hardhead Harry in the fall, however satisfying a crack it made. The idiot teacher grabbed me by the scruff of my neck and hauled me off the snivelling wretch.

"What's your name boy?"

"Patrick Rees, Sir."

"Well, Rees, boy, man descended from the trees millions of years ago. You apparently didn't. You can count yourself lucky you can still stand. The Headmaster's office! Now! Whilst I phone for an ambulance for Master Stockwell."

I stood outside the foreboding door of the headmaster's office trying in vain not to tremble so visibly. It was a total injustice.

"I told you not to climb that tree."

"Oh, hello, Danny. Some lookout you turned out to be. What did you go and lead Hardhead Harry onto me for?"

"I never! But I did tell you not to climb that tree. It's too late now I know but I thought you might want to hear the real reason."

I sighed. "Not especially, but I suppose you're going to tell me anyway."

"That tree's been there a long time, you know. Long before there was a school here. Do you know what's buried underneath it?"

"Nothing."

"Wrong. This is the real reason why they don't let you play conkers. A long time ago there was a ferocious warrior. They called him the Demon because of the fury he used to fight in. Do you know what his favourite weapon was?"

"Of course I don't! I've never heard of him, I mean come on!"

"What do you call those metal balls on chains? The ones all covered in spikes and you swing them on a chain. He had one of them. He used to whirl it around and smash people's heads open with it."

"Yes, very interesting but what's the relevance?"

"When he was finally killed they wanted to forget about all the horrors he'd done so they didn't mark his grave. They just dug a hole in the ground and threw him in. That would have been it if a conker hadn't chanced to be dropped there. It was ages later but that conker grew and took up his spirit. It's our horse chestnut, Patch.

That's why you mustn't take its conkers. You'll let the Demon into you."

Danny and his folklore, he really freaked me out. "Don't be stupid," I said unconvincingly, "if that was the case they wouldn't let us take the conkers home would they?"

"You'll soon see I'm right," said Danny, "the Demon's bound to go for you. You see, he only had one eye as well. Goodbye, Patch."

Away he went. My best friend supposedly and he left me with a messed up head. I stood waiting for the Headmaster to arrive, fingering the prize conker in my pocket. Funnily enough, the prospect of having to face him on only my second day didn't seem so bad any more. Not when I had the Demon to worry about. Oh, hell, what was I going to do? The sound of footsteps approaching gave me the immediate answer to that question. I was going to follow the Headmaster into his office and get shouted at.

"You are Rees?"

"Yes, Sir."

"Follow me, boy." He opened the door to his office and went in. I followed.

The Headmaster closed the door behind us, made me stand on the spot and strode round to his desk and sat down.

"You were present in school yesterday?"

"Yes Sir."

"You were made aware of the ban on climbing the tree?"

"Yes Sir."

"So why did you climb the tree?"

"I don't know Sir."

"That's not good enough." Neither of us spoke for what seemed like an age. "The ambulance man said it looks like Harry Stockwell has broken his neck," he said at last.

"Sir?"

"He may be left in a wheelchair. What have you got to say for yourself?" I said nothing, fingering the conker on its string. "Hand out of your pocket!" the headmaster snapped.

"Sorry Sir."

"Give me that conker. Now, boy, give it to me. You're already being suspended. If you don't want a week of detention when you come back, give me that conker."

"No, I can't Sir. The Demon."

"Don't try my patience boy! Give it to me!"

And I did. Lashing out and sending it flying through the air. His head cracked like a nut and I recoiled at the sight of his brains squelching out on the floor. I ran and ran and ran to the nearest toilet, bent over the wash basin and was sick. Again and again. Shaking I grabbed hold of the basin and tried to steady myself. I looked at myself in the mirror, the face of a killer staring back at me with his one flashing eye. It wasn't my face I saw. Apart from only having one eye, Danny hadn't gone into detail about the Demon's appearance but he didn't have to. I knew it was him looking back at me and I knew I was in his power. With a cry I turned from the mirror and locked myself into one of the cubicles, adamant that I was never going to come out again. That would have been just madness.

I stayed in the cubicle, trying my best to shut out the world beyond it, but I couldn't blot out the voices. How did the girls do it? I'd never understand their ability to talk nineteen to the dozen without even stopping for breath. The thought was nagging at me for some minutes before I realised why. I was in the wrong lavatory! In my haste and being in such a state in view of what the Demon had made me do to the Head I had run into the nearest toilet not realising it was the girls' loo. Any other day and this would have been the worst thing imaginable but being under the power of a spectral warrior really helps you put things like that in perspective. I'd have to wait until they'd gone and then find a boys' toilet to lock myself in but that was the least of my worries. I sat tight and waited for them to go. They didn't seem to be in any great hurry to do so. Now why was that? I wondered. Then slowly it dawned on me. Through the partition between the bottom of those stupid partial doors they always used in school cubicles and the floor I saw the direction of their feet and realised that I was the main attraction. Suddenly long trousers weren't such a good idea after all. Socks and shins could just as easily be his or hers but muddy hemlines were a dead giveaway.

"Who is it in there?"

That was all I needed. Debbie. Wouldn't it just have to be a total injustice like that? Now what was she doing? Oh, hell she was climbing up to look over the top.

"Patrick, what are you doing here? Couldn't you see the sign with that patch on?"

"Go away. All of you leave me alone," I shouted. Then I rushed out of the cubicle brandishing my conker. "Go now before I kill the lot of you! I mean it, I've already killed the Headmaster. It's the Demon, he's got me. The other girls just looked at me like I was some kind of weirdo but Debbie seemed genuinely concerned.

"Patrick, don't be stupid, demons don't exist."

"This one does, come and see for yourself. See what he made me do to the Head." A part of me really wanted her to see all the blood and gore and watch her go hysterical. Or maybe that part of me was the Demon, I can't say, but I insisted that she come. Then the Demon would claim his next kill.

"Patrick we'll be late for class."

"I mean it!" I grabbed her hand and practically dragged her away with me, hastily filling in the details of the story as I went. "If I didn't crush his head why didn't he chase me? Answer me that?" I said triumphantly as we approached the Headmaster's door. I knew all too well that she couldn't answer and neither could anyone else. "There." I pointed.

"The door's closed."

"Look at the blood spilling out underneath! Can't you see?"

"Patrick stop it, I want to go to my next class. The bell's gone."

Angrily I swung the conker at the door, seeing it splinter to matchwood. "Can you see now?" I screamed before swinging the conker at her head and running off. I ran straight into the path of the idiot teacher who'd sent me to the head in the first place.

"Patrick Rees, boy, stop right there!" He grabbed me by the scruff of the neck again which was a total injustice. "Your mother is waiting at the school gate to take you home. You are suspended."

I've seen Mum looking cross several times in my life but never to the extent that she was then. She snatched the conker out of my hand, putting it in her handbag, and practically threw me into the back seat of the car.

"Just wait till your father hears about this!" she screamed as she drove away.

I wasn't too bothered to be honest. Now I'd been separated from the conker, the Demon could no longer reach me, I was safe. Whatever punishment Mum and Dad inflicted on me would wear off in time. I was free of it. But then a sickening thought hit me. I might be free but Mum wasn't. She would take the conker out of her bag and what would stop the Demon taking her over as he had me? At least I knew about the danger but Mum didn't. I couldn't let it happen. There was only one honourable thing to do, get the conker back. Mum's handbag was sitting on the front passenger seat. I undid my belt and lunged for it. "I must have it! I must have it! The Demon! The Demon!"

"Patrick!" Mum screamed as she lost control and skidded into a lamppost.

I could tell by the looks on people's faces as I told them my story that they didn't believe me. I understood why, of course, it was their job not to believe me. Their brief was to dissuade me of my own veracity and convince me otherwise. Why was the psychiatric profession's mind so firmly closed? Did it never occur to them that just once in a while they'd come across somebody who was telling the truth, who wasn't mad, who hadn't had a breakdown and hadn't cracked up? Did they never stop to think that maybe that someone was me? Apparently not it seemed. I learnt of course, how to play these people. I had to pretend that I agreed with them and that no, I wasn't a demonically possessed murderer. This wasn't easy because in order to convince them I first had to convince myself. It was a Herculean challenge but eventually I managed to persuade enough of them that I had convinced myself they were right. But it was several years since the fateful day that I climbed the tree that they finally agreed to stop seeing me and accept that I was rid of my inner demons.

I wasn't of course. There never were any inner demons, just the Demon himself and he was external. But he haunted me still. I would walk around the streets with my left eye scrunched shut, not that it showed me much when I had it open these days. I would screw the eyelid up to try and stop him seeing out of it but it was no use. I knew there was only one way I was going to free myself. To do that I was going to need to get myself an axe.

Highfield had undergone some changes in the years since I'd left but in other ways it was the same old place I'd been all too briefly acquainted with. I walked purposefully into the grounds, the axe gripped firmly in my hands. Yes, just as I had known it would be, the horse chestnut was still there, still casting its baleful shadow over my life. Well not for much longer. I hoisted the axe and set about it with a frenzy.

"You! Stop! What are you doing here?"

I turned round and found myself face to face with the Headmaster. I must have looked as if I'd seen a ghost because he backed away looking concerned. Or maybe it was my axe that frightened him.

"Oh, my God," he said quietly. "I recognise you. Patrick Rees." The one who went mad was the unspoken suffix he didn't add.

So this was the Demon's plan. He could possess you through the conkers but they weren't really weapons, that was just his visions. It was all part of his scheme to manipulate me into obtaining a real weapon with which he could really kill someone. Well I wasn't going to let him. I closed my eyes and saw his contorted face exhorting me on. My every sinew fought to turn the axe on the tree again whilst his crazed voice sounded in my brain, urging me to turn on the Headmaster and raise my axe for the kill.

Double Standards

by Manus McDaid

Freelance Tea Dance – well, not total – there were certain concessions: depping musicians (contractual). You have to get in the mood; how much free tea can one consume. As a Dep (Deputy: stand-in) I was personally propping up the bar quite early on, ostensibly running through the pad: block of music notation in numerical form i.e. song 'number', trying to get motivated. The band from Basildon – *The New City Stompers* is to be of the old-fashioned *'Trad Jazz'* variety – not my type, really. I felt like I'd been blown-in from Mars, actually, so I was pretty damned chuffed to see Paco breeze into the venue: Paco Pastorius - the 'Modern Jazz' trumpet player (also depping – also early) @ Club 'M' (for murder).

The 11th hour deal with me, as a replacement for their regular banjo-bloke, was to turn up with my standard (no effects) "electrical" guitar and 'go for it.' Due to the increased versatility of this 6-stringed instrument I would get to solo on each number (same as Paco, although not necessarily at the same time of course)...

...Of course not. However; old Paco and me had a bit of catching up to do and after a couple of pints and much reminiscing, the mischievousness started to kick in. We made a tacit agreement that when I got to blow on *Honeysuckle Rose,* come the second chorus (complete harmonic cycle: I was generally taking two) I would launch into the contemporary Parker part - (Charlie 'Bird' Parker, late, great alto sax man – definitely in his own parallel orbit) *Scrapple from the Apple* as the Bird re-titled it. Paco would pick it up, note for note,(with an enigmatic, trumpeterial flourish) in unison; buy one get one free – the poor old Stompers were astonished: double whammy – well beyond the confines of the regular, anachronistic *Traditional Jazz* and the flatulent, old brass sections/new town marches (Mardi`farts). Mind you, even Pac' was sounding sonically grim, like a muffled old wassail-bowl and it wasn't even half time yet.

Things weren't going well, overall. We had to try (at least) to be prudent and the pair of us decided to rein it in a bit during the break – *slowdown.*

Showdown

Seconds out – we have a guest: Norah Yorke from New York, so [good] they named her twice and she definitely didn't like our little shtick; the effect on the band, the stolen dynamic; the stolen moment(s) from a swollen ego – heartbreaking! Over she came, a real blowhard – 'You guys are takin' the fanny out of [my] group – this is a [*fuckin'*] Earl Gray... NOT... ... a [fuckin'] runaway Greyhound [Gray – sorry 'one' forgot there for a moment] bus and it ain't Coltrane-gravy either. Not when Norah gets up > there: this lady sings the blues! Here's the charts > learn-em [ah-hem]'. This is *a* gig, "honey bunch".' She appeared to be addressing the pair of us in some sort of American singular plural – *sour grapes* kind of thing (thanks a bunch).

(?) *Agog/* My God...

...Got a red pen?

Highlight the party tricks (tricky bloody parts), not many; not as far as Greenwich Village, technically, but Norah was biting into her green witch self-belief (tract). My opposite number: Paco was falling all over her less than more at this stage - don't look back, cover it. *Somebody's going to get hurt.*

Off the rack, the band is good; not great... they're a unit, an entity, **solidly doing one thing** (not their own... which is good; not great) very industriously - the leader being rather like a shop steward type of bloke. We went back on and so it came to pass. We were chugging through the cha cha, *Tea for Two* when Paco turned slowly to tip me the wink and lo and behold – out shot this cellophane wrapped cheese roll, in B flat, right at New York's crown, as she was fronting the band you see. I'd been wondering about Paco having to blow so hard but with Norah, the *New [Yorke] City Stomper* it was different:

it was sounding like an old 78 rpm wind-up. I mean, for all I knew she could've been the *Nightingale from Berkley Square,* but through this PA she was stuck in *Birdland* – with us. A mixed metaphor she could probably have done well without: Paco's missile was the catalyst that caused her to stomp off stage – albeit humiliated. When I asked the drummer, Knut Sproat what sort of "system" it was he replied with mock modesty, 'I made it myself.' *Oh dear: she didn't stand a chance.*

'Who did it?' Couldn't of been me, I was struggling as well – when the red spotlights fired up they completely neutralised my highlights, so I was on the floor in hysterics; C major 7 ringing out rather dissonantly in light relief/disbelief. That Paco is such a slob – he just bungs (operative word) everything into his battered old case after a gig and this cheesy thingy must've got wedged inside the bell of the trumpet last night. Great shot though, I thought – a real rollover. We all played a lot better after that, though; 'cept for Yorkey who was in a dis-united state on a bar stool somewhere over the rainbow (we were still getting over it). In fact, I do believe the band called a union meeting later that night – it's like we put a spell on 'em in our duplicity: double standards; topped off with a salutation to the diva – Paco's greatest hit!

The magic of 'Bird' eh? His variations were probably once improvised and then analysed to find the motifs from which longer passages were developed re-harmonising the standard song-forms of the day. That's the trick – they sound like well constructed solos. I'm sure he would have loved our rendition of his take on *Tea for Two* - free cheese roll included.

The proprietor certainly enjoyed the melodrama – he framed it; one for the local press, "The Bird of Consciousness Shakes down Princess @ the Club 'M'; Hard Cheese!" – and invited the two of us to shtick around for a bit, gave us a special password by way of dispensation – 'anything you want from the bar just order it up and say "*Delaney said*".' Simple as that – *crapulent us.*

I think 'Delaney' might've had something to do with Eric – the great old American jazz drummer; or was it 'Delano?' (Franklin. D. Roosevelt) < whichever it derived from it turned out to be a very hospitable code indeed – some tea party eh? So glad I learnt those Parker be-bop tunes when I still had half a brain – good for the double act: the governor burst out laughing every time he set eyes on the pair of us. I'm sure he thought we staged it, theatrical verisimilitude and all that jazz.

Ms Yorke breezed back to Basildon Bond to write some new stuff; on a roll apparently and that was that, as they say – *roll on*. Cheese and wine: next time… and a Tannoy.

A Ring Cycle

by Carey Barlow

Marion had not known Alan Wakefield personally, so it was with some reluctance that she went to his funeral. Wakefield had been a business acquaintance of her husband William, and Marion was starting to get tired of funerals. Although, naturally, she would not have mentioned it to William, Marion could not help but notice what an extraordinarily large number of the men in William's circle had died over the last few years. Nor had their deaths been from the normal things like heart attacks or strokes. These men had all been victims of the most astounding accidents. Wakefield, for example, had been chopped into a multitude of little pieces by the 18.45 down train from Edinburgh, although his head had survived well enough for identification to be both immediate and certain. What made it odd was that no one could remember having seen him in the area before the accident, and Wakefield had been the type of man who made his presence quite uncomfortably felt.

The widow, whom Marion knew slightly, and honestly liked, sat hidden in a mass of veiling, at the front of the church. Her shoulders quivered with emotion. This was particularly so during the eulogy which shamelessly implied that Heaven should feel honoured to receive the likes of Wakefield. For one brief and guilty moment Marion wondered if the loss of William would affect her quite that deeply, though of course, William was a perfectly wonderful man. Immediately rebuking herself for her lack of circumspection, Marion burst into song along with the rest of the congregation. The set of William's eye brow checked her. She lapsed into silence.

After the ceremony William made it understood that he had an urgent appointment which prevented him and Marion from attending the gathering which was being held at a nearby hotel. In this he did not appear to be alone, as well over half the small company flocked off to their cars. Marion was shocked by this obvious defection. Leaving William to free himself, and the car, from their narrow parking space, she ran back to the widow, who by now was standing alone. Marion had no idea what she was going to say, but the widow saved her from that particular embarrassment.

Turning her back on the mourners, the widow raised her veil, and, to Marion's consternation, winked. Seeing Marion's reaction, the widow's vast amusement bubbled into gales of silent laughter. Then, before Marion had time to think that perhaps the widow was hysterical, she thrust an envelope into Marion's hand.

"Pass this on when you have finished with it," she hissed, lowering her veil. Then with complete composure, she turned back to the few remaining mourners.

Marion could not ask her what she meant because William, who detested to be kept waiting, was now hooting from the car. Stuffing the envelope into her bag, she hurried through the lychgate. William rebuked her for leaving him like that, particularly when he was short of time, but as soon as he had driven round the corner from the church, he discovered that his appointment was less urgent than he had thought. He decided instead that Marion could give him lunch before driving him to the golf club. She must pick him up from there when he telephoned her later. William, a pillar of the community, was punctilious about not driving after drinking alcohol. It would never do for a man in his position to be seen to break the law, especially since he had become such a senior member of The Rotary Club.

So, it was quite late in the afternoon before Marion found the envelope while she was emptying her bag. William liked her to be organized, and to take care of her things. With the way the cost of living was forever rising, they must be made to last. Since Marion only used this bag for funerals, it must be put away until the next such tragedy. The envelope was small and pink, and Marion was astonished to discover that it had her name on it, although she had been sure till then that Clara Wakefield had acted solely upon impulse when she gave it to her. Nor was Marion any less surprised to discover that the envelope contained nothing but a ring.

The ring was beautiful. Reddish gold, which had the oily look which only comes from absolute purity, was etched with patterns which looked almost like some kind of oriental script. A strong claw setting clutched an exquisite blue stone. Marion stared at it. The stone was obviously not a sapphire, but set in gold like that, it must be very valuable, and women do not give their female acquaintances precious jewellery. Yet, Clara Wakefield had obviously not done so by mistake. Although every time they met, the two women had enjoyed each other's company, that had been as far as it went. There had never been a hint of any impropriety. Nor would there have been time for any, because William did not like his wife to hold conversations with the wives of his dwindling band of colleagues. Small talk must be the order of the day. Too much familiarity, he said, might undermine his standing within the local community. In fact, Marion now remembered that William had been quite abrupt when he broke up her chat with Mary Maynard.

Mary was a widow now. Although no fault had been discovered in the wiring, her husband had electrocuted himself while surfing some rather nasty web sites on his computer. Mary had been sketchy on the details because she had been away that weekend, looking after her mother, who had suddenly gone frail. Marion would have liked to get to know the widowed Mary better, but it had been impossible to pursue the friendship. Mary was now living in Bermuda with her mother, a sprightly lady who had made an excellent recovery.

But reminiscence would not help to solve the problem of the ring. While it was not within the normal range of conduct to accept such a thing, surely Marion would be even ruder if she returned it. And, clearly, since Clara had distinctly asked Marion to pass it on elsewhere, she did not expect it back. It was more as if she had been entrusting Marion with some type of custodianship, though Marion had not the least idea of where the ring must be passed on to next, nor even how one finished with it, whatever that meant. She was baffled.

When the perplexities of life with William particularly distressed her, Marian had learned to find comfort in watching the visitors to her bird table. Life with William was not easy for someone whose intellect was as limited as William had made her understand that hers must be. She was so stupid when it came to pleasing him that she had learned to keep the bird table well supplied with nuts. Even William could not balk at that expense. Winter and summer, the table had become a positive cornucopia for all her little feathered friends. And her friends brought friends of their own to share the feast. Marion's bird table was now a well known assembly point for every bird for miles. Their antics could always be trusted to console her as she watched them through the kitchen window. One day she would buy a bird book, and learn about them properly, only it would be unpardonably selfish of her to buy it just now. As William constantly told her, the price of everything was rising fast. He talked a lot about inflation.

Marion had heard that blue tits are the most acrobatic of all our garden birds, and it was quite amazing what she had seen them do. Take that one, for example. It was hanging in the air, completely without moving, and yet it did not drop. Marion moved closer to the window to admire it. The bird stayed still and airborne, its little wings outstretched, and with its claws stuck forwards, ready for the perch. So used to doubting her own judgment, it took Marion some time to realize that, within the laws of nature as she knew them, this bird's achievement was impossible. It took even longer for her to decide to go down into the garden to have a closer look.

Once outside, Marion noticed that there were none of those tiny movements among the leaves and things which she always took for granted. The air was absolutely still. Then Marion noticed that a mouse which had been stealing nuts had stayed, unmoving, on the table. The bird remained hanging. Marion, who had never been so close to one before, was astonished to see that it had tiny eyelashes. She was awe-struck by the bird's perfection. Wonderingly, she put out her hand, and plucked it from the air. It was as she stroked the feathers, not soft as she had imagined them to be, but on the wings quite hard and sleek, that she realized that she had inadvertently slipped the ring onto her finger.

This would never do. William was always telling her she must take better care of things. Money does not grow on trees, and to wear such a ring into one's garden was obviously unwise. If Clara asked for it again, she would never be able to replace it. Marion must take the ring off at once. In order to do so, she released the bird. It stayed where she let go of it, some few inches above the bird table. The moment that Marion pulled off the ring, the bird fell, corrected itself, and flew off in a panic. The mouse forgot the nuts and ran away. A sudden breeze played gently with her hair as Marion returned to the house. She was not surprised. She was used to nothing making sense. After all, William said a lot of things were only her imagination.

Marion put the ring away among her knickers because William did not care to touch these fripperies.

But when William was not there, Marion enjoyed looking at her ring. Beyond the thin wedding band, William had never bought her jewellery. He had told her that it was a bad investment, and with the way inflation was heading, she must not ask for any. Since Marion had not thought to ask, she was shaken now to see how flattering this ring was on her hand. Her sensibly clipped fingernails achieved a new elegance and her fingers looked quite sensuous and slender. She waved her hand about, admiring it from every angle. Then, holding it in artistic poses by her face, she looked into the glass.

The moment that she saw herself in her new glory, Marion wished she had a hat. In fact she wished she had a lot of other things which had not occurred to her before. It was different for William, of course. He had lots of lovely suits, and his shirts were all handmade in silk. But this, as he had explained to her, was entirely so that he might dress himself in keeping with his position in the community, and not look out of place on the many evenings when he attended vital business meetings. He was seldom home on Saturdays as well.

It was on one of these Saturdays that Marion, resplendent in her ring, happened to glance out through the bedroom window, and notice someone on a bicycle in the road outside. His hair and coat were streaming out behind him as if he were travelling at speed, and yet he was not moving. Marion, who had cycled quite lot when she was young, knew beyond doubt that bicycles fall over if you do not pedal them. Perplexed again, her thoughts rushed to her bird table. For once it brought no comfort as she remembered the astounding blue tit. Marion sat down on the bed. Presently she got up again, looked at the cyclist, and took off her ring.

The cyclist shot off down the road. He did it with no slow gain of speed, only an instant rapidity. It was as if a film which had been left on hold, had been switched back on. When Marion again put on her ring, the cyclist stopped. Then she took it off, and let him go. When the cyclist turned left at the top of the road, he was replaced by a car which Marion also caused to make spasmodic progress. The driver and his passenger appeared to be unaware of

231

what was happening to them. Marion, enthralled by now, kept on her ring and crept downstairs into the road.

The couple in the car did not move as she approached. Nor did they react when she tapped on the window. The woman held a piece of chocolate tantalisingly by her open mouth. The man was in the middle of a sneeze. Neither moved as Marion inspected them closely. A nearby cat, which hung in mid-leap off a wall, took no notice, either. Marion stroked it idly for a while before she went back home, and pondered. Even to an intellect as under-used as hers, it was obvious that, somehow, time became suspended when she wore the ring. Although she was tempted, despite the evidence, to believe that such a thing was impossible, she rapidly got used to the idea. Marion experienced her first tremors of delight.

How useful such a thing would be. How invaluable, in fact on the days when no matter how hard she tried, she could not make the house as immaculate as William required that it should be. With all the windows and the paint work needing to be washed each week, this calamity happened shamefully often. It was a big house, and as William had explained, they could less and less afford to pay the wages of a cleaner. This meant that Marion had no time to rest, and her increasing tiredness often slowed her down. There had even been one memorable occasion when William's supper had been half an hour late. Marion cringed with shame at the memory of that evening. She slipped the ring back in among her knickers, and ran to the telephone.

When Clara answered, Marion thanked her joyfully for making it possible to finish all her housework. From now on, she would make sure that William had no cause for complaint against her. Clara was less pleased than Marion had anticipated. In fact, Marion got the distinct feeling that Clara was annoyed with her. This did not astonish Marion, who knew that she was irritating. Had not William often told her so?

Next day, while working with the ring on, Marion found that her new powers were not as simple to control as she had anticipated. For example, machinery did not work unless she powered it herself. This meant that she could not use the vacuum cleaner or washing machine. Nor would water leave the tap because it was propelled by motors at the pumping station. On the other hand, a bucket of sponges which had been soaked in advance worked well, and the water in them did not cool. There was also the advantage that things stayed where she put them. Ornaments would not fall and shatter, and William's books, she found, could be stacked on air while she washed down the shelves. But here was an unexpected problem because the stillness of the air prolonged the drying time. This phenomenon had puzzled Marion while she towelled them dry, but she soon began to find it entertaining to work out what she could and could not do.

That evening, when the house was immaculate, Marion indulged in a nap. Then, rested and serene, she took off the ring, ready to welcome William when he drove home from the station. From now on she would be the perfect wife.

William was not pleased. A wife with energy was less restful than the previous version. True, she was quicker when he told her to fetch things for him, but there is only a limited number of things that a man can think of for his wife to fetch. Also, she annoyed him by interrupting with consoling remarks while he relayed his catalogue of complaints about the day, a thing that she was normally too dazed by then to do. Then, as the evening progressed, William began to worry in case his wife might still be feeling frisky when it came to bed time. He had enjoyed his grievance that she was invariably too tired to enthuse about her bedtime duties. William had performed them earlier that day to the satisfaction of himself and, possibly, his secretary, and was dismayed to think that he might appear less masculine before his wife. He had never been required to contemplate such a predicament before. But Marion, the perfect wife, was full of sympathy about his sudden headache. She encouraged him go to bed with a good tumbler full of whiskey, and then she lay and smiled into the darkness. She knew that William did not love her, but was sure that, very soon, thanks to the ring, she would be worthy of his favour. She must try harder.

Next day, for reasons which she never quite managed to explain to herself, Marion put the ring into her pocket when she went to the supermarket. Thus, when she saw a glossy magazine whose cover showed a place setting which she was sure would win her husband's love, she hid behind a display of cheese and slipped the ring onto her finger. Then she hid the magazine beneath her coat.

233

Her housekeeping did not allow her to afford such luxuries, and with the way that prices were rising everywhere, she knew it would be hopeless to ask William for an increase, even for a special dinner. Emboldened by the frozen state of the people round her, Marion helped herself to two mangoes, a lobster and a box of liqueur chocolates. She did not take off the ring again till she was round the corner and alone. The whole thing had been an impulse, and as soon as she had time to think, she was horrified by her own conduct. But it would be worth it if it pleased her William.

It did not. After a week of gorgeous meals served in charming styles, William's only response was to cut her allowance to deter any future extravagance. He had already dined superbly at lunch time, and his stomach reacted badly to this plethora of food. From then on, with her meagre budget cut so deeply, Marion was left with no alternative but to steal. To salve her conscience, she stole a bicycle as well, in order that she might spread her pillage over the widest possible area.

The other effect of the magazine was that it reminded Marion of how much she had enjoyed reading in the years before her marriage. Now she could indulge herself. Within days, magazines gave way to thrillers, and soon Marion was back among the classics which had lit up her youth. Within the month she had joined the library so that she might keep up to date with the latest trends in literature. She spent what must have been many hours each day, wearing her ring, and rediscovering how good it felt to feed her mind. She had seen with humiliating clarity how boring she must have been for all these years, and it pleased her to think that she would soon become a companion who was worthy of her husband's intellect.

William was not pleased. To be sitting at a charmingly presented meal in a spotless house and confronted by a scintillating wife made him feel tired and inadequate. Having had a stimulating day, the last thing he wanted was a lively evening. He had always known that his wife was too clever for her own good, which is why he had so kindly done his best to thwart it. A woman was so much happier with nothing but domestic thoughts to occupy her mind. He had other things to think about.

The Rotary Club's Summer Fête was looming on his

calendar, and every year more and more of the responsibility for it fell to William's lot. A few months prior to Wakefield's death, Al Benson, who always ran the candy floss machine, came to a sticky end inside a vat of boiling tar belonging to his road surfacing company. Now his wife was living in Paris, when by rights she should be running the white elephant stall. Miles Baxter was another loss since the previous year. His accident with a chain saw had been comprehensive, and the widow, far from showing loyalty to her husband's position as chairman of the Parish Council, had vanished off to Florence to admire the art, and would not be coming back. With Marion being of so little use, William did not know how he would manage to keep the Fête up to its usual high standard. He thought about it constantly.

One morning he was so preoccupied with drawing up a mental list of the equipment which must be ordered well in advance of the great day, that he forgot to eat his breakfast at the normal speed. This was a disaster since, through the years, his routine had become accurate and perfectly adapted to his needs. This morning's small delay put him in real danger that he might miss his train, and he was sure he had a particularly busy day ahead of him at the office. Marion must drive him to the station so that he might make up the time by not having to find a space to park the car.

Unfortunately, people have set times for leaving every morning, and Marion drove out into the later traffic which William's group of drivers always missed. William, already stressed, became convinced that Marion had intended to delay him. He lost his temper. Marion was distraught. Although her recent achievements had lifted her morale to such an extent that she was able to recognise that she was not to blame for William's lateness, she dreaded the next twenty minutes which must be spent with him while he waited for the later train. Worse still, the torrent of William's fury was making her increasingly nervous, and it was affecting her driving. The car was slowing down, and her ring could not be used to stop the train because the car would stop as well. All that Marion could achieve was to deliver William, purple faced with rage, to the station forecourt just as the train drew out.

Then, as William paused briefly to draw breath for further invective, inspiration struck. Marion put on her ring. William at once

235

became immobilised, with a particularly unpleasant expression on his face, and the train stopped as well. Marion got out of the car, and searched the station for a luggage trolley. The one she found had been rained on in the night, so she lined it with newspapers from the book stand. She balanced William on the trolley, tying him on firmly with a length of flex which she found beside the fence. Then, pausing only to take money out of William's wallet to pay for the newspapers, she wheeled him to the train. There she found a seat for him, and heaved him into it. She returned the trolley, and sat down in the car before she took off the ring. William was carried safely up to town while Marion drove home in a state of shock.

This was because she had discovered how much money William carried in his wallet, and even more so when she realised that the wallet, which, naturally, was made of the finest crocodile skin, was slightly stretched. This showed that the profusion of its contents was the usual condition. Apart from the money, there had also been a large assortment of credit cards, although William had told her many times that such things led to debt and ruin. Presently, her shock gave way to rage.

She was furious with herself. She could not imagine how she had allowed herself to be so easily deceived, and for so long. Why, until she put William on the trolley, had she never really looked at him? How had she failed to notice the petty malice which was his habitual expression? It had always been apparent in his conduct. What on earth had led her to imagine that such a man might be capable of love? Moreover, why should she care that he was not? He had lied to her about everything from their financial position to his own intellectual capacity. When she looked back over the bleak years of her marriage, she recognised them as bereft of joy.

After having lived for so long in a state of illusion, she could go on this way no longer. This was her chance to re-evaluate her situation. Since she had already started to re-estimate herself, she knew she had sufficient brain to understand whatever her finances might turn out to be. Yet, she knew she could have found out long ago if she had not allowed her self respect to be destroyed. William, secure in the knowledge that his wife would never touch his things, had merely filed the bank statements and the lists of comfortable investments, and left them in an unlocked cupboard. That she had treated William's cupboard with a respect which bordered upon reverence was entirely of her own doing. Marion could blame no one but herself. It was only moderately consoling to know that many people have been duped by pompous fools. But duped she now refused to be.

Fortified by a strong cup of coffee, she made copious notes on all she saw. Then she went to the public library to swat up on everything financial.

All day she studied stocks and shares, and trust funds and the like. Then she checked out a lot more books to work on when she got back home. Having admitted to herself at last that her paint work and windows looked just as clean as they had the previous week, and that there was no reason why their cleanliness should not last for several months, she settled down to cook her own favourite supper. Her anger had subsided into icy calm.

This was not the case for William. Having no memory of anything that had happened in between his sitting, railing at his wife while he watched his train draw out, and suddenly, indeed inexplicably, finding himself inside it, he was very puzzled. Nor had the other people in the carriage done anything to soothe him, being both startled and offended by his presence. His first few words to them had been decidedly unflattering, since he still imagined that he was speaking to his wife. Then his reaction to discovering his changed situation had not been couched in the phrasing which he normally used while addressing his peers. Finally, to make matters worse, his seat was in reality the preserve of a banker who was only waiting for the train to move before he flushed the toilet. William found himself bewildered and unpopular. Since he was not used to upsets in his routine, even the blandishments of his well-paid secretary failed to rouse him from his depths. He passed a miserable day, looking for a victim on whom to vent his spleen, but had found none. Naturally, he was less than charming when Marion fetched him from the station. It increased his sense of dislocation to find that Marion did not seem to care.

True, she was perfectly polite, but there was something in the tilt of her jaw that suggested an inner confidence which he had not seen for years. William retreated behind his large newspaper to evaluate the situation. Marion, who had wanted, if not a confrontation, at least some kind of explanation from him as to why he had misled her, was suddenly annoyed. She went into the kitchen and put on her ring. She seized the kitchen scissors, went back to William, and cut a vast hole in the centre of his newspaper. Then she returned to the kitchen, put the cuttings in the dust bin, and took off her ring. Her anger subsided, and she giggled.

When she returned to the sitting room on the pretext that William might like another cup of coffee, she found him in a state of panic. It had never occurred to her that William could be capable of doubting his own sanity. Yet, the face that she saw peering at her through the hole was so severely undermined that, if William had been a nicer man, she might have pitied him. As it was, she just enjoyed the quietness of the evening, and, apart from the regular looting of his wallet, Marion never played a prank on him again.

She was surprised when, over the succeeding weeks, William in his shaken confidence, began to speak to her. He did not expect any contribution of ideas from her, only a perpetual confirmation that his own ideas were right. While once she would have welcomed his attention, seeing it as love, she now was irritated by his heightened expectations of her tolerance. Even so, she might have felt some flicker of affection for him had this new slant on their relationship prompted any honesty from William, but though he still wafted hints of costly ladies' scents, he remained as tight fisted towards Marion as ever.

Each evening now, he followed her about, constantly rehearsing his concerns about the coming fête. When the appointed day was a mere month away, William's anxiety verged on the hysterical. Clara Wakefield had not hired the grand marquee and cricket field as she had in other years. Nor had she bothered to mention it to William. He only found out when Marion received a postcard from the widow which she sent from her pretty new villa perched on a hill in Tuscany. She confided to Marion that she had bought the villa with part of the proceeds of her late husband's life insurance.

William was almost apoplectic before it occurred to him that he could telephone to enquire about the tent and field himself, and it was in no way due to his diplomacy that they were both available at such short notice. Since they had been used on the second Saturday in August for almost thirty years, and the owners had liked Clara, they had assumed that this year's application had been lost in the post, and booked the fête as normal. Marion watched William strut, then rang up to thank them later

As a direct result of this episode, Marion spent several evenings convincing William that it had been his own idea to hold a meeting of the dwindling group who ran the fête. She was already recognising, in the way that William's colleagues looked at him, a wariness similar to the way in which they had latterly regarded Wakefield, Maynard and such other short-lived men. It was arranged that the committee would meet on the following Thursday, and they would bring their wives. Marion would keep an eye on the proceedings while the duties were re-allocated, and she would provide delicious canapés, and petite fours. She had discovered an excellent baker in a nearby town, and only needed to find a way of carrying the fragile pastries on a bicycle. But Marion was learning fast. A quick dip into William's wallet ensured a prompt delivery by van on the appointed day. Marion arranged the chairs in a charmingly intimate circle in the living room. Each chair was provided with an occasional table, where a pencil and writing pad was laid out for each guest. William had the biggest chair, flanked by some lovely flowers. If the evening did not go well, it would not be through any fault in Marion.

William, puffed with a sense of his own authority acted as an able chairman. The jobs were soon assigned to those who were considered most capable of doing them. The fete would be as good as ever because some previously excluded wives declared themselves eager to take on new tasks, and even offered to both hire and run a bouncy castle. Ben Hardy and his wife would do the toys and lucky dip between them, while Harry Greenling announced that Sylvia his wife would be delighted to dress up as a gypsy and tell fortunes at a pound a time. Then, on account of the splendour of the canapés and petite fours, it was considered a compliment that Marion should be put in charge of the teas, which would be served inside the marquee in case of rain. William's status was restored.

It is impossible to know if he credited any of this success to Marion. Certainly he never said so, only mentioning that he thought she had overdone the icing on the petite fours. With the way the cost

239

of food was going up, she must learn to be less wasteful. Since she apparently had so much surplus cash in her allowance, it was only fair that he should cut it. When would she understand the problem of inflation? In one evening, William had returned to normal. Marion had not. She was well aware that the national rate of inflation had fallen by half a percent over each of the two previous quarters, but she held her peace.

The day of the Rotary Club Summer Fete arrived. It was dry and bright. Little puffs of pure white cloud rolled gently in the deep blue sky. From early in the morning Harry Greenling strutted round the field organising other people as they toiled to put up tables. William organised, then organised again, the most suitable place for the erection of the bouncy castle and for the machine that pumped it It was vital for the air intake on the machine to be as unobstructed as possible for the castle to remain properly blown up. Marion and the other wives staggered in with home made cakes, boxes of produce, soft toys and strange vases. Husbands moved the tables several inches to the right. Marion was enormously admired for the way she had set up the teas. She had done it all in no time, and yet she managed to look fresh and rested. Then everybody left the field to go and grab an early lunch. The fete began at two.

At three o'clock, Marion, along with several teenagers who had been dragged in reluctantly to help her, watched the festivities from the tea tent. The stalls were doing splendid trade, and the children on the bouncy castle were hopping up and down like popcorn. Everyone was having fun. Only Sylvia Greenling drooped at her card table. She was preposterously dressed and painted, while an enormous Christmas bauble masqueraded as a crystal. Harry Greenling sniggered, and went over to enjoy the joke with William, who, complete with an enormous cylinder of helium, was in charge of the balloons. The balloons all carried labels to be returned by any lucky finders. One year's winning label had arrived in France. Marion put on her ring.

In the ensuing stillness, she went to William and his cylinder of gas. She took the gas hose out of his hand, and rammed it down his throat as far as it would go. Before she left to do the circuit of the fête and steal some candy floss, she turned on the tap to full. Finally, when she reached the tea tent, she resumed the pose she had been in before she left, and took off the ring.

Seconds later, William exploded.

Marion draped herself in black for William's funeral. The outfit had been expensive, but she would soon collect lavishly on the insurance which she had taken out so few months before her husband's tragic death. When the money came, she would move to the Maldives.

The only thing still left to do was to put the ring into the envelope which she had addressed to Sylvia Greenling. Harry Greenling's sphere of influence was wide, and it was time the ring moved on to conquer other fields. It was with some amusement that Marion wondered how long it would take Sylvia to discover the ring's true use. As well as eschewing fortune tellers and the like, Sylvia's rather rigid chapel group might well object to murder.

Hindsight

by Emma Melville

Inspector John Marshall watched the Scene of Crime team carefully manoeuvring equipment. Dr Trent crouched by the body while Hickson and Marks gingerly stepped round her, photographing bloody footprints and spatter patterns and dusting every surface for prints. It was a process he had witnessed a hundred times before and he was always slightly horrified to realise that he was bored. He wanted to get on and though he knew this painstaking investigation of the body and its surroundings was necessary, he had long ceased to be fascinated by the technical wizardry which told him where the killer had stood and what he had used. That was particularly the case, as here, where it all seemed blindingly obvious. The blood, the carving knife and the large holes in the victim's chest told John Marshall all he really needed to know.

"Well, doctor?" Liza Trent had finished her examination.

"All done. Take him away."

"Knifed to death, I assume?"

"Looks that way. Victim is late teenage, was attacked from the front and put up some struggle but didn't stand much chance. Been dead about four or five hours. I'll have more for you after the post mortem."

"Thank you, doctor." She nodded briefly and left, her sensible shoes making no noise on the hard floor.

Marshall looked round. The back room of 5, Primrose Street was a fairly standard suburban dining room. A French window opened out onto the back garden and a hatch in the side wall allowed food and plates to be passed back and forwards to the kitchen. A small round table with four chairs sat in the middle of the room though it had been knocked off centre by the falling victim. A dresser ran along the length of the wall opposite the hatch though Marshall would place money on it being mahogany effect rather than real wood. A single door led out into the hall.

The force of the knife blows to the victim's chest had spread blood far and wide and someone – presumably the killer – had left bloody footprints across the wooden flooring.

"What can you tell me, Hickson?" The inspector had waited for the removal of the corpse before asking to allow Hickson and his partner time to perform their intricate routine.

"Well, he was facing the hatch and the killer stood in front of him so was presumably already in the room when the victim entered. If the killer had entered the room second, then you'd expect the victim to be facing the other way or to have been stabbed in the back."

Marshall had already sized up the situation himself so he nodded. "That makes sense. So, a disturbed burglar?"

"Possibly. Though we can't find any sign of forced entry."

"What else?"

"The knife doesn't match the block in the kitchen though it has the look of being from a set, therefore I think either the victim or the killer must have brought it with them. And then there's this oddity."

"Go on."

"Look at the footprints."

A line of prints led away from where the corpse had lain towards the hatch to the kitchen.

"Our killer put something through the hatch?"

"No. Come here." Hickson crouched by the wall.

Marshall picked his way carefully across the room and bent down beside the other officer. Very clearly against the wall, a heel print stood out. He frowned. "That's not possible."

"Not without taking your heel off your shoe, cutting it in half and ramming it up against the wall. Not something the average killer does in the middle of a getaway." Hickson smiled. "It gets better, follow me."

He led the way out of the room, down the small hall and into the kitchen. The line of bloody footprints continued across the kitchen, starting by the hatch, and out of the back door into the side alley. Hickson again crouched by the wall. "Here."

There, under the hatch, was a toe print.

"So what does that tell us?" Marshall was nonplussed.

"Well, judging by the regular stride length and the piece missing between heel print and toe print being about the correct width, I'd say our killer walked out through the wall." Hickson was obviously enjoying this.

Marshall nodded practically, refusing to join in the joke. "So, you're looking for a false door here, round the hatch."

"No." Hickson shook his head, suddenly serious. "We've looked. Solid brick. He or she walked out through a solid wall."

The inspector crossed the hall to the front room where Constable Helen Lovell was sitting with a well-dressed young woman. They were drinking tea which Marshall always thought was no real cure for the horror of finding a corpse. He noted the contrast between the two of them, Lovell in her comfortable trousers and severe white blouse with her hair pulled back into a neat bun and the other, dressed in an expensive looking trouser suit, glittering with jewellery and with her dyed, blonde hair hanging in beautifully sculpted waves to her shoulders.

"Mrs Sutherland?" Marshall sat on the settee next to his colleague. "This must have been a terrible shock for you."

She nodded. "Yes, I was just telling your constable. It's quite creepy because I must have been home half an hour before I found him and all the time he was lying there." Her voice shook a little but was almost immediately brought under control. Marshall judged this to be a rather capable young woman who was managing to take even the horror of finding a dead body in her dining room fairly well. Judging shrewdly, he wondered how capable. Perhaps she had found a live body in her dining room and dealt with it accordingly.

"Half an hour? What were you doing, if you don't mind going over it again for me?"

"Well, I came in and went straight up, as I normally do, to shower and change after work. I was early today because we were going out tonight to celebrate. I've just got a promotion. I took a bit more trouble over getting changed and make up and so on. Then I came down to have a cup of tea while I waited for Jez and I thought I'd draw the curtains in the dining room. I normally do it after tea but we weren't going to be eating in there." She stopped as if realising that he probably didn't need that sort of detail. "Anyway, I went in and there he was."

"Can you tell me who he is?"

"Me? No. I've never seen him before in my life. I sort of hoped, inspector, that you could tell me what he was doing in my dining room."

"So, we have an unknown young man, repeatedly stabbed with some considerable force by a killer who then walked out through the wall." John Marshall looked at his team who were gathered in the incident room. "Time of death is lunchtime, say midday to one o'clock, so can we check that Mrs Sutherland was at work and didn't come home even earlier than she's making out and surprise him. Better check on her husband too and I want house to house enquiries down Primrose Street. See if neighbours saw the youth or anyone else entering the property or anyone leaving it. Helen, check missing persons though after so short a time there probably won't be anything useful and contact the press. I shall give them a statement for the late news appealing for information." There was a small silence while Marshall thought through his instructions but they'd all done this before and he was sure of those who worked for him. He didn't keep people on his team unless he was sure of them. "Let me know what you find." He dismissed them, calling after Helen, "And get me an appeal line set up, would you Constable?"

He retired to his desk and the difficult task of drafting a statement for the press that said just enough.

The appeal made the early evening news. Marshall, feeling as uncomfortable as he always did in front of the cameras, had managed a brief statement which omitted any real facts of interest and then asked for the public's help. He thought, watching it later in the staff canteen, that he looked stilted and awkward but Mark Sherbourne, his sergeant and deputy of ten years standing, nodded approvingly. "Good one, John. You do sound professional doing that."

He looked at the older man. "I hate it, Mark. That was about the fifth time I'd said it because…oh, I don't know, the wind wasn't right or the light or the noise or something. I just think I sound bored of saying it."

"You were fine, Sir." Helen Lovell assured him, not yet having been with him long enough to risk the use of first names.

245

There were just the three of them in the canteen. Marshall had called it a day and everyone else had gone home but Sherbourne and Lovell had stayed to see the television appearance. Mark because he knew his boss would want to and that he didn't take his work home; Helen because she was still young and keen and wanted to make a good impression with the boss without knowing him well enough to realise that she already had.

By this time they knew that Mrs Sutherland had been at work until four in an office with seven other people, that Mr Sutherland had been defending a client in court all day and that either the inhabitants of Primrose Street had been particularly unobservant or there really had been nothing to see.

"You'd think," Mark Sherbourne noted, "that a killer who walked through walls would make some sort of impression."

"Hickson work out how that was done yet?" Marshall had a worrying feeling that this was going to be one of those cases that went nowhere fast.

"Nope. He still claims the killer walked through the blasted wall."

"And no idea who the corpse is?"

Neither answered what they assumed had been a rhetorical question.

Marshall sighed. "All right, let's sleep on it and hope the appeal brings us in something over night."

Helen Lovell was in before him in the morning. Marshall found her leaning back in her chair sipping coffee while the computer screen flashed through a search.

"Morning, Constable. What did the appeal line give us?"

"Three possible identifications, twenty-seven descriptions of possible killers none of whom were actually seen in Primrose Street but they were all – according to the reports – acting suspiciously at midday yesterday, and one double glazing salesman."

"No pets stuck in trees or old biddies who are convinced their neighbours have buried someone under the new patio? I am impressed."

"Oh yes, sorry Sir. A librarian who thinks her glasses have been stolen."

"There's always one." Marshall sighed, it looked like the appeal line had been even less helpful than normal.

"On the other hand," Helen peered at the computer which had stopped scrolling, "I do know who the victim is."

"Yes?"

"We have a match on the system for his fingerprints. One Ryan Bradby."

"Ryan Bradby?" Mark entered the office on the tail end of her remarks. "That's a blast from the past. Right little shit he was. Loud mouthed, violent, lost his licence years before he was old enough to own one. Then he vanished."

"Vanished?" Marshall asked in surprise.

"Yep, full missing persons act, the lot. Before your time, John, I was still in uniform so it must have been... fourteen...fifteen years ago."

"Fifteen." Helen confirmed, still reading the screen.

"Probably a file still open on him somewhere 'cos we never did find the little toe-rag."

"Well we have now." Marshall told him. "He's our corpse."

"Can't be."

"Yes, I've run his finger prints." Helen objected.

"But, John, you said it was a teenager."

"Yes, twenty at most."

"Ryan Bradby was seventeen when he vanished and that was fifteen years ago. It's just not possible."

"OK, sergeant, you go and tell forensics they've sent us the wrong bloody fingerprints. Constable, start a check on these three possible identifications from the helpline and I'll..."

"Sir," Lovell interrupted, "the odd thing is, Ryan Bradby's last known address *was* 5, Primrose Street. Lived there with his mum."

"In which case, I'll go back to Primrose Street. There could be a connection, whoever the corpse is. I'll see if I can find someone who was there fifteen years ago. Mark, once you've blown forensics out of the water, see if you can find the file on the missing Ryan Bradby."

247

Marshall was just pulling up in front of 5, Primrose Street when his mobile rang. It was Mark sounding very subdued.

"You're not going to believe this."

"Try me."

"They're the right fingerprints. I ran down the file too and there was a picture in it that we used at the time. Our victim does seem to be Ryan Bradby."

"OK, track down the mother for an identification. I'll ask if anyone remembers him from this end and saw him yesterday. Then we need to go through that file and locate anything which might explain this."

Having rung off, he stared unseeing out of the windscreen at the light drizzle. Gaining facts normally made a case clearer but he honestly couldn't say that of this one. The identification of the corpse cleared up a couple of things. Obviously, if the victim had once lived here, then he may well still have had a key and so been able to let himself in. That explained the lack of a break in. Judging from what they had on the lad, it might also explain the knife, he sounded like the sort of person who may well bring one with him. He made a mental note to check with Mrs Sutherland whether the door had been unlocked when she arrived home. Had she then disturbed the victim in his burglary and ended up stabbing him? Unfortunately that didn't really fit with the timing of death but her shower could have been to wash away more than the grime of a day's work. He rang Hickson and suggested he come and take a look at the Sutherland's shower though he had to agree that it didn't explain why the footprints led out of the house and not up the stairs.

"She could have done that as a bluff and then taken the shoes off and come back in without them. You probably want to check her dustbin too." He told Hickson.

"Why on earth would she make it look like she walked through the wall?" Hickson was not convinced. "Surely she would have walked through the hall and out of the front door if she wanted to lay a false trail. You're assuming she pretended to walk to the wall, ripped her shoe apart to create a false impression, then walked round into the kitchen without leaving any trace of blood – we checked, there wasn't any in the hall – and then she continued her charade with the shoes in the kitchen. That's just not possible, John."

"I know, but currently it's the best I've got so just go and check the shower, OK?"

"Fine, but it's a waste of time." Hickson rang off.

Marshall opened the file on the passenger seat. It contained all the witness statements taken in Primrose Street the day before. Most were unpromising; married, middle-class couples who had been out at work all day. A couple were better and one stood out. Mrs Kathleen Ascott at number 12 had lived here 'all my married life' according to her statement and then on into widowhood.

"She'll do." Marshall muttered, getting out into the damp, October drizzle.

Kathleen Ascott was a spry eighty year old with white hair set in neat curls and a twinkle in her bright blue eyes. She ushered Marshall into her front room and then bustled into the kitchen to make him tea.

He peered through the window while he waited. This gave him a clear view up and down the street. Number 5 was across the street and up a little way though it took him a moment to work out. It was quite difficult to tell the difference. Even with their individually painted garage doors and the small bits of lawn done in personal tastes, the houses still looked like identical boxes. Not like the modern roads on his own estate where the developers had gone to some trouble to mix and match the styles and make every house different to its neighbours.

Mrs Ascott arrived back with a tea tray. "Here you go, inspector. Do sit down."

She poured tea into bone china mugs and offered him a biscuit from a neatly arranged plate.

"Now, how can I help you? I did tell the young man yesterday that I hadn't seen anyone. I was probably in the kitchen having lunch at about the time you're interested in."

"Yes, I have your statement. I was actually interested in something that happened fifteen years ago. A young lad went missing from Number 5."

"Ah yes, inspector, I think that was the last time I had the police knocking on my door wanting my help."

"You remember him?"

"I'm afraid so, inspector. I'd prefer not to if I'm honest with you. He was not a nice young man at all. Mind you, I think the parents are the ones really at fault when I see children turning out like that. Of course, she was distraught when he vanished but she should have expected it really."

"His mum, you mean?" Marshall noted that Mrs Ascott, despite chatting away cheerfully, also had one eye on the goings on beyond her windows.

"Let's face it, inspector, he spent all the time that he should have been in school stealing and racing cars that he wasn't old enough to drive. It was only a matter of time before he killed himself or was locked up."

"You think he's dead then?"

"Oh, I expect so, inspector."

"So you didn't see him here yesterday?"

She shook her head. "Of course not, Inspector."

"So his mum moved out and the Sutherlands moved in?" He tried changing tack.

"No, Inspector. It was the Fieldings who bought off Mrs Bradby. Susan and Trevor. Nice couple, they were there about ten years and then they had three babies in three years and, of course, the house wasn't really big enough so they moved on. I still exchange Christmas cards with them which is more than I can say for the new pair. They're hardly ever here, out at work all day and keep themselves to themselves.

"And yesterday?"

"Everything as usual except I think she got home slightly earlier than normal. And then your lot started arriving." She smiled at him. "More tea?"

"I'd love to but I'm afraid I ought to get on. Let me take this through to the kitchen for you." He picked up the tray and followed a familiar route across the hall to the kitchen. Whole street, he thought, all the same inside and out, as if the builders had thought everyone was the same.

Stepping into the kitchen, he stopped in surprise.

"Mrs Ascott?"

"Yes, Inspector." She had followed him in.

"When I was in number 5 yesterday, there was a hatch through there." He pointed at the open archway which led through to the dining room.

"Oh yes, some people have had them bricked up. It gives you three living rooms, you see, for the estate agent brochure. Puts the price up, Sue Fielding told me."

"So the Fieldings had the arch in Number 5 bricked up?"

"That's right, Inspector. Is it important?"

"I don't know. Probably not but sometimes little details like that give us a bigger picture."

He arrived back at the station as Mark was escorting a lady out to her car. She was lighting a cigarette with shaking hands and her eyes looked red and tear stained.

He waited until she had driven off before crossing the car park to join his sergeant. "Mrs Bradby?" Somehow the died blonde hair scraped back into a pony tail and the over-made-up, haggard face had been appropriate to the picture Mrs Ascott had given him of a mum unable to control her child. That was, he reflected, stereotyping which wasn't always helpful but, more often than not, accurate. Mark nodded to him.

"Yeah, she recognised him straight off. Said a funny thing, actually."

"Not funny, 'ha-ha' I take it."

"She said 'he hasn't aged a day' and then burst into tears."

"Has she seen him at all then in the last fifteen years?"

"She said not."

Marshall nodded. "And I suppose she had no idea what he was doing in Primrose Street either?"

"No."

"This case is full of dead ends. Let's go and have a look through Ryan's file and see if it gives us anything."

Instead, they were greeted by Constable Lovell who was replacing the phone as they entered the office.

"Anything, Constable?"

"That was the librarian again, Sir."

Marshall snorted. "Found her glasses now, has she?"

251

"No, but she says she knows who took them."

"Oh for Christ's sake." Marshall laughed. "Tell uniform. Let them deal with the old bat."

"OK, Sir…"

"There's a 'but' in that sentence, constable." Marshall had a great deal of time for Helen Lovell and her intuition. It was one of the reasons he had made it a priority to get her on to his team. "Spit it out, what's bothering you?"

"She gave me a name. Alison Miller."

"And?"

"I ran it through the system. No form but fifteen years ago her two year old son was run down outside their home. A hit and run driver who deliberately drove across their front lawn."

"Fifteen years ago?" Mark asked. "Do you have a precise date?"

"Same day Ryan Bradby disappeared and only a couple of streets away – Twenty Seven Tulip Drive."

"Is there anything to suggest that Ryan was involved in her son's death?" She'd caught Marshall's interest now.

"No-one was ever caught for it but it was a stolen car which was used and it was found burnt out at Five Oaks. No forensics to speak of and definitely no finger prints."

"But it is his MO." Mark sat down beside her. "Steal a car, do as much damage as possible and then torch it. He took to doing that after the first time we caught him and made the mistake of explaining it was because his fingerprints were all over the steering wheel."

"Does this get us anywhere?" Marshall asked, allowing them to run with it.

"I could see if I can track her down – this Alison Miller." Mark offered. "If we can get a picture of her then we could take it back to Primrose Street and see if it jogs some memories. Maybe she was seen yesterday but people discounted her. They do that if it's a respectable looking woman."

Marshall nodded, he knew witnesses tended to look for what they wanted to see but it all seemed an awfully long shot. Not to mention, a hell of a way from a librarian who thought this woman may have stolen her glasses. On the other hand, cases were often built on such coincidences.

"All right." He was reluctant but they couldn't really afford to ignore any possibility, however slim. "The two of you see if you can find her. Ask her where she was yesterday. At the very least then we can eliminate her from our non-existent list of suspects." He smiled. "Ask her about these blessed glasses while you're there, save uniform the job."

"What are you going to do?"

"I'm going to go and ask a librarian what possible relevance she thinks her stolen glasses can be to my murder investigation. If the answer is good enough I might even refrain from arresting her for wasting police time."

The Smith Foundation Library on Museum Street was a square stone building with massive oak doors and a discreet bronze plaque which told him that the librarian was a Miss J Williams.

The elderly spinster he was expecting turned out to be a young woman barely out of her teens. Pale, corn-coloured hair fell in waves to her shoulders and deep blue eyes suggested a greater experience than her age would allow.

"You called about some glasses Miss Williams." Marshall produced his badge. "I'm Inspector Marshall and I wondered if you would be so good as to explain why you think this information is at all relevant to my investigation."

"Certainly, Inspector." Her voice was soft and in no way concerned by his abrupt tone. "Come through to the office."

She led the way to the far end of the library away from the front desk. The small office was crowded with old books and parchments and full display cabinets. An ornate, full-length mirror hung on the back wall looking a little out of place.

The librarian cleared a space in a chair on one side of the table and then took a seat across from him.

"So, what do you know of my investigation, Miss Williams?"

She said nothing for a moment and then smiled. "I know nothing about your investigation, inspector." Marshall couldn't have said why, but he was sure she was lying. She continued, "I know that

253

I have a very special pair of glasses missing and I believe they..." she searched for the right word, "...came to the lady who took them in response to what you would term an improper need."

"Would you care to explain that, Miss Williams?"

Her blue eyes met his seriously as she leant forward. "Alison Miller started coming to the library a few weeks ago looking for solace after the death of her husband. She told me he eventually died of a broken heart due to the death of their son. She blamed the man who ran down their son for her husband's death as well." She paused and gave a small smile. "I know, Inspector, that you will not believe this but sometimes the library listens to people's needs and provides information or objects which may help."

"The library does?"

"Yes, Inspector. The library does."

"So it 'provided' Alison Miller with your glasses?"

"The glasses were kept in here, Inspector." She pointed towards a case on the wall which seemed to be filled with a variety of objects. "They are rather valuable and fairly unusual and I think Mrs Miller may have felt they could help her."

"And do you think they could help her, Miss Williams?"

"I really couldn't say, Inspector." Marshall had the feeling that she was lying again, though he really couldn't put his finger on why.

They sat in silence for a while. The librarian seemed quite content to allow it to continue having told her tale.

"Was there anything else, Miss Williams?" Marshall said eventually.

"No, Inspector."

He got up and headed towards office door.

"Inspector?"

"Yes, Miss Williams."

"If you need peace or answers then the library is open to you. It may be able to help."

"I'll bear it in mind, Miss Williams." He made no attempt to hide the sarcasm.

"Anything for me, Sergeant?" Marshall strode back into the office.

"Librarian a wash-out then?"

"You know me too well."

Mark laughed. "You only ever call me 'sergeant' when things are going badly."

"She claims the library 'gave' Alison Miller a pair of glasses which could help her in some way with her son's death."

"You're joking!"

"No, what's more, neither was she."

"A looney?"

"The trouble is, Mark, if she is then so is Hickson who claims our killer walks through walls and Dr Trent who is claiming our victim is late teens when we know he has to be early thirties." Marshall slumped into his seat. "I saw that body, Mark. There was no way it was a bloke in his thirties, so maybe I'm crazy as well."

After a minute, Mark said. "Well, we did manage to track down Alison Miller. She was at work so we said we'd call in at her home later. It might give us something."

Marshall sighed. "It's probably a waste of time but we don't have anything else. Hickson find anything in the shower?"

Mark tossed a piece of paper across to him. It was a report with 'I told you so' scrawled across it.

Marshall laughed. "I suppose I asked for that. What's Helen doing?"

"Going through old files - Ryan Bradby's, Luke Miller's death."

"We're clutching at straws, Mark."

"I know."

Alison Miller was small and trim, her dark hair cut in a neat bob and a subtle layer of make-up expertly applied. She was dressed in the dark suit and cream blouse she had obviously worn to work. Her greeting at the door was warm but wary.

"Do come in, Inspector, Sergeant. I've only just got in myself." She led them into a large, open kitchen with a pine table at one end. This was a much larger house then the Primrose Street one with a beautifully landscaped garden visible through the kitchen window. Marshall noted the pictures on the window ledge. One was of Alison Miller with a man who must have been her husband and which looked like it had been taken fairly recently. The other showed a much younger version of the pair of them with a small boy. The younger Alison Miller had had nearly waist length hair and an even slimmer figure than the current version that faced him across the table.

"I'm sorry to have to trouble you, Mrs Miller and it's probably nothing but we believe you may be in possession of a pair of glasses belonging to the Smith Foundation Library." Marshall wasn't sure what had prompted him to start this way and he could feel Mark looking at him oddly though without comment.

"Why, yes." She got up and removed a pair of thick-rimmed spectacles from the handbag on the side. "I believe I picked them up by mistake the other day. I've been meaning to return them." She handed them over to Marshall who put them into his pocket with barely a glance as she sat down again. He was more concerned with how he ought to approach the next question, his eyes straying to the picture of the happy family group.

Mark leapt in. "This is a nice place you've got here, Mrs Miller. Have you been here long?"

"Fourteen years now. We moved after the accident. We couldn't bear the memories there."

"Of course." Mark nodded and Marshall was impressed anew by the effortless way his sergeant could approach sensitive topics with such delicacy. He had attempted to push Mark a number of times into going for inspector but mostly he was glad that Mark remained with him, bringing his gentle fatherly air to these difficult questions with fragile witnesses. Mark continued gently. "In fact, we have had a development in the case. I wonder if you remember anything that might help us about the driver of the car?"

"I told the police at the time. All I remember is seeing this bright red car leaving the road and then Luke flying through the air. I rushed out as he started to scream and then I sat holding him in the road until the ambulance came. I don't know what happened to the car and I don't even know who phoned the ambulance. People kept saying things to me but all I could hear was Luke…"

"I'm sorry."

"…and the dog."

"What dog, Mrs Miller?" Marshall asked curiously.

256

"Our dog, well Luke's really. She was barely a puppy and she was shut in the garden when I rushed out and she just howled and howled. I'm sure she knew something was wrong, animals do you know but I couldn't get up. Funny isn't it, inspector, the things that hurt most. I can forgive myself for his death because he should have been safe playing in our garden while I made a drink but I can't forgive myself for not letting Poppy out to say goodbye. She just howled and howled and howled and I couldn't move. I'm not sure she ever forgave me either."

"I'm sorry." It seemed such an inadequate thing to say.

She nodded. "Don't be, I live with it." They sat in awkward silence for a minute and then she said brightly. "You said there might be a lead. To do with this driver?"

Mark drew a picture of Ryan Bradby from his pocket. "Do you recognise this man at all?"

She looked at it for a long moment before handing it back. "Should I?"

"We really don't know, Mrs Miller. This man was found dead yesterday but he vanished on the day your son was killed and he did have a record for stealing cars and wrecking them. There is a possibility that he was the driver of the red car."

She gave a small smile. "I told you, Inspector, I didn't see the driver."

Inspector Marshall stood up. "Well, thank you for your time, Mrs Miller. One further thing, would you mind telling us where you were yesterday lunchtime."

"I was at work, Inspector."

"Would you mind if we borrowed a photograph, Mrs Miller? Just so we can check your story."

"By all means." She handed him the one from the window ledge. "I had this taken with Robert a couple of months ago, shortly before he died. It's probably the most recent I've got. I will get it back, won't I?"

"Of course." He shook hands and followed Mark out of the house.

"Well," He told Mark as they got into the car, "you better check her alibi but I imagine it will stand up."

257

"Back to Primrose Street?" Mark asked. "Now we've got the picture?"

Before Marshall could answer, his mobile rang. It was Helen Lovell.

"I found a couple of interesting things in the file about Ryan Bradby's disappearance."

"I'm listening, constable."

"Well, firstly, when he vanished his mother was asked if any of his things were missing and she said nothing of his but she was missing a carving knife out of the block in the kitchen. Forensics took a picture and I'd say the knives are identical to the one we recovered yesterday."

"Interesting. And the second thing?"

"There's a statement from a Mrs Ascott on the day of the disappearance claiming that she saw a strange woman leave number five that day."

"Really? I've met Mrs Ascott. I think we ought to go and pay her another visit. I seem to have asked the wrong questions"

Mrs Ascott was more than happy to see Marshall again and ushered him and his sergeant through to the front room.

"Can I be of further help, Inspector?"

"We hope so, Mrs Ascott. Would you look at this picture for us, please and tell us if you've seen the woman in it before."

"Oh yes, inspector."

Marshall exchanged glances with Mark, they were getting somewhere. "She was here yesterday, in the street?"

"Yesterday? No, Inspector."

"No?"

"No, but last time the police were asking questions, when the Bradby boy went missing. She was here that day."

"Are you sure? That's a long time ago."

"Oh yes, she was coming out of number five. She followed him up the street and into the back alley at about half twelve and then came out again about ten minutes later."

"She had longer hair then?" Marshall hazarded.

"No, Inspector. She looked just like your photograph except for the glasses she was wearing. Large, dark things which

258

were much too big for her face. I'm glad she took them off for the picture."

Marshall took the glasses from his pocket and showed her. "Like these?"

"Precisely those, inspector, I remember noticing the odd white blob on the nose piece and thinking that I would have got them mended if I were her." Marshall took a better look at the glasses. They had thick black rims and there was a white dial on the nosepiece. It looked like the scrolls used on library date stamps before computers took over.

"You're absolutely sure?"

"Yes, Inspector. I saw her as clearly as I'm seeing you now."

"Thank you, Mrs Ascott, you have been a great help."

"Just how is that a help?" Mark leant against the car. "Fifteen years ago Alison Miller was sitting three streets away caring for her dying son. There's no way she was here killing Ryan. She didn't even know it was Ryan who had killed her son. In all honesty, neither do we. Not to mention the fact that if she did it fifteen years ago what happened to the body for fifteen years, how did she preserve it and..."

"Hold it, Mark. Mrs Ascott didn't see the Alison Miller of fifteen years ago. She saw the one from the picture."

"That makes even less sense."

"Not if the librarian is right about the glasses. I have a thought but I'm struggling to believe it." Marshall pulled them from his pocket. "Look at these. Why would they have a date scroll on them?"

"John..."

"No, just suspend your disbelief for a moment. Let's consider what fits the facts. If these glasses could take you into the past then we solve an awful lot of our problems. Alison finds them, puts them on and discovers she is here with the man who killed her son. So she follows him and kills him. The footprints therefore go through the wall because there was no wall fifteen years ago. The knife vanished because it re-appeared here next to the body. It explains why Mrs Ascott saw her wearing them...."

"But it doesn't explain how she knew it was Ryan who was driving the car, or how the corpse ended up here and not fifteen years ago and as your original premise rests on being able to step into the past…" Mark shook his head.

"I'm going to go and check something out, Mark. Will you go and bring Alison Miller in."

"You want to arrest her on *that* sort of evidence?"

"No, I just want to ask her a few questions." He paused. "I tell you what. Take her to the library, Miss Williams said I could find answers there." He ignored Mark's look of concern. "I'll join you there."

"I don't understand."

"Trust me, Mark."

Mark took the car and Marshall set off on foot for Tulip Drive where, fifteen years ago, a small boy had been run over. The houses here were almost identical to Primrose Street. A whole estate of sixties houses built to replace the bomb damage of the war.

Marshall stopped outside number twenty seven. The front lawn was now a block-paved drive and the garage door painted a bright blue. Feeling a little silly, he took the glasses from his pocket. The date on them was already set to the 4th June, fifteen years earlier. Taking a deep breath, he put them on.

The air shimmered and then he was looking at a neatly trimmed lawn surrounded by an ornamental mini fence across which two tyre tracks ploughed a dark scar. A woman sat sobbing in the road, her arms wrapped around a still form in her lap and somewhere a dog howled.

As he watched, Alison Miller – the older version – appeared in front of him watching the tableau in the road. She stood there for half a minute and then reached up to remove the glasses he was now wearing and vanished.

Marshall nodded, he'd seen enough and now he needed some answers. He reached up to remove the glasses and then hesitated. With sudden resolution, he walked over to the side gate and pushed it open allowing the young Labrador on the other side to charge out into the road.

Mark was just pulling up outside the library when Marshall stepped from the taxi he'd called. Alison Miller sat beside the sergeant looking as neatly turned out as earlier though she had had time to change into a more casual skirt and top.

Marshall held the car door for her and then ushered her into the library.

"Inspector." Jenny Williams came round from behind the desk. "I was about to close for the day. Please go through to the office."

"A bit late to be open, Miss Williams."

"I don't keep very regular hours. Who knows when the library might be needed?"

He nodded and led the way to the office at the back. It was tidier than his previous visit and there were already four comfortable chairs set around the fire place to one side almost as if they had been expected. Marshall found he was unsurprised.

The librarian joined them almost immediately. "What can I do for you, Inspector?"

"We found your glasses." He removed them from his pocket but didn't hand them over.

"Thank you, Inspector. Did you bring Mrs Miller here just to apologise?"

"I want to ask her some questions but I don't think we need an interview room. You said the library may answer a need for me."

She looked at him thoughtfully. "You seem to have had a change of heart since our last meeting, inspector."

He nodded briefly.

Mark, who had sat in silence watching this exchange with a look of confusion, leant forward. "John, are you sure this is wise?"

"Yes, Mark. Put your notebook away and keep quiet. You're just here as a witness to this." He turned to Alison Miller who sat silently watching the fire. "Mrs Miller, I have a few questions for you."

She nodded but didn't take her eyes from the dancing flames.

"You went out to Five Oaks?" He had taken a slight detour on his way here, he knew she had.

261

"Yes, Inspector."

"You knew that was where the car had been found?"

"Obviously, Inspector."

"You followed him home?"

"Yes."

"Did you plan to kill him?"

"Yes, Inspector."

"The perfect crime because at the time of death you were known to be at the hospital with your son."

"Yes, Inspector."

"So how did the body end up here?" The only question he couldn't yet answer for himself.

"He caught hold of me and we struggled. The glasses got knocked off. I found myself back here but I had hold of him so he was too. It was too late by then as well, he was already dying. So I left him and fled."

"You put the glasses back on to leave?"

"I'm not stupid, Inspector. I couldn't be seen leaving a house where a corpse was about to be found so I left in the past."

"You *were* seen." Though, Marshall thought, she may as well not have been for all the help it had done either investigation.

They were all silent for a couple of minutes.

"One last question, Mrs Miller. If you knew you could go back, why did you not save your son?"

Then she did look at him. "Don't you think I tried? I set the date and it took me back to midday. I tried several times and it was always midday, always ten minutes too late. So revenge was all I had." She burst into tears, burying her face in her hands.

Jenny Williams crossed quickly and placed her arms around the shaking shoulders of the older woman.

They sat by the fire half an hour later once Marshall had sent Mark to take Alison Miller home.

"You'll let her go then?" Jenny Williams had made coffee for the two of them.

"I think she's probably suffered enough. Besides, the CPS would laugh me out of court if I produced that story as evidence. It will have to go on file as an unsolved crime." He held out the glasses. "I believe these are yours."

"Thank you." She took them and replaced them in the display case.

"Is it always midday?"

"For some people, Inspector, life doesn't move forwards past a certain point and they cannot see back beyond it."

"They work like that?"

"*We* work like that, Inspector."

They sipped in companionable silence for a while.

"I thought you said, Miss Williams, that the library gave people what they needed."

"What they need, Inspector, is not always what they think they want." She paused. "Perhaps it was not Alison Miller's need that was answered here. Maybe this youth needed to pay or maybe we needed to appreciate each other's skills." She shrugged. "Or maybe it was her need after all."

"But what did Alison Miller need if not to save her son?"

"I think she needed to lay her ghosts to rest and, possibly, to forgive herself."

"But she said..." He looked into the very blue, very knowing eyes of the young librarian.

"You did let the dog out, didn't you, Inspector?"

An Open and Shut Case

by Sarah J Bryson

The hospital trolley was hard. Dressed in a white gown and covered by a white cellular blanket, Penny lay waiting to be transferred to the theatre. Her hair had been pushed up into a paper cap, and her left ring finger felt stiff, constrained by the protective tape wrapped around her wedding band. Her mouth was dry. She wanted to turnover onto her side and curl into a foetal position, but the trolley was too narrow. Her heartbeat seemed to shake her whole body.

So this was it.

The surgeon, in theatre greens, arrived and looked down at her. His distant voice swam its way towards her.

"Have you said goodbye to your family?"

The porters wheeled her into the lift and she struggled to gain a sitting position, opening her mouth to speak. There was a lump of panic in the pit of her stomach rising up, blocking her words. A hand grabbed her shoulder, pushing her back. In slow motion as the doors started to close she saw the consultant turn to the junior doctor, overheard his words:

"I'm very much afraid that this is going to be an open and shut case."

The doors buffeted together and the lift's mechanics whirred, creating that familiar lurching in her stomach, as they descended into the depths of the hospital. She became aware of a rushing in her ears and with a gasp she pulled herself back. Her breathing was rapid, her pulse racing, she felt damp from sweat. Each time she resurfaced to reality the prospect of surgery was closer.

After a moment to order her thoughts she spread out across the bed to discover that Alasdair had already gone. She opened her eyes. He had roughly pulled back the curtains to reveal a cold, grey early-morning sky.

At least the mornings were getting a little lighter.

She sighed deeply and sat up, reached for the dressing gown draped over the foot of the bed and pulled it on. A cup of tea would be good. She lay down again, drew up the covers and closed her eyes.

February. Not a good month for her, especially over the last six years, marking the anniversary of her mother's death. She felt heavy limbed and lethargic. Maybe it was her age? Or something else? She counted silently to ten. She pushed the thoughts away with the duvet, put her legs out and felt around for her slippers.

In the kitchen she filled the kettle while staring out into the unkempt garden. Nothing had been touched since October. There was a dense fog obliterating the view beyond the fence. Yet the snowdrops under the apple trees had resurfaced, showing their small white heads against the green-white tufts of the frosted grass, and a few aconites boasted acid yellow patches amongst them. Even a few very early crocuses had braved the cold. The birds would soon have them. Especially the yellow ones. But the stirrings of spring had not yet touched her. She felt as though she was a bystander, waiting.

The cat mewed loudly as she went through to the utility. She rattled a few biscuits into his dish, and then stepped over neatly dissected small mammal innards deposited in the middle of the floor. She scooped up the remains with a piece of tissue, holding her breath and flushed it down the toilet. The cat hunched over his bowl, crunching.

She was daydreaming when Alasdair came into the kitchen: he did not notice her but started distractedly searching, aimlessly lifting yesterday's newspaper, checking the notice board, opening his briefcase....and she watched him as he went back out into the hallway, turning things over in a half-hearted way.

"Has anyone seen my keys?" he called out redundantly as he found them. "Aha!" He straightened his tie checking his reflection in the mirror. Then he looked at her.

"Morning, lazybones." He walked over to her and encircled her in a hug. "The boys are fighting over the bathroom... you may have to wait." He paused, releasing her to look at her properly. "You look a bit peaky. Are you OK?"

She reached up and kissed his cheek, smiled at him.

"What's on today?"

"Meeting in Birmingham this morning, then lunch with Matthew: I'll try not to be late," he said, as he looked at his watch. His lips brushed the top of her head. "Don't forget we're going out tonight." He slammed the door as he left.

Later, after the boys had gone for the bus and the house was quiet, she went into the bathroom and weighed herself. She had only recently started taking any notice, but now for the fourth week running the scales registered a little less. She felt touchy and tired, had lost her appetite. The beginnings of medical problems perhaps? As she lay in the bath she felt around in the space between her pubic bone and jutting hip bones. She had said nothing, not even to Alasdair. Especially not to Alasdair. She thought of her mother. By the time she had gone for investigations the tumour had spread into the wall of her bladder, attached itself to her bowel, and inveigled itself into the structure of her ovarian artery. It had silently become an inseparable, incurable malignant mass. An open and shut case. The treatment she had been offered was purely palliative in the hope that therapy might shrink the tumour, maybe give her a few extra months. Instead it made her life a misery. Penny had asked her mother to live with them, turning the dining room into a temporary bedroom. In the turmoil of small children she cared for her, desperate to re-form a bond which had been eroded over the years. But her mother had been unable to connect with her. Her feisty nature was lost, she transformed into a withdrawn, passive, sad old lady.

Dressed for work Penny looked at her watch and then made herself another cup of tea. She added a few grains of sugar and stirred it vigorously, creating a deep vortex, stopping the spoon abruptly to watch the swirling pattern disintegrate into chaos. She tapped the spoon decisively on the edge of the mug and put the mug down.

A telephone call secured an appointment for 11:30 am. She was fortunate, or so the receptionist told her, slightly resentfully, as she had taken 'the last emergency slot.' Penny rang through to work leaving a message to say she should be in later.

When she arrived at the surgery she found the stuffy waiting room full. She stood in the corridor assiduously reading the entire notice board, listening out for her name to be called, isolating herself from the possibility of conversation until she was called.

Dr Broadhurst listened to her symptoms with little comment. He remembered Mrs O'Conner, and the difficult situation Penny had found herself in, looking after her mother with small children at home.

"Is it hereditary?" she asked.

In response he said, "Let's have a look at you," and swished the screen across the couch. She hated this. It reminded her of the times she had endured countless examinations while she and Alasdair had been investigated for infertility.

"Chaperone to room two please," she heard him request as she lay down.

That would not be necessary if Alasdair could be here, she thought. An impassive third party, she felt, however silent and reassuring somehow formed a barrier between doctor and patient. She prepared herself and tried to relax. Deep breaths. The chaperone arrived. Dr Broadhurst gently examined her belly while she studied the ceiling. The chaperone departed.

"How long did you say this has been going on?" he asked.

"Oh, weeks: before Christmas I suppose...."

He paused,

"From what you say, your mind has understandably been preoccupied with your mother's illness," he said gently, "so this may come as a bit of a shock." He paused, "Penny ... has pregnancy crossed your mind?"

She stepped out into the frozen, still, foggy day, dazed. It had not occurred to her that the scanty, almost non-existent periods had been anything but a symptom of her weight loss. The doctor had filled out forms, made a referral to the midwife and telephoned through to the hospital requesting an "urgent dating scan." He had jotted down a date and time, stressed its importance, handed her the paper. Pregnant.

She had not been looking for it.

When she arrived home she rang through to work, "No, nothing serious," she said, "Yes, back on Monday or Tuesday," then she filled a glass of water and went upstairs. She lay down on the double bed, fully clothed and pulled up the covers. For a while she stared out through the window at the still grey wintry sky, watching the floaters in her eyes, her mind blank.

It was nearly four o'clock when she woke. She had slept without moving and realised that she had no recollection of any dreams. The sun had at last broken through the grey clouds and sent long shafts of low afternoon light in through the bedroom window illuminating gently moving dust motes in the air. She lay there for a moment gathering her thoughts, watching the floating particles before rousing herself, forcing her enervated body to get up. Ben and Jonathan came home not long afterwards, ravenous. She poured squash and produced cake.

"What's for tea, Mum?" asked Ben.

"Can we watch 'The Simpsons?'"

She took her tea into the sitting room to be with them, enjoying their laughter. Jonathan came to sit next to her, curling up comfortably.

Just like any other Friday.

That evening, a party for a friend's fiftieth birthday passed in a blur. She found herself observing the group rather than being part of it. Their conversations focussed on their children's progress, school choices, holidays, home improvements, job opportunities or career changes. The women were all what her mother would have called 'well preserved': women who had reclaimed their lives as their own now that their children were more independent. Penny felt annoyed with herself. Why did she so often see other women through the eyes of her mother? Was she turning into her? Then another thought flashed through her mind. *I can't do all that with a baby again.*

She looked at the men. They ranged from paunchy to very fit; balding, greying or both: but all had had an air of confidence and stability. They looked established, self-assuredly settled. Alasdair was one of them.

Once or twice Alasdair looked across at her to catch her eye and she saw a slight anxiety in his glance. She switched on a smile to reassure. Later he appeared at her side, and slipped his arm around her waist, pulling her gently towards him.

"Are you thinking what I'm thinking?" He spoke in a mock whisper, out of the corner of his mouth, his slightly inebriated attempt to make her smile.

"Probably not," she replied, but allowing her body to be pulled in closer to his.

"I'm thinking," he said, "of suggesting it's home time. Are you ready?"

In bed he wrapped his arms around her: her back to his front.
"You smell good." He nuzzled her neck. Then, "Are you on a diet or something Pen?" he asked, "Skinny ribs." He squeezed her. "Look arms twice round you! ..." His joking stopped as he realized that Penny was crying.

She had not known what his response would be when she told him. Not at all. She had not really decided how to tell him, how to prepare him, but in the end it juddered out between sobs, the lack of appetite, the weight loss, the lethargy and how she'd been scared, and the doctor's appointment; and he lay there just holding her. Saying nothing. The sobs subsided. Neither said anything. Then a deep remote voice that did not sound quite like Alasdair said,
"What do you want to do?"
"Do?"
"Well.... do you want the baby? Or..."
"I don't know," she replied.

In the morning Alasdair slipped out of bed well before it was light. Penny did not move. She heard him go downstairs and rattle about in the kitchen. Around and around in her head chased the alternative scenarios. *Life with a new baby, life without a new baby, life with, life without.... now you see it, now you don't, who's got the baby? Who's got the baby? Oh! Where's the baby? I can't see the baby...*

Alasdair woke her later with tea and toast. He pulled back the curtains. It was another foggy, frosty day. He perched on the side of the bad.
"Bad dreams?"
She nodded.
"How are you feeling?"
"So-so... what about you?"
He took her hand.
"I can't take it in. I mean the boys are getting so grown up, it's difficult to think of a baby..." He cleared his throat, then looked away as he spoke. "I don't want to think of a baby: a baby would upset the balance, the whole family...things wouldn't be the same."

269

The alternative hung in the air between them, unsaid.

"I have a scan booked," she said. "It's on Monday. Can you come?"

The weekend passed quietly, and they treated one another gently, almost reverently. She slept a great deal. No more dreams. The children crept around, and argued quietly; uncomprehending, but alert to the charged atmosphere.

On Monday morning the boys went off to school with Alasdair, after missing the bus. She watched them disappear into another foggy day, the car's exhaust creating huge clouds in the cold air. Still her mind was unfocussed and she felt as though she was in a trance. After her bath she stood naked in front of the mirror and studied her profile. There was a slight swelling of her lower abdomen. Not a malignant growth. Her breasts were fuller, her nipples darker. How had she not noticed? Her appetite had started to return, just as it had when she had been pregnant with the boys. Did that mean that she was already twelve or fourteen weeks?

Alasdair came back from work at midday. They drove to the hospital in silence. In the crowded waiting room full of women of various sizes and ages Penny surmised that she was easily the eldest there. Eventually they were called. In the dimly lit small room they were greeted by the radiographer.

"I'm Sheila." She looked at the card in front of her. "A dating scan. Have you had scans before?"

"My youngest is eleven."

With her belly exposed, and knickers pushed down she reached out for Alasdair's hand.

"This will be cold," said Sheila, a moment too late as she spread a dab of lubricant on Penny's belly, over her full bladder. "Just a bit of pressure while I find the right spot... there." The noise from the monitor changed from a general shushing and formalised into a rapid heart beat. The image on the screen showed the heart pumping. As they watched the baby kicked out.

"Well, there you are," said the radiographer, "it looks to me as if you might be about fourteen or fifteen weeks....."

Alasdair pressed Penny's hand against his mouth.

Outside the stifling atmosphere of the hospital the day had turned blustery. In the biting wind tiny crystals of snow were buffeted about, but here and there in the sky there was a streak of brightness where the sun might yet break through. The unspoken possibilities hung between them, solid. Penny glanced at Alasdair. It was impossible to see what he was thinking.

"We need to talk," she said. He did not reply. "It's all still such a shock," she said, "I don't know how to start thinking about it, not properly."

They had nearly reached the car.

"This time last week," she added, "I was convinced I was going to die. Like my mother. And now instead...." Alasdair stopped and looked at her. "Alasdair, I need you to talk with me." He nodded. Penny said, "I know what you said... on Saturday...." but he still said nothing. "Is that it?" said Penny, her voice rising, "Talk to me. Tell me what's going on in your head. I can't...think straight. Something's blocking my brain."

"Shall we have lunch out?" he said, "What about the White Horse, we haven't been there for ages."

During the drive the clouds opened out, revealing a pale blue sky. They didn't speak. The sun shone on rooftops, melting the frost where it struck, leaving the shaded areas white and glistening.

"What made you think of this pub?" Penny asked.

"Oh, you know....old times sake or something I guess," he answered, not concentrating, his mind elsewhere. As they approached she remembered evenings out, just the two of them. This place had been in walking distance of their first house. A true local. Alasdair opened the door and held it for her. Inside it was warm, with a log fire blazing. As they waited at the empty bar Penny quietly said,

"I know what we *should* do... maybe what most people in our position would do..." when Alasdair suddenly laughed and put his arm around her shoulders.

"I was just wondering," he said, "what the boys will say when we tell them?"

Pretty Words

by Judi Moore

Hils stood beside the French windows in the drawing room and watched Jocie trudge across the lawn towards her. There was a large man's handkerchief clutched in Jocie's fist: it fluttered like a flag of surrender.

With a sigh Hils went through to the kitchen and put up a cafétiere. Jocie would need coffee. And sympathy. Again.

It wasn't Jocie's fault that Daniel had left her - no more than it was Hils's fault that Win had left her. People moved on. Or died. Hils missed Win more than she could say. And for her there wasn't even the marginal comfort of being able to rail at him and heap scorn on the tarty piece he had gone off with. Win was beyond recrimination or communication of any kind. Hils often thought she saw him in the village, or heard his cough at a concert, or glimpsed him in the garden, but that was neither here nor there. Win was dead and existed now only in her head.

Jocie's Daniel, on the other hand, kept turning up for real. He'd ring to ask where his favourite cuff links might be, or turn up on the doorstep and say he was just going to get a couple of things from the shed if that was all right. Sometimes The Bimbo would be sitting in his car in the drive while he went and ferreted out whatever it was he wanted. Hils was fairly certain that if anyone had told Daniel that Jocie wept buckets after every one of his incursions he would be amazed. She was completely certain that the information wouldn't stop him popping round. He wasn't callous, but he was thoughtless of anybody's needs but his own.

Nevertheless, Jocie needed to be getting over his departure – it had been nearly a year ago, after all. She should be out meeting people – men. But just as she was getting to the place where she might be able to do that, Daniel would turn up like some sort of jovial ghost and force her to relive the eighteen years they'd been everything to each other. It ripped Jocie to pieces every time.

When he'd been in touch - and sometimes when he hadn't - Jocie would need her good friend Hils to tell her woes to, slipping through the gate at the end of the garden that Win had always said they should get a lock for, and making her way tearfully up to the French windows where she would tap miserably, like a damp puppy wanting to come in out of the rain.

By the time Jocie had made it up the steps Hils was back on station at the French windows. She had thrown them open anyway on this beautiful day. June was such a happy month – her favourite. Such a shame that Win had decided to trim the yew walk last June, fallen from the ladder and broken his neck.

The full beauty of an English country garden was spread out before her, glowing in one of those incomparably fresh, sunny mornings of an English summer. The twin arcs of the rose beds in front of the semi-circular patio were a riot of blossoms so fiercely coloured that they hurt the eye, their scent was wafted to her on a capricious little breeze. Across the lawn the Robinia's froth of leaves towered up like a plume of yellow smoke. Squirrels played there, making the branches bounce and the leaves shake.

Hils loved the garden as it turned through autumn to winter too – the smell of a bonfire, the russet colours of the fallen leaves, the filigree of frosted cobwebs covering the lawn early in the morning, the absolute peace of it then. And spring was a delight, as the bulbs came up through the vast lawn and covered it with tiny halcyon blue croci, narcissi and daffodils. She loved it all.

As Win had done – even the beastly yew walk.

But she had it all to do now. Here she must bide: this was her lot.

Jocie plodded up the patio steps. She had barely reached the threshold when; "Oh, Hils - he wants the boys for the whole summer, and ..."

Hils missed the rest. It washed over her as she looked at her friend aghast. Jocie's eyes were so puffy. The dark circles surrounding them looked as if they were dyed into the skin. Her hair was an unkempt thatch. The hem of her skirt was coming down. Her blouse looked as if she had worn it for a week and not been hanging it up at night either. She still had her slippers on.

273

Something must be done. This woman was going to the dogs. Indeed, if something weren't done soon even the dogs wouldn't have her.

Hils held out her arms and Jocie fled into them like an arrow seeking its target. She clung with such force that Hils had to take a step backwards to keep her balance. For long minutes Jocie did nothing more than sob. Hils rubbed her back and stroked her hair by turns. Jocie had never been as bad as this before. Hils was afraid for her. It had been a year now, and Jocie was sinking deeper and deeper into her mire of loss. Seeing her so distraught, Hils began to wonder if living in that big old cottage across the lane with so many memories was going to drive her out of her mind.

When Daniel had gone off with The Bimbo he'd insisted that the boys go to boarding school. He'd said Jocie wouldn't be able to cope on her own. Jocie – and Hils – had been furious. But he had been right: Jocie had shed many tears over the weedy flowerbeds, many more over everlasting piles of ironing and expensive silk shirts she'd ruined in the wash. Daniel had organised everything – the gardener, the housekeeper – and had paid for it too. Now that he had two boarding school places to pay for and two households to maintain he was keeping his expenditure on Jocie to a minimum, despite the exorbitant amount he earned. He had separated out the upkeep of the boys and made Jocie an allowance that funded neither gardener nor housekeeper. When the boys came home in the holidays they found the house filthy, the drive overgrown and the lawn knee high. They did their best – they were good boys – but it wasn't much to come home to. And now Daniel wanted to take them for the summer. The boys might even have suggested it. There wasn't much fun to be had at Hope Well Cottage in the holidays, with nothing but burned toast to eat and their mother weeping over it. Hope Well: what an ironic name that had turned out to be.

Eventually Jocie grew calmer. Hils eased her onto the sofa and went to fetch the coffee. She wondered what Jocie had had to eat recently. Very little by the look of her. She added her freshly baked chocolate cake to the tray.

Coming back into the room she found Jocie slumped over the arm of a sofa, still clutching the disgusting handkerchief. Hils could see the 'D' monogram on a down-hanging corner. Bloody man. Nobody should have to be so flattened by circumstances.

As she busied herself with the crockery she tried to think of some way to help her friend out of her misery. Nothing came. The circle seemed unbreakable – Jocie when miserable sought unquestioning sympathy from her friend then, cheered, went home where everything reminded her of what she had lost and misery returned.

Seeing poor Jocie so unhappy made Hils feel less unhappy herself. Life had to go on. One could fall off a ladder tomorrow and break one's neck. She ministered and coaxed.

Jocie drank her coffee and nibbled a slice of cake. Then she had another piece of cake and, finally, a third. Slowly she became more cheerful; then, as it got towards lunch time, more miserable again. She stayed for lunch. Then, as Jocie still showed no signs of going home, Hils suggested they go into town. Jocie cheered up at once.

In the expensive department stores Jocie spent a lot of money that Hils knew she didn't have. It seemed callous to remind her of her situation, however, so Hils kept quiet unless asked for an opinion about colour or fit, and good-naturedly helped her carry her purchases.

After they'd had a cup of coffee in Debenham's, Hils suggested that they get their hair done. Jocie sorely needed something done in that department. But they couldn't get appointments until Thursday. Hils would much rather have hers done by the local woman, who knew what she liked and how to deal with her wiry, obstinate hair. She thought she might cancel the appointment when she got home. Then she remembered that Jocie had no car now. The rural bus service was very good, but Jocie wouldn't use it. Hils supposed she felt it to be the final degradation.

Hils wasn't able to get Jocie away from the shops until they were closing. Fortunately it was too early in the week for late night opening. Hils finally dropped her off at Hope Well Cottage a little before seven, having had to wrestle with the rush hour traffic on the motorway. Still Jocie lingered:

275

"Are you sure you wouldn't rather I came back with you? I could, you know, easily. I don't like to think of you in that great big house all on your own."

Hils choked back laughter and forbore to mention that Liv was coming over this evening - soon, in fact.

"Oh, I've got things I really ought to attend to," she said. And then something made her add, "but thank you for the offer."

When she got in Hils, exhausted, headed straight for the sofa. She'd make herself a sandwich in a minute. Then Liv would be here.

It had been like this for nearly a year. She was getting nothing done. She hadn't even finished sorting through Win's things. Jocie came round every day. Two or three times a week she would arrive in despair. More often than not she stayed for lunch. Sometimes she lingered until Hils invited her to stay for dinner too. It was entirely too much. Hils couldn't bring herself to say anything - either about the constant intrusion into her life, or the dreadful state that her friend was in. She'd ask Liv. Liv was so sensible.

Liv. The things they did to names in this family: Hils, Win, Liv. Hils had asked her once if she minded. After all, they had chosen Olivia, her given name, with great care. It wasn't as if they had called her Ethel or something, in the hope of being remembered in the will of some ancient aunt. Hils had promised that if Liv was bothered by the contraction that they would start calling her Olivia. Liv had laughed.

"You'd never make it stick, Mum. I mean - you hate Hils, but I've never heard anyone call you anything else. You even introduce yourself as Hils."

"That's why I'm mentioning it now. Before it's too late and you're stuck with it. Your father did it to me. He called me Hils on our first date, and that was that."

"It's too late already, but I love it. Think about it: Liv. What could be a better reminder to have the best time you can, leave nothing unexplored, *carpe diem* and all that? Olivia is a beautiful name Mum - a wonderful starting point. But Liv is the distillation. It's who I am. Who I always want to be."

This had given Hils pause for thought. Not only because her daughter was so passionate in defence of those three little letters, but also because she was so clear about who she was. Hils herself had always been a foil for somebody else; wife, lover, gardener's mate and hostess for Win; mother, sounding board and (in the dark days of puberty) whipping post for Liv; a shoulder to cry on for Jocie. Amongst all those demands who, exactly, was Hils? Well, Win and his demands were gone and Liv's would reduce when she married Gus (Oh God – Liv and Gus!) That left Jocie.

The way things were going Jocie could end up moving in with her at The Beeches. She was surprised that Daniel hadn't suggested it. It would cut down his maintenance commitment even further, she thought uncharitably.

No, she needed concerns, goals, of her own. She was dismayed to find that she had no idea how to gain these things. Hitherto they had been thrust upon her. Now that she was free to choose her own she realised that she'd never had a chance to acquire the skill.

Nor, she reflected, had Jocie. Ah, she thought, returning to her recent contemplation of names, that pretentious 'c'. Jocie had inserted it into her name since Hils had known her, although long ago now. It was meant to imply that Jocie was short for Jocasta, whereas actually Josie was her given name. She had substituted the 'c' when Daniel had begun to move in the kind of circles that might include a Jocasta. Neither of them was out of that drawer, but both were ambitious: Daniel for power and Jocie for what went with power – money. Someone who was what Daniel pretended to be would never leave his ex-wife with so little. He owed her a little generosity, if nothing more.

So what did she, Hils, have to look forward to? Penury and old age, that's what. Win's life insurance had been surprisingly meagre. She was only fifty (well, fifty four if you wanted to be precise). Win shouldn't have gone so young. The best part was yet to come: Liv was off their hands, there was the wedding to look forward to, then grandchildren would arrive. She and Win should have drifted quietly down to his retirement from the practise, enjoyed the garden, taken trips abroad. The good life had been beckoning. And then the daft bastard fell off a ladder. Suddenly fifty four, instead of being the start of something glorious, was the end of everything. Every new and inexplicable little pain, every headache,

277

every shortness of breath seemed to say 'This will only get worse and there is nobody to bring you an aspirin. This is what's left'.

Hils sighed and levered herself off the sofa. Her shoes were pinching, she'd go and take them off. Then she'd make that sandwich. Then Liv would be here to cheer her up. She was being silly. There would always be Liv. Unless *she* fell off a ladder.

She hoped her dark mood was simply the result of having to be cheerful for two all day. Then again, perhaps it wasn't.

The next morning Hils glanced in the long mirror on the landing on her way down the stairs. She stopped with her right foot hovering over the descent; her reflection was certainly arresting. Caught like that, in profile, it was horrible - just horrible.

The light streaming in from the window above the landing took all the peach blonde out of her hair and left it dead and white. The same unkind light demonstrated every tiny streak and blob in her *maquillage* of light foundation and translucent powder. Her face looked like a badly put together mask.

Below the dead hair her two slumped shoulders threw her stomach out and dragged her breasts down to meet it. The buttocks drooped in sympathy. There was so much of everything, and it was all arranged in an awful, collapsing S. It was like looking at a semi-melted wax figure. And she had had the nerve to think unkindly of Jocie's appearance! How long had she been like this?

She straightened and stepped out of the sunlight. Instantly she looked twenty years younger. Well, several anyway. For some minutes she tried combinations of awfulness, slumping and straightening, stepping in and out of the sunlight. She couldn't make up her mind which of the various iterations was really her.

She was still stepping backwards and forwards on the landing when the door bell rang. Quickly she trotted down the rest of the stairs and peeked through the little window in the hall. On the doorstep stood Mr Skinner.

Hils's heart sank – not at the sight of Mr Skinner, which was extremely pleasant, but at the probable reason for his call. He wanted his money. Mr Skinner, the local odd job man, had kept The Beeches from falling around her ears since Win had died. A number of surprisingly expensive jobs had needed doing: the flat roof of the garage had had to be recoated, the window frames on the north-east side of the house had had to be replaced, all the rest of the exterior woodwork had had to be painted, the upstairs loo had ceased to flush and one of the steps outside the French windows had started to crumble. In all she owed him over a thousand pounds. She didn't have it.

If only he had let her settle up after each job. If only she had insisted. But each job seemed to have led on to the next. He had always said 'that's all right. I'll do you a bill for next time I'm over.' And he never had.

Now there he was smiling on her doorstep, holding a rather dirty envelope.

"Hello, Mrs D. I'm sorry its taken so long to get this to you."

The yew walk needed cutting back again, and something must be wrong with the pitched roof on the annex, because a patch of damp had appeared in the corner of Liv's old room. A big, old house was just a money pit.

"Come in," she said.

Mr Skinner was about thirty, tanned from working out of doors. His smile was a gorgeous thing, revealing many absurdly good teeth and crinkling the corners of his blue eyes. He had a full head of curly light brown hair, locks of which wisped over his collar at the back in a ridiculously sexy way. He wore a check shirt with the sleeves rolled up to expose muscular, sinewy forearms and a pair of denims which appeared to have been sprayed on to extremely well-made buttocks and thighs. Hils noticed that he wore a belt with a big silvery buckle in the shape of a bull's horns around the waist of his jeans. She wondered how he got the jeans on and off. In her mind's eye he managed it, and she felt her face grow hot. She'd just bet he didn't wear Y-fronts.

As her imagination ran wild he wiped his feet carefully and stepped inside. She noticed that his boots were filthy and changed her mind about where to have this interview. It would have to be in the kitchen. The Chinese rugs in the drawing room were not up to Mr Skinner's boots.

He stood beside her waiting for directions.

"Go through to the kitchen, won't you, Mr Skinner?" she said, and watched the jeans undulate across the hall in that direction.

279

Once there he put the envelope on the table. Gingerly she picked it up and opened it. With dismay she discovered that it was for even more than she'd expected. She'd forgotten about VAT.

To give herself time to think she went and filled the kettle.

"Cup of tea, Mr Skinner?"

"Yeh, great." He sat down at the kitchen table. "Call me Brad."

"How do you like it, Brad?"

"As it comes thanks, Mrs D."

It was difficult to think with Brad Skinner sitting so close to her. If she took two steps backwards she could be sitting on his knee. He really was beautiful. It was a mind-numbing beauty. Although, of course, her inability to think sensibly what to do about the invoice could just be that there wasn't a solution. And then what?

She brought him a mug of tea, and the sugar bowl. He put three big spoonfuls in and stirred with the spoon from the sugar bowl.

"You look tired, Mrs D."

"Do I?" She was surprised, both at such an observation from him and at how accurate it was. "Yes, I am rather. I had a friend over for the day yesterday."

"Mrs Bannister, was it? I see her coming over here a lot, seeing as how I live just up the lane from her. It's a shame."

"Yes," said Hils, "it is." Whatever he had meant by that, it certainly was.

"You shouldn't wear yourself out over other people's troubles. You've had enough of your own."

"Well," Hils said, surprisingly herself, "it does make one feel better somehow about one's own misfortunes. It seems to be true that there's always someone worse off."

"It's good you can think that way Mrs D., but you want to look out for number one. You lost Mr D, what, a year ago now? You're an attractive woman Mrs D, always so smart and lively. If you'll pardon my saying so you want to get back in the swim now, not spend all your time helping lame ducks. You've got this lovely house for a start, and your health and you always look a picture. I bet any man in the village would be honoured if you'd look his way. You could have your pick."

"I certainly miss having a man about the place," Hils said, very conscious that a very attractive man was sitting at her kitchen table paying her compliments, and beginning to wonder where this conversation was going. Somehow she did feel ten years younger. Energy that she hadn't had for - oh, a year at least - was flooding through her. She wondered what she was going to do with this sudden vitality. Clean the windows probably.

"It can't be easy for you, on your own. All you have to do is whistle you know, and they'd all come running. I'm surprised you haven't been beating them off with a stick since your husband died."

She laughed, embarrassed and pleased.

"It's hard for a woman to be on her own. Women have needs, same as men. It's a new Millennium, right? We're all modern people, honest people, right? I'll be honest with you now, Mrs D. Of course you're lonely, but you don't have to be. Take what *you* want. You deserve it." And his right hand, that had been clasped with its partner round his tea mug, crept across the table and covered her left hand where it lay beside her cup and saucer.

Hils first reaction was to snatch her hand away, but she didn't. She held his gaze. One of his eyebrows shifted upwards quizzically. Still Hils looked at him. She didn't know if she was playing up to him or imitating a rabbit caught in car headlights. She did know that if she held his gaze, stood up, and continued to hold his hand, that next stop would be bed.

He gave her hand the merest squeeze.

She looked down, finally, at their joined hands lying on the table top. No, she wouldn't go to bed with him – though the idea was enormously tempting. She could feel the old, familiar ache of desire deep in her body. It had been a long time since she'd felt that. But this sort of flirtation was just a form of small talk for someone like him. He must do this all the time. If she went to bed with him she would lose the services of a very useful odd job man – and the opportunity to flirt with him whenever he came round to do those odd jobs. If she went to bed with him she (and this was rather a degrading thought) she probably wouldn't have to pay his horrible, big bill. So she must find a way to pay him. Perhaps she could persuade him to let her pay in instalments? Making her eyes moist and her voice tremulous (the latter needing very little pretence) she set about a little flattery of her own.

It worked. Hils fluttered and simpered and flattered, enjoyed herself hugely, and extracted from Brad the concession that she could pay off her bill so much every month. Apart from relief at having solved the problem she was delighted at the prospect of seeing him at least once a month.

Hils was surprised at what a fillip the flirtation had given her. She realised, of course, that Brad must do this with all the women he worked for. He was in an ideal position, sorting out minor building work for women on their own. She would be surprised if he had actually bedded any of them. It was almost certainly all a big bluff – and one that was never likely to be called.

She regaled Liv with the story that evening. She made it sound outrageous and told it against herself. Liv laughed, as she was supposed to do, but it was a small, strained sort of laugh – not the roaring gales of merriment Hils knew Liv to be capable of. Her daughter was genuinely shocked. Mothers didn't flirt. Mothers, especially widowed mothers the wrong side of fifty, did not contemplate casual sex. They did not, even in jest, consider paying off a debt with sexual favours. They took to pastel hair colours and shapeless clothes in olive and taupe and behaved themselves. Hils began to regret that she *had* 'behaved' herself.

On Thursday morning Hils phoned Jocie and reminded her about their hair appointments. After they'd been coloured, cut and styled Hils suggested lunch. After lunch Hils suggested a little light shopping. This time Hils had some purchases to make on her own account. She bought a pair of red shoes, a long, red silk scarf and a pair of red gloves. Altogether these items cost almost as much as her first instalment to Brad.

Jocie made no comment about Hils's discreet little bags on their way back to the car: neither did Hils. Despite her new hair do - which looked very good indeed - Jocie was full, as usual, of her own woes. Hils listened to the diatribe as if from far away on the top of a high hill. Poor Jocie was still down in the valley of Despair. Hils had new red shoes and a man had flirted with her.

When they got back to the village Hils offered coffee. Jocie accepted, of course. As Hils came into the drawing room with the laden tray the lovely late afternoon sunlight poured through the French windows, making everything warm and honeyed - Jocie's new hair, the cream suite, the beech coffee table. Hils felt something … sensuous – no, sensual – ripple up through her body. It was a very similar sensation to the one she had experienced when Brad covered her hand with his. She so wanted to share this with Jocie, to show her that life went on - but how? Send Brad round? Jocie had even less money than Hils. And Jocie might be fool enough actually to go upstairs with him. How to start Jocie healing? What had been so marvellous about Brad's attention? Hils poured the coffee and reflected. Ah, now perhaps she had it. She handed Jocie her coffee and said:

"Your new hair do looks super, dear. You look years younger."

Jocie put her hand up to touch the new hair, as women always do when a compliment tends that way.

"Yes, doesn't it. I don't know why I didn't get it done before."

"The colour suits you perfectly."

"Yes, they're good in there."

This wasn't right, Hils thought. There's no *frisson* here, it's just two women talking about hair. She sat down beside Jocie on the sofa. How had Brad done it? She tried again.

"You've been looking so tired since Daniel went. And that's a long time ago now. You don't want to let yourself get dragged down by all that. You need to look out for yourself now. An attractive woman like you, you could have any man you want. I'll bet any man in the village would be delighted if you looked twice at him. You ought to be beating them off with a stick."

Jocie laughed lightly.

"Well," said Jocie, "I guess I'm not in my dotage yet."

"You're a very attractive woman. You've got your whole life in front of you."

The Brad-ese seemed to be coming out better now. Hils reached over and covered Jocie's hand with her own and tried to remember what came next.

283

"Its very hard for a woman to be on her own, Jocie. Women have needs, same as men. It's a new Millennium. We're all modern people, honest people. You must be lonely over there in that big place without Daniel and the boys – but you don't have to be. Take what *you* want. You deserve it."

Jocie looked up and into Hils eyes. Hils held that gaze, as Brad had done, and saw a smile come into Jocie's mouth. It had been a very long time since she had seen that. There had been so much pain in that face that the smile sat oddly, but it remained.

Hils hoped that Jocie wouldn't ask her *how* she was to take what she wanted, because Hils had no idea how to do that. For herself the beginnings of something new had come in the purchase of red shoes, scarf and gloves. She hoped that Jocie would be able to make her own start in her own way. For Jocie it probably wouldn't involve buying things. Jocie had been buying things ever since Daniel had gone. It was for her like comfort eating was for some people, and had done her absolutely no good. All she had to show for it was a big credit card bill that she couldn't pay.

But Jocie said nothing, just sat there with her hand under Hils's and a dreamy look on her face with its smile. They didn't say anything for a while. Then Jocie said;

"I think I'll go home now. I've got some things I want to do. I think I'll turn out the spare room. Chuck out some of his things, and the stuff the boys have grown out of."

She stood up and the contact was broken. Hils stood too. Then Jocie reached over and gave Hils a hug.

"Thank you," she said. She drifted over to the French windows, through them and out into the balmy June evening. Hils watched her walk across the lawn. There was a purpose to her step that hadn't been there for a long time. Hils wondered how long it would last.

The effect on Jocie wasn't quite what Hils had expected. The next morning Jocie was tapping on the French windows before Hils had finished dressing. Fearing the worst, Hils hurried down. But the Jocie that stepped through the draperies was anything but depressed. Her eyes were bright, her cheeks were flushed. She had on a fresh white summer frock, a clean white cardigan and a pair of little white pumps.

Hils had her face set ready in an expression of tender concern. Before she could regroup to take account of this unexpected turn of events Jocie was saying, "I've been thinking about what you said, and it's all quite true."

Jocie grasped her friend's hands and continued breathlessly, "The only thing is, I don't know how any more. I've forgotten how to flirt, how to attract a man. You must help me, Hils, you simply must. You've obviously had experience. I'd never have guessed before, but you were so practised, so easy yesterday. Please tell me how it's done?"

Hils - easy and practised? She'd put on a good act, apparently. She began to regret recreating her conversation with Brad in the kitchen. It seemed to be leading to more than she had bargained for.

"I ..." she began, "I ... I'll go and put some coffee on."

This was supposed to give her time to think, but Jocie followed her through to the kitchen and began to run through her wardrobe for Hils's benefit, asking what of her many clothes might best attract a new man. Hils let this wash over her and thought desperately. She had a bad feeling. Sure enough, as she carried the tray back to the lounge Jocie finished up with, "But what do I *say*? I used to know, but somehow, its been so long, I've forgotten. And what do they say to me? I'm not sure I'd recognise a chat up line now if I heard one. Please, Hils?"

Hils poured the coffee. Their play-acting the day before had made her uneasy. She didn't want to get into a conversation that might lead to it happening again. But Jocie's eyes were shining, and she was persistent. Finally Hils said; "Well, men pay you compliments. For instance, that's a beautiful dress you're wearing. It sets off your hair. It makes you look like a girl again."

Jocie giggled and shrugged her shoulders. Hils noticed that what she had just said was, actually, true.

Hils threw caution to the winds.

"But if they really want to get close to you they start complimenting more personal items of clothing. Like earrings."

"Oh bother, I'm not wearing any."

"It doesn't matter. We can pretend. Or they might draw attention to a little curl of hair and say something like …"

Hils located a suitable tendril in the fringe of Jocie's neat page boy and stretched out her hand towards it. Jocie flinched ever so slightly.

"Sorry."

"Sorry."

Hils drew back her fingers as if she had burned them.

"Well – something like that."

"No, go on. I'm sorry. That was silly of me."

Hils stretched out her fingers towards the tendril again and thought fast.

"It's like the sun is caught in your hair," she said and brushed it oh so gently back into Jocie's fringe.

"Oh," Jocie breathed. "If only someone *would* say something as beautiful as that to me."

Jocie's eyes were riveted on Hils's face. Hils couldn't look away. Some sort of electricity was fizzing through her fingers from Jocie's hair. Hils felt shaken – powerful and vulnerable at the same time. The fizzy feeling ran up her arm to the nape of her neck and made the hairs there stir. It spread out across her shoulders as a tingle, and ran down her spine to that place deep in her body where desire was rooted. The whole thing was bizarre, she knew that, but she didn't want to - couldn't - analyse it. She felt so *alive*. This was what she had been without for so long. Her hand wandered from the strand of Jocie's hair, across her forehead and caressed her cheek. The sensation was delicious. Jocie's skin was lovely – like taut, cool silk. Hils found herself looking deeper and deeper into Jocie's skin. There was no flaw, she was beautiful.

Then there was a scraping step outside the French windows and Liv walked in on them.

"Ah, I thought I'd find you in here," she said. "What's the matter? Has Jocie got something in her eye?"

The two women sprang apart.

"No," said Jocie.

"Yes," said Hils.

It was a bit of a shock to be thrown back into her own reality like that. Suddenly she was back to being Hilary Dowdeswell – a woman on the wrong side of middle age, widowed, with one daughter. And the daughter was here. Refreshment must be offered, interested enquiries made, feelings damped down.

While she fetched a cup for Liv and made a fresh cafétiere of coffee, Hils tried to order her thoughts. It was just a game, a role play to help Jocie. There was nothing wrong in a few pretty words. They were two grown women. They could do what they wanted. But she saw again in her mind the dreamy look in Jocie's eyes as she submitted herself to Hils's hand and felt her own face grow hot. It had nothing to do with the steam from the kettle.

The next day Jocie came over again. A cheerful Jocie was, apparently, no less needy than a depressed one.

"I've got earrings in today, see? You said men sometimes make remarks about earrings. What do they say, Hils?"

Hils suppressed a sigh. She really didn't want to play this game again. It had been … disturbing, the day before when Liv had walked in on them. But Jocie was insistent and Hils was used to letting her have her own way.

The earrings were pretty pearl drops. It would be no lie and no hardship to pay them a compliment.

But Hils couldn't find any words, not straight out like that. She had to think herself into the powerful, tingly place she had been in yesterday. It had been a wonderful place, and she knew she wanted to find it again.

She drew a breath and began.

As she stretched out her hand towards Jocie's earring she found she was trembling slightly. She hoped Jocie didn't notice her hand was quivering.

The pretty words came easier this time;

"Such beautiful earrings, like your skin. Such a bloom …"

Hils's hand strayed from the earring to Jocie's cheekbone and cupped it. She leaned in towards Jocie.

"And your eyes …" Jocie's eyes had been puffy and bloodshot for so long, but no longer. Now they were large and deeply blue, like a baby's. "Such a baby blue." She found herself repeating that, "baby, baby blue." You could drown in those eyes, as big and blue as the deep Atlantic ocean.

287

And now somehow Jocie's lips were on hers, like a butterfly's wings and this, now was *definitely* a mistake.

The same thing obviously occurred to Jocie. The two women sprang back and retreated to opposite ends of the sofa. Hils inspected her nails, then picked up her coffee cup. Her hands were really shaking now, so she put it down again before she spilled what remained in it. Jocie, had something in her eye, perhaps. She fished around in her sleeve for a handkerchief, made a show of removing whatever it was, patted both cheeks – which were flushed – and finally blotted her mouth, hard. Hils wondered if she had Jocie's lipstick on her. Almost she put out her tongue to taste.

They didn't speak half a dozen words more before Jocie was gone.

Hils felt very flat sitting on the sofa by herself in front of the used coffee things. She took the tray through to the kitchen, but that reminded her what Liv had caught them doing yesterday that had led to ... *this* today. She was still shaking. Washing up the cups was impossible. Some sort of electric current was running through her. She found herself wandering the house. She tidied things that didn't need tidying, pinched a few dead heads out of the flowers on the hall table. Finally she wound up in the attic. She stood at the window in the gable end and looked out over that great lawn that would need cutting tomorrow if the weather held. At the end of the lawn was the hedge with the side gate in it. Beyond that she could just see the roof of Hope Well Cottage.

She realised now just how much of herself she'd invested in Jocie since Win had died. In some way Jocie had replaced him. The two women had suffered their losses so close together. They were just victims of other people's thoughtlessness, that's what had led them to ... what *had* it led to? Hils looked down at her still shaky hands. This one had cupped Jocie's face, tenderly, lovingly. It had been so ... she still didn't know what it had been. Did she *love* Jocie? In *that* way?

No. She had liked Jocie well enough, as a neighbour, as a guest, as half of a couple when she herself had been half of a couple. Then she had felt sorry for her. Then she had become a project. And if truth be told she had felt sorry for herself as well and had badly needed the Jocie Project.

288

Well it looked as though the project was complete, because Jocie wouldn't be coming back. Hils could see her blotting her lipstick in her mind's eye. She had never seen that most womanly of gestures done with revulsion like that. She cringed inwardly at the thought of seeing Jocie again. What could they ever say to each other after this? Hils would have to find another friend.

She still felt shaky, and now she felt tearful as well. She didn't want to mow that absurd ocean of a lawn, or trim the yew walk, or get damp patches fixed in the eight rooms she didn't use, or worry about the bills any more.

She didn't want to be able to see Hope Well Cottage through the gable window.

She didn't want always to be an empty vessel, to be filled at somebody else's whim. Win and Liv and Jocie and Brad had all done it, and she had let them. All her life she had let people do that.

But not any longer. She'd put the bloody house on the market. She'd have a really nice holiday somewhere expensive and warm. Then when she got back she'd find some voluntary work to do in town and join an evening class in something exotic that she'd never done before, like Russian. And when she told Liv what she was doing she would try to make her understand why she was doing it without having to tell her what had happened when she'd spoken those damned pretty words to Jocie.

She went downstairs and got out the local paper.

A House Officer's Diary

by Dr Emma Morgan

Monday May 22nd
Number of meals: 2 (not bad)
Number of hours sleep last night: 7 (again, not bad)
Number of patients dead: 0 (excellent)

20.00

I woke with a start this morning. It was very light in the room and I had a feeling of panic as I fumbled for my phone to see the time. It was 9.30am. Pants. I was late for work. As I hurried onto the wards my bleep started going off again and again. A nurse dragged me towards one of my patients. The patient was sitting forward gasping for breath.

"What's wrong with him doctor? What are you going to do? What are you going to do doctor?!"

BEEP BEEP BEEP. My bleep was going off again. BEEP BEEP BEEP. I woke with a start. It was my alarm. I had been dreaming. I've got to stop dreaming about work; it can't be healthy.

When I did get into work I picked up the cardiac arrest bleep and started the morning ward round. After seeing the first four or so patients the bleep went off.

"BEEP BEEP BEEP cardiac arrest on the medical assessment unit level one BEEP BEEP BEEP cardiac arrest on the medical assessment unit level one"

It was a long run from the wards on level seven to level one and I was one of the last to get there. The anaesthetist had just turned up and took over from the nurse, Simon. I took some blood and busied myself with sending it off to the lab. By the time I came back the patient was breathing and waking up. This didn't happen very often; most arrest calls were not successful.

As I hurried back up the stairs to join my ward round my phone rang.

"Hello darling!"

"Mum I'm at work."

"Oh are you darling? Well I just wanted to call to remind you to write those thank you letters."

"What?!"

"You know, your Auntie Celia sent you that lovely jumper for your birthday and you haven't said thank you yet."

"Mum I'm at work. I haven't really got the time for this right now."

"Well, this is very important."

"Okay Mum. I'll write that thank you letter tonight. Now I've got to go...bye."

"But...."

"Bye Mum." I hung up. When I was younger I imagined being a doctor. I imagined striding around the hospital in a white coat making important decisions and doing complex surgical procedures. I did *not* imagine my Mum would still be phoning me up reminding me to write thank you letters!

I hate to admit it but by the time we got to our 30th patient they were all blending into one. A confused old lady with a 'water infection', she lives on her own and couldn't cope....and so it goes.

"She may have constipation. Emma could you do a PR and decide whether she needs an enema or not?"

"Sure." There's another thing I didn't imagine - sticking my finger up some poor old lady's bottom. It's so glamorous being a doctor.

03.00

Swas somehow purswaded to go to pub with Kate and Co...swish I hadn't staid out so late thugh.

Tuesday May 23rd

Number of meals: 6 (little and often is the key to a hang over)

Number of hours sleep last night: 4 (not good at all)

Number of patients dead: 1 (v. bad)

Oh boy I felt so sick this morning. I had to guzzle water surreptitiously in between patients. Feeling ill is always so much worse when you know it's self-inflicted. Several patients down the line I couldn't stand it any more. I felt hot, sweaty, light-headed and incredibly nauseous.

"Excuse me." I rushed to the nearest toilet, which seemed like miles down the corridor. I got there just in time.

When I rejoined the ward round I was greeted with the sympathetic words, "you're not pregnant are you?" this from my consultant.

"That's all I bloody well need - a pregnant house officer!"

"No no I'm not pregnant." I reassured him.

We finished off our ward round down on level one in the medical assessment unit (MAU). While I was on the ward the emergency bell went off. As I hurried into the cubicle I saw Simon starting chest compressions; he looked flushed and excited. I took over opening the airway and asked Simon what had happened. He'd come in to check on the patient and found her not breathing. Soon after that she'd lost her pulse and he'd started chest compressions. Although it seemed like forever, it was only a few minutes before the crash team turned up and took over. This time the resuscitation was not successful. After 10 minutes everyone was in agreement and we stopped.

Wednesday 24th May
Number of meals: 1
Number of hours sleep last night: 5 ½ (bad)
Number of patients dead: 0 (v. good)

I was at work until late last night and had to go in early to prepare for the ward round. Being tired makes a difficult day even harder. After the ward round I started to see patients in the medical assessment unit.

I saw a sweet old lady, Mrs Williams, who'd come in with chest pain. I was really touched by her story; she was 75 and had never been to hospital in her life until today. Mrs Williams' granddaughter brought her in and they were obviously very close. Fortunately she didn't seem to have much wrong with her; the ECG and blood tests were all normal. Hopefully she will be able to go home tomorrow.

292

I left late again tonight. It's weeks like this that make me feel that all I do is work, eat and sleep (without much of the latter two).

Thursday 25th May
Number of meals: 2
Number of hours sleep last night: 6 (not too bad)
Number of patients dead: 1 (terrible)

I went in to work early this morning to see Mrs Williams. As I walked into the cubicle I knew something was wrong. Simon was standing fiddling with the drip; he turned as I walked in and he looked worried.
"What's wrong Simon?"
"She's not looking good this morning. She's having difficulty breathing."
He was right. Mrs Williams looked terrible. Within seconds her breathing slowed and then stopped. She became blue. I pulled the cardiac arrest cord and Simon started using the mask to give her breaths. I felt for a pulse, there was none and I started chest compressions. Other staff from the ward turned up with the crash trolley. The rhythm on the heart tracing was completely flat and so the defibrillator was useless. By the time the crash team arrived it was fairly obvious that our efforts were futile but we continued for a while longer. Finally we stopped and the crash team left.
I was the last one there. It was suddenly quiet as I stood there amongst the wreckage of the cardiac arrest. Mrs Williams looked very peaceful amongst the chaos of the room, almost as if she were asleep.
A nurse poked her head round the curtain "Mrs Williams' granddaughter has come back from the canteen. Do you want to talk to her now?"
"Yes. Take her to the relatives' room and I'll be in in a minute."

It was one of the most difficult things I've ever done. As I explained what had happened to her grandmother Miss Williams, Anna, broke down in tears. She described how the two of them had lived together in the same house for the last ten years. She didn't have a family of

293

her own and the two of them had looked after each other. Anna couldn't imagine life alone.

I know I should distance myself from my patients but I particularly liked this family. I found it hard getting through the rest of the day.

Friday 26th May
Number of meals: 2 (okay)
Number of hours sleep last night: 7 (good)
Number of patients dead: 0 (v. good)

When I went into work the next day there were police officers interviewing various members of staff. They wanted to speak to me too.
"Dr Hughes. In your opinion, what did Mrs Margaret Williams die of?"
"What is this about?"
"Please answer the question Dr Hughes." The police officer was a particularly unpleasant character and it clearly wasn't going to be easy to get any information. I did however manage to discover that they had carried out a post mortem on Mrs Williams because her death had been so sudden and there wasn't a clear explanation for it. At post mortem they had not found any evidence of a heart attack, stroke or any other obvious abnormality that could have lead to her death. What they did find were high levels of diazepam in her blood. Later in the day Simon explained to me that the police suspected foul play. It turned out that Mrs Williams was extremely wealthy and Anna Williams was set to inherit everything. So she had a motive and that, it seems, had made the police suspicious.

The suggestion that Anna Williams might have killed her grandmother infuriated me. I just could not believe it. I had seen the misery on her face as I told her the bad news.

Just before I left for home I went to the MAU to finish off a few jobs. I noticed Anna Williams standing around nervously biting her nails. I walked up to her.

"Oh Dr Hughes, I was hoping I would find you here. I need to talk to you."

"Of course. Come through to the relatives' room."

Anna looked terrible. She explained that she'd spent most of the day in the police station. The police did indeed suspect her of killing her grandmother. They had found a bottle of Mrs Williams' sleeping tablets (diazepam) in Anna's handbag. The bottle had only two tablets left in it. She had brought all her grandmother's tablets with her to show to the doctors but that bottle had been left behind. According to the GP's records there should be half the bottle remaining. Anna couldn't explain why Mrs Williams had used more than she should. Mrs Williams had been in charge of her own medications. Additionally one of the nurses had reported to have seen Anna hurrying out of the cubicle just before Simon had gone in to find the old lady struggling to breathe. I didn't know what to say. I believed that she had not killed her grandmother but by the same token the evidence was quite damning.

Saturday 27th May
Number of meals: 3 (oh boy I love the weekend)
Number of hours sleep last night: 6 (too much thinking)
Number of patients dead: 0

I just couldn't sleep last night. I couldn't stop thinking about Anna Williams and her mother. I'd seen many daughters, granddaughters, sons and grandsons told that their relative was dead and few times had I seen anyone quite so devastated. But that wasn't all; there was something else playing on my mind. When I closed my eyes I could see the cardiac arrests I had been to. At each one a particular face was present.

I got up early and went into the hospital. I must be crazy. This weekend was the first weekend I'd had off for three weeks and yet I chose to go into the hospital. There was something I wanted to check out. I looked up the details of the cardiac arrest calls for the last month. In the last week alone there had been five primary respiratory arrests i.e. the patient stopped breathing first before their heart stopped. Respiratory arrest is uncommon so to have five in one week is exceptional. I collected the notes of the patients on the list and sat down in the library to study them. There was one connection between the patients. They had all been nursed by Simon on the day of the respiratory arrest. The idea that had been forming itself in my mind suddenly took shape. Could Simon have killed Mrs Williams? And if so how many others had he killed?

Monday 29th May
Number of meals: 2
Number of hours sleep last night: 6 (again, too much thinking)
Number of patients dead: 0

First thing this morning I took the information I had found straight to my consultant, Prof Griffiths. Unfortunately he was not convinced. He told me in no uncertain terms that there was not enough evidence and that I should not make accusations that I cannot back up. If that was what he thought then it is likely that the police will think the same. I knew I would have to find more evidence.

Throughout the day I kept finding excuses to go to MAU, writing up intravenous fluids here, requesting an x-ray there. I watched Simon very closely but I could see nothing that would support my theory. It was so frustrating; I was sure I was right but how could I prove it? Could I really wait for someone else to die?

Tuesday 30th May
Number of meals: 2
Number of hours sleep last night: 7
Number of patients dead: 0

19.00

I tried the same technique today. I tried to spend as much time in MAU as I could, watching Simon like a hawk but still I couldn't see anything suspicious. I was asked to clerk in a patient and it was a good excuse to stay in MAU so I agreed. He was a really sweet old man who'd fought in the Second World War. He was a fighter pilot and had some amazing stories.

296

As I sat down to write up the notes I opened the nursing folder. I froze mid-sentence as I read the name on the nursing notes. Simon was looking after this lovely man. He'd managed to survive what was probably the most dangerous job in the Second World War I couldn't let him be killed now. I couldn't let another innocent person die.

I called my consultant and told him there was something very important I had to show him in MAU. He was not very pleased but, when I wouldn't give up, he eventually agreed.

Simon was behind the curtain when Prof Griffiths arrived. I was taking a huge risk and I was shaking a little as I opened the curtain. Simon was leaning over the patient and was reaching into his pocket.

"Simon, let me look in your pocket!" I said loudly.
"Dr Hughes, I hope you know what you're doing." Prof Griffiths warned me.
"Simon let me look in your pocket!" I repeated.
I put my hand into his pocket and pulled out an empty syringe.
"An empty syringe?" Prof Griffiths said incredulously "an empty syringe? I bet you've got an empty syringe in your pocket. I bet she's got an empty syringe in her pocket." He pointed at a nurse walking by.
"You brought me all the way down here for this?! I'm so sorry Simon."
As Simon walked away from us I spotted a dark patch on Simon's uniform. His uniform was wet around the pocket.
"Wait!" I couldn't believe I was doing this. If I was wrong then this was probably professional suicide.
"Wait. Whatever was in the syringe is now in his uniform. Please just test the liquid on his uniform."
"Dr Hughes, you are making a fool of yourself....I'm sorry Simon but if we let her have this one then maybe she'll shut up."
"What? What are you talking about? This is ridiculous." Simon looked panicked but, despite his protestations, Prof Griffiths took the shirt. I squeezed out the liquid from the shirt and sent it for analysis.

That evening I left the hospital late and walked outside to find my bike. I was so tired that I couldn't remember where I'd left it. I hunted in the main bike racks but had no luck there so walked through to the secluded bike rack at the back of the hospital. I eventually found it by spotting the grotty plastic bag tied over the seat. As I unlocked my bike I thought I heard a noise behind me. I turned but there was nothing to see but blackness. The wind whipped at the trees that encircled me and I felt a chill down my spine.

I jumped onto my bike and cycled away. My route home took me along a tree-lined path out of the hospital grounds and then along a narrow road with high walls either side. As I passed through the tree-lined avenue I heard a twig snap and when I looked behind I thought I saw a shadow move between the trees. I cycled faster and was relieved when I reached the road. Then I heard what sounded like footsteps on the tarmac but I didn't dare look behind this time I just cycled even faster, my legs pumping. I continued at this pace all the way to the accommodation block and when I got there my heart was racing. I felt a little ridiculous when I reached the safety of my flat. It was probably just someone else making their way home after a late shift. This business with Simon had really got me nervous.

02.00

I was woken from a deep sleep by my mobile phone. When I answered it there was silence at the other end and then it rang off. Was it just a wrong number?

After checking the door was locked I turned the light off and got back into bed. As I lay there I suddenly became aware of noises all around me; my senses were heightened by fear. There was rustling in the hall and I sat bolt upright in bed. A door creaked but was it the front door opening or simply my flat mate going to the kitchen for a drink? Next there was silence for a long time and I was beginning to think that I had imagined it all. I relaxed a little and settled back under the covers. Then I heard what sounded like footsteps in the hallway. I wanted to turn on the light but I was too frightened to even get out of bed. I had a child-like instinct to stay hidden under the covers. There was more rustling that sounded very close to my door and then there was silence.

I eventually drifted to sleep but it was a very restless sleep punctuated by terrifying dreams. After about an hour I was woken by my phone ringing. Again it was a 'no number'. My skin tingled with fear but I answered the phone. There was silence at the other end and I hung up.

04.00

My phone rang five further times. It cannot be a wrong number.

Wednesday 31ˢᵗ May
Number of meals: 2
Number of hours sleep last night: 5
Number of patients dead: 0

07.30

When I opened my bedroom door there was a note on the floor just outside. It read simply,

"Just you wait."

Simon had been in my flat. If he could do that, what else could he do? I have to find enough evidence to get him arrested or I could be his next victim.

19.30

The first thing I did when I got into work was check the computer for the results from Simon's uniform. They were 'pending'.

When I had jobs to do on MAU I ventured onto the ward with a feeling of trepidation. I tried to finish my work as quickly as I could and get out of there. When I had finished I walked along the corridor back to the lift lobby. MAU is in the basement of the hospital and the long corridor is completely dark in places. The lights are supposed to turn on with movement but they've never worked. I heard a noise behind me but when I turned around I couldn't make anything out in the darkness. I walked a little faster. I heard a noise again, closer this time, so I started running. I ran up the stairs to level two and out of the hospital. I sucked in gulps of fresh air and tried to calm myself. I had become a nervous wreck.

I spent the rest of the day at the computer clicking on 'refresh' and every time it said 'pending'. At 4pm I clicked on refresh and the results were finally there. The liquid on Simon's shirt contained diazepam and vecuronium (a muscle relaxant that paralyses the muscles of breathing). Simon had discharged the syringe, with a fatal concoction of substances, into his pocket. I quickly printed out the page and ran with it to Prof Griffiths' office.

When I arrived at his office there were already two policemen inside. I walked in with the results in my hand.
"I know Dr Hughes, I have the results here."

The police arrested Simon and took him away.

The hospital and the police investigated Simon further and found 17 suspicious cases of respiratory arrest. Two of the patients died (including poor Mrs Williams). He will stand trial in August charged with two counts of murder and 15 counts of grievous bodily harm. Anna Williams was cleared of all suspicion.

This story was inspired by my own experiences and those of my colleagues however, the characters depicted are entirely fictitious.

The Pin Man

by Brenda Ray

The doll lay on the dressing table next to the trinket box, small, smooth and metallic. It had slit, slanting, empty eyes, a microscopic mouth, and no nose at all.

"Where on earth did that come from?" I asked my mother.

"I don't know," she said.

"I thought we'd got rid of that years ago." I picked it up, and its tiny, jointed metallic limbs swung heavily beneath its out-of-proportion oval head. It couldn't have been more than two inches long. For a thing of its size, it was surprisingly ominous.

"So did I," she said.

I put it down again, quickly. An icy hand clamped itself firmly round my subconscious. And I remembered something I had seen in Rhys and Rosa's house a long time ago.

Rhys and Rosa's house was exactly opposite ours. From our front bedroom on Quilley Road, you could look right down on Rhys and Rosa's bungalow and see straight through their windows. One of the earliest things I could remember was the sound of Rosa slamming them in a vain effort to prevent the neighbours hearing the kids screaming and drumming their heels on the lino. It always failed, of course and up and down the road, you cold sense the neighbours quietly sniggering to themselves. Newcomers might possibly have wondered if something dire was going on, but it wasn't true. The plain truth was that Gina and Gwyneth were spoiled rotten, and the merest whiff of the word 'no' was likely to ignite a tantrum of horrendous proportions.

Rosa was the grand-daughter of Italian immigrants, who had settled in Britain in the 1900s and set up a local ice-cream empire. She was dark and dumpy, her wavy hair crimped short and rigid into one of those flat-topped fifties hairdos which made everyone look ten years older. She was also becoming fat. Despite their names neither she nor Rhys had any trace of an accent. Rosa rarely mentioned the Ronchetti family. To me, the idea of foreign relations was exciting, but Rosa always soft-pedalled it and the Ronchettis seldom visited. But maybe they were just too busy making ice-cream.

Rhys was matchstick thin, mild mannered, dark, with Brilliantined hair, horn rimmed specs and slightly protruding teeth. Rhys wasn't proper Welsh – his English mother departed early on to the Other Life or another husband, depositing Rhys at some minor public school. His father had set up a company that produced prefabricated housing shortly after the Second World War and raked in a load of money, although when we first knew them, not much of it had filtered down as far as Rhys.

Every Saturday night, my parents and Rhys and Rosa would meet up to chat and play cards, while we children were put to bed in whichever house they were in. I never really liked sleeping at Rhys and Rosa's house, perhaps because their bedroom was on the front so that headlights shone through the windows and people walked past at a stone's throw from the bed. There was also a clock with a luminous dial that looked like a face and ticked in an ominous and erratic manner. Everything in the bungalow was brown or beige, except for the bathroom, painted a nauseous shade of peach, the thought of which still gives me migraine.

Gina was tiny and dark, her features marred by an almost permanent scowl. Gwyneth was plumper, fairer and more placid in appearance, but as we all know, appearances can be deceptive. Gwyneth could scream and kick with the best of them. Compared to Gina, however, she was positively cherubic. Without a doubt, the Lampeter sisters were the most ill-behaved children known to man, and whatever the occasion, Gina and Gwyneth could come up with a performance of Oscar-winning awfulness. Both of them by today's standards might be considered disturbed. Not because they were deprived, but because they had, in fact, too much. Too much affluence, too much freedom. Perhaps the reasons for this dated from the War when both parents had spent six years in the armed forces, making the very idea of discipline repugnant. Or maybe public schools had something to do with it. But the sad fact was that the Lampeter children were completely unmanageable, and anyone who crossed their path was playing with fire.

Despite the fact Rhys and Rosa were so lenient with their children, they were surprisingly undemonstrative, and all the years I knew them, I never remember seeing them kiss or hug their children. The Ronchetti grandparents, on the other hand, treated them like infant royalty, lathering them with ice cream and stuffing them with sweets, while Rhys's father, Mr Pugh Lampeter (Rhys had long since dropped the Pugh), bestowed an endless supply of toys and cash. Mr P.L. Senior, as he liked himself to be known, was a thunder-voiced, beetle-browed Welshman of the hellfire and brimstone variety who doted on his grand-daughters, none the less. All the Lampeters and Ronchettis had appetites like horses, even Rhys, who remained matchstick thin all his life, and was renowned for the enthusiastic sneezing which accompanied his hay fever. The final member of the household was a cross-looking Persian with a dodgy digestion called Felicity, which ate anything that moved.

Gina and Gwyneth had two dolls called Nola and Lola. Nola (or it may have been Lola) was an old-fashioned doll with a pot head. This was replaced regularly due to having been chucked into the fireplace or against the nearest wall, so she seemed to suffer from a permanent identity crisis. Lola (or possibly Nola) was a modern, more pliant kind of doll, made of whatever they made dolls of in the 1950s., and seemed slightly more stable. But neither of the girls played with dolls a lot, which was probably just as well. Gina had a tricycle on which she used to hurtle down the road like a very tiny bat out of hell, while I tried to keep up on a scooter made of wood. However, the Lampeter girls were three and four years younger than I was, so our actual playing together days were few. It was really the parents who were friends, and we children who just tagged along while they played tennis, or kicked a football about in the back garden. Every other Saturday, Rhys and my dad would go to the match together and spend the evening discussing it ad infinitum, while Mum and Rosa chatted. Then they'd play cards. My parents usually won, which bugged Rhys no end, so the stakes were kept to the minimum.

One Saturday night, the younger two had been put to bed and I was sleeping in the front bedroom at Rhys and Rosa's house. Suddenly I awoke, or thought I did, to see a strange figure standing at the foot of the bed. Whatever it was resembled an animated drawing more than a person, luminous, with a whitish, silvery glow. It was a child's idea of a skeleton, minus bones or detail, rather like the drawing of The Saint in books I was yet too young to have read. A pin man, in fact. Its head was a featureless oval, and with its non-existent eyes, it was looking at me. As I lay there, frozen with terror, it began to jump up and down, as if on springs. As it gained momentum, leaping like something on a trampoline, I started to scream.

After the ensuing mêlée had died down (which soon involved all three of us, as my screaming had woken the other two) it was simply assumed I'd had a nightmare, and my parents took me home. To this day, I've never known exactly what I saw in that room, and I was always afraid to sleep there again. Although I was still put to bed there, I'd stay awake, going round the room with my eyes, making sure it wasn't lurking. The clock was the only rational suspect, but stood nowhere near where the creature appeared, and in any case, the numbers on its dial were clearly visible. Eventually, I'd fall asleep out of sheer exhaustion, terrified of waking up in case it was there. Then one Sunday after Gina and Gwyneth had slept in my parents' room, by the bedroom door was a scrap of paper. I picked it up. It was a child's drawing of a pin man. Suddenly sick, I screwed it into a ball and threw it into the boiler.

I said nothing about the Pin Man. Gina and Gwyneth weren't the sort of children you could talk to about anything delicate. They'd only snitch on you. And I was honour bound not to describe what I'd seen in Rhys and Rosa's bedroom. Gina and Gwyneth were so protected they weren't even allowed to watch The Cisco Kid. Since they owned the only television in the street, this was a sore point with me – but Rosa said no, and that was that. It was a word she could say to me, but not to Gina or Gwyneth. So I stewed and brooded over pin men and skeletal apparitions until a few weeks later, when I was allowed into the house to watch Heidi, or something more wholesome. By the dining room door, scribbled in pencil on the wall about three feet from the floor, was a pin man. I probably went pale, but said nothing. And under the little table where the telephone sat, there was another. Gina and Gwyneth, obviously, were the sort of children who were allowed to draw on walls, and frequently did, their art-work eventually painted over, or hidden by items of furniture. But why pin men?

One Sunday morning a few weeks later, I went in to my parents' bedroom, and there on the dressing table was the doll. Not a friendly doll for playing with like Nola and Lola. This was the oddest thing I'd ever seen. A tiny, jointed figure made of metal, with a too-large head, slanting, empty eyes, tiny mouth, and no nose at all. Apart from being solid, its resemblance to the figure in the bedroom was chilling.

I picked it up, and it felt cold. The metal was a curious curdled colour, as though it had been burned or oxidised. But its very strangeness made it memorable. It was heavy, too, for a thing of its size, and something about it was quite disconcerting. I showed it to my mother.

"I don't know where that came from," she said, "but I don't like the look of it. Where did you find it?"

I told her.

"Must be something Gina and Gwyneth left," she said. "Better take it back."

I picked it up and put it in my pocket.

When I got to the back door, I could hear Rosa rattling her wooden spoon against the side of a basin. Felicity was on the lawn, masticating something in greedy, enthusiastic gulps. Rosa opened the door, wiping her hands on her apron.

"Oh, it's you, Andrea," she said. "What is it? I'm busy just now."

"I think Gina and Gwyneth left something at our house," I said.

"Gina, Gwyneth!" she bawled. No-one appeared. "Oh Felicity, you are disgusting! – Well, what is it?"

"This," I said, displaying the object I'd put in my pocket.

"That's a nasty looking thing," she said, squinting at it. "I'm sure it doesn't belong to the girls. Just then, Gina appeared, followed by Gwyneth. " – Girls, Andrea found this. Is it yours?"

Both looked at it and back at me with egg-like blankness.

"No," they said, in chorus.

"I told you it wasn't theirs," said Rosa. "Well, I don't like the look of it. Give it here."

She took it off me and dumped it unceremoniously in the bin.

"That's the end of that," she said. "Must get on. Bye." And she shut the door.

As I went back, stepping over Felicity's regurgitated offerings, I saw the girls watching from the dining room window. The next day, the doll was back on the dressing table.

"I thought you'd got rid of that," said my mother.

Next time I looked, the doll had gone. After a day or two, it reappeared. It lay on the dressing table gathering dust until one day my mother put it in the PDSA collection bag. Several days later, it was back. It seemed to be making a point, somehow. Slightly sorry for it, my mother dropped the doll into a box with other bits and bobs. Unclaimed and unidentified, it disappeared into a dusty corner somewhere and was, for the time being anyway, forgotten.

One day I went round to the house and heard raised voices through the dining room window. I paused.

"Daddy, Mummy keeps saying I've been drawing on the walls!" This was Gwyneth. "Well, I haven't!"

"Yes you have!" This was Gina.

Then Rhys's voice: "Have you Gwyneth?"

"No, I haven't. It's Gina!"

"No it's not!"

Rhys: "Well you're both too big for that sort of thing now. Whoever it is, stop it."

There was a moment's silence, then somebody started screaming.

It would be Gina. Then Gwyneth joined in. And for once, I heard Rhys add, "And you can stop that, as well!"

I decided it might be an inappropriate moment to knock on the Lampeters' door and went home. Felicity, with a set of legs hanging out of her mouth, paused for a moment, then carried on chewing. As I went out onto the pavement, I heard the sound of a bucket being emptied into the drain and a scrubbing brush being thrown after it.

Time moved on. I passed my eleven plus and went to the local grammar. Gina and Gwyneth had been sent to a private school, so we saw each other less and less.

Gina and Gwyneth still threw tantrums on a regular basis. And I still had qualms about sleeping in the Lampeters' bedroom so I was relived when my parents decided I was old enough to stay on my own and listen to the radio instead. However, Gina and Gwyneth still came to our house every other Saturday and, grumpy and complaining, were deposited in my parents' bed.

Sometimes though, when we children were older, we would stay up for a while and play cards or board games with our parents. One of these was a word game using cards, called Lexicon. Everyone had a hand of cards with letters on, from which they had to make a word. Naturally, with Gina and Gwyneth, this led to violent arguments as to what was a proper word and what wasn't, usually ending up with Rhys or Rosa saying, "Oh go on, let them have it, to some verbal chimera, which rather went against the point, but it was either that or compulsory deafness. However, it was me who really put the cat among the pigeons. One night I noticed I had a P, an I, and an N, then to my sudden malicious delight, another N, an M and an A. It was simply too good to ignore. Slowly I spelled out P.I.N.M.A.N. There was an ominous pause. Then Gina shrieked, "I don't want to play any more! I hate this stupid game! Everybody's always getting at me!" And she stormed out of the room. Predictably, Gwyneth also began to wail: "It's not my fault, it was Andrea!" she howled.

Rhys said, "Gwinnie, bed. That's enough."

This was about as adamant as Rhys ever got. From the bedroom, the sound of wailing and mutual recrimination could be heard for some time.

"They're over-tired," Rosa said.

For once in my life, I felt quite guilty.

Later that night, some inner mischief made me creep to an upstairs window and look down at the Lampeters' house. For a second, in the space between the glass of the window and the drawn bedroom curtains, I thought I saw a silvery skeletal figure, and then it was gone.

When I was fourteen, Mr P. L. Senior died, and Rhys and Rosa moved to a larger house a mile or more away. Without the screaming and sneezing and the more homely sound of Rosa's spoon rat-tatting against the side of a basin, the road became a quieter if less entertaining place. A new family with children moved in, but they seemed pallid compared to the Lampeters and I never heard any yelling or mention of strange apparitions. Rosa's family retired to Italy, and the Lampeters began spending holidays there. Our parrnts still met up on Saturday evenings, but as Rhys took over the family business, Rhys and Rosa were acquiring richer and more influential friends. We still did some things together, and I was pleased when Rhys suggested that I might go with Gina to tennis lessons on a Saturday morning. Gina and I didn't have a lot to say to each other these days, but it meant a trip into town then an hour or so of tennis before a free ride home, which usually involved Rhys stopping somewhere and buying us an ice ream or bag of sweets. For all his alleged tight-fistedness, Rhys was never stingy where children were concerned.

Tennis lessons were given by an eccentric lady with long teeth called Mrs Laporte, on a small private court on the edge of town. Nearby was a stretch of no-man's land, heaps of thistly earth and lumps of concrete and a disused clay-pit with KEEP OUT signs flapping in the dusty wind. The tennis court was a green oasis hemmed in by high hedges, but there was an odd feeling to it, like somewhere fixed between one world and the next. I always found it unsettling and I think Gina did, too. Perhaps it was this very quality that made me say out of the blue one day, "Gina, did you ever see the Pin Man?"

Gina went white. "I don't know what you mean," she said, "you're just being stupid!" But I knew she did. By her very insistence, she'd given herself away.

As I got out of the car outside our house, I heard her hiss almost inaudibly: "And don't you ever, ever mention that to me again!"

The next lesson, Gina was very moody. Rackets were thrown and tennis balls kicked. "I hate Mrs Laporte," she said, when Rhys came to collect us, "I don't want to come here any more."

"You will," said Rhys, "because I've paid for the lessons. You are going to give it a go."

"Don't talk to me like that!" said Gina, as though she was the adult and he the child. I looked down at Gina's smooth brown legs and the splintered top of her racket, feeling embarrassed.

However, next week, Gina was moodier than ever. She yelled at me, Mrs Laporte, and Rhys in the car on the way home, and the following Saturday, rackets were thrown again. When Friday night arrived, Rhys appeared to say a trifle sheepishly that Mrs Laporte had written to say she was unable to offer Gina any further lessons. So that was the end of my private tuition. I went back to bashing a ball about at school and Gina went on to become personal coach to John McEnroe. Well no, I made that up. But for years, the reaction in our household to any display of awful behaviour was, "Doesn't that remind you of Gina Lampeter?"

As time went on, the families drifted further apart. Rhys, I felt, had grown particularly pretentious, and instead of going to football matches was now a golf aficionado, though this seemed to involve more elbow-lifting in the clubhouse than club-lifting on the course. Rhys invested in a fancy hi-fi he couldn't tune and a load of classical records, and lined the living room with leather-bound books. I picked one up once and was amused to find it had uncut pages. Intrigued, I picked up another and found the same thing. My parents smiled a sad but 'told you so' smile. I knew my father mourned the Rhys he used to know, the funny, footballing Rhys, not the Rotary Club Rhys he was now. I missed them, too. I'd always liked Rhys, though Rosa could be brusque and hurtful. But I missed her all the same, her spoon-rattling in the kitchen and her funny rumbling laugh, like a road drill at a great distance. But the girls, did I really miss them? No, I don't think I did. And I'm certain they never missed me.

I left school, got a job in the library service, had boyfriends, wrote stories. Gina and Gwyneth left school too. Gwyneth went off to teacher training college. Gina went to work as a hairdresser. I later heard she was sacked from one establishment for whacking a client with a pair of scissors (an accident, obviously.) So Rhys bought her a salon. Around this time, my mother became seriously ill. She recovered, but neither Rhys nor Rosa called or phoned, or even sent a get-well card. Our friendship with the Lampeters was clearly over.

One Saturday morning, as I was leaving work, two girls came out of the wedding boutique, laughing and chatting. Gwyneth and Gina. Gina was getting married, apparently. His name was Jeremy. He was a chartered accountant. That should keep Rhys happy. In fact, for once even Gina looked happy, although when I passed on the news to my parents, sad to say, their sympathies lay with the accountant. None of us got an invite, but the pictures in the county magazine showed Gina looking vivacious and Italianate in frothy white lace.

It was several years before I had news of the Lampeters again. My father died suddenly. I received a little note from Gwyneth saying how sorry she was, and what a good time we'd had together when we were children. After the funeral, as the cars pulled away, among the people leaving the church, I saw Rosa. She didn't see me, but she looked distinctly upset. From Rhys and Gina, I heard nothing at all.

Then one day as I was passing through town, a news placard caught my eye. 'Young Mum Stabs Husband', it screamed. I bought a paper. The young mother in question was a Mrs Gina Moorhead. Mrs Moorhead, it stated, was the daughter of well-known local businessman Mr Rhys Lampeter. "Oh bloody hell!" I said.

According to what emerged later, Mrs Moorhead had been cutting up raw meat in the kitchen. Mr Moorhead offered to help. Whereupon Mrs Moorhead, who had recently given birth and was of a nervous disposition, hit him across the hand with the carving knife. When Mr Moorhead tried to take the knife, she stabbed him several times before panicking and phoning for an ambulance. On the wall, daubed apparently in Mr Moorhead's blood, was what seemed to be a childish drawing of a pin man.

Luckily, the unfortunate accountant survived. The story about the drawing on the wall, with its bizarre implications, was quickly quashed. There would still be a case, however, since the charges were serious.

It occurred to me that during my lunch break I might be able to sneak in to the court. After all, it was free to anyone, no questions asked. However, just my luck, the court had also adjourned. It was a pale spring day, and the wind whipped up cold from the river. As I went down into the public gardens, I saw a small figure huddled disconsolately on the steps.

"Gwyneth?"

The figure looked up, bemused for a moment, eyes red and puffy with crying.

"Andrea?"

"Yeah, it's me. Heck. I'm sorry. I really am."

We sat and shared my sandwiches on the steps.

"She didn't mean to do it, you know." Said Gwyneth. "Half the things Gina does, she never really means to do. Grandpa P. L. used to have a terrible temper like that. And the Ronchettis used to should and yell a lot. But it didn't actually mean anything."

"There's something awfully positive about sticking a knife in your husband, though, isn't there?"

"I suppose so."

We threw our crusts to the ducks.

"Do you think she'll get off?"

"God knows," I paused. "Gwyneth," I said, "was it true about the drawing on the wall?"

"You heard that, then? I don't know. By the time the police got there, somebody had wiped it off. There was blood all over the place. Some from the meat and some from Jeremy. It was awful."

"But it was the Pin Man, wasn't it?"

Gwyneth paused. "Yes, it was," she said. "It was Gina who used to do it, you know. She always blamed me, but it was really her. Mummy and Daddy sent her to a psychiatrist in the end. It was driving us all bats."

"When did it start, do you remember?"

"Gina found this thing in the garden. She dug it up behind the rockery. She used to frighten me with it. Then one day she said it was real. She said it moved, like it was human."

"The doll? That little cracker-doll thing?"

"Yes, that. It was hideous. We were always trying to get rid of it."

"I know," I said.

"It went in the end. I've often wondered what happened to it."

"I could tell you exactly what happened to it," I said. Gwyneth wasn't listening.

"She used it to frighten me. If you don't do something, the Pin Man will get you. She said it grew big and came out at night to haunt people. She started seeing it in the day, as well. Eventually she could see it all the time. She said it made her do things. She thought it was taking her over, like The Body Snatchers, or something. We thought she was going crazy."

311

"Maybe," I said, "but I don't think so. She could be freaky, but I don't think she was crazy."

"They've taken the baby off her, you know. I hope to God she doesn't ever tell them about the Pin Man or she'll never get it back. They'll put her away, or something."

"Gina isn't nuts," I said. "I saw it too."

And for the first time ever, I told someone what I'd seen in Rhys and Rosa's bedroom at the bungalow in Quilley Road.

The Island

by Claire Follett

Although he saw with the eyes of many, he spoke the words of the few. He wished he could play the tunes others played, dance their dance. He saw them, he tried to walk their paths but always as an island in the midst of isolated seas.

His heart yearned to be a part, even a small part of the whole, whatever that was, but always some part of himself withdrew. His mind was deceived but a little slice of his soul knew the truth of the illusion. Because in truth all was an illusion but one so real, so tangible, that its density deceived him. For so many years he had deceived himself and cocooned himself in a cloak of interminable hue, of darkness that fooled even the master of deception.

A part of his being danced a fandango of furious passion in a union of understanding and empathy, he was coalesced into an eternal contentment and awoke from sleep still inspired by night fancies, but to face another day as the island. He joined them in the local bars and drank as good as the next, cracked jokes that made their faces crease but behind the sides of the corneas could be detected some stale sadness that bagged his eyes, that no amount of sleep or lotion could remove.

Around the headland he would spend many an hour lost in the rocks watching the breakwaters, the sentinel monoliths of warped wood that appear and reappear with the tides. Always standing silent and on each tide slightly, ever so slightly changed, eroded by the salt waves. And in time these too would go to the water and become part of the beach. He felt empathy with them and on each encounter his soul would refill as the tide filled the little rock pools. He was always drawn here to the sea, although he couldn't quite say why, maybe it was because he was composed himself of eighty to ninety percent water, so he had read somewhere. Or perhaps it was some unfathomable lunar pull that beckoned.

Then one day he had to go way. Leave his solace and go to the city. The thought aggrieved him, although he knew it would all await his return. But what if it didn't, if for some reason it was gone, what then? These thoughts vanished from his mind quickly as he took the rattling, rolling stock up to town. On return he stepped back onto familiar terrain and cycled down to the beach with a rucksack of water and chocolate. This time he took his camera. They were all there, his old friends, half submerged in a spring tide. They seemed to smile at him, he felt their embrace. They seemed to be taking him with them. He wanted to be with them.

It was exactly one year later that the coastguard was on his morning's lookout over the channel.

"Here Jack, what's that out over there? Looks like something floating out over Beachy Head way."

They looked, the binoculars making red rings round the flesh so their eyes.

"Reckon it must be one of them from last night, Jack, better take a look."

The lifeboat flares sounded. The men were out of the harbour within minutes and as they approached the dark mass, expecting to see lifeless faces from last night's incident, noted something unusual.

"That's strange Bill, never noticed that there before." Bill's eyes tried to focus on something that had not been there as far as he had been aware, and he had patrolled the shores these last twenty years. An island swam into view, craggy, grass-covered. He couldn't quite pin it down, it seemed to dance before his eyes glinting in the sun, surrounded by a circle of old breakwater posts.